From Caribb[ean] [...] **simple tales** [...] **teenagers,** *Gr*[...] **will enrich the lives of both you and your children. Here is a sampling of the books you'll find inside. . . .**

For toddlers and preschoolers . . .

Bright Eyes, Brown Skin **by Cheryl Willis Hudson and Bernette G. Ford.** Full-page illustrations of black children at play and at school that reinforce a positive self-image.

Jaha and Jamil Went Down the Hill **by Virginia Kroll.** Favorites from Mother Goose retold against a beautifully illustrated African backdrop.

Children ages four to eight . . .

Abby **by Jeannette Caines.** A young girl's curiosity about her adoption leads to a deeper understanding of family, acceptance, self-esteem, and love.

It's Raining Laughter **by Nikki Grimes.** Spirited poems and accompanying photographs celebrating life's simple joys.

Eight to eleven . . .

. . . If You Lived at the Time of Martin Luther King **by Ellen Levine.** An accessible history of the civil rights movement.

Kids' Book of Wisdom **compiled by Cheryl and Wade Hudson.** Inspiring quotes and proverbs drawn from black culture and tradition.

And young adults . . .

Sounder **by William H. Armstrong.** The award-winning classic about a Georgia sharecropping family and a boy and his dog that teaches the virtues of loyalty and the power of faith.

The Parable of the Sower **by Octavia Butler.** Science-fiction adventure set in twenty-first-century Los Angeles that is ideal for both boys and girls.

PAMELA TOUSSAINT is the co-author of *Mama's Little Baby: The Black Woman's Guide to Pregnancy, Childbirth, and Baby's First Year*, which garnered glowing reviews from *Essence, Emerge, American Baby,* and *Today's Black Woman* magazines. A former editor at *Essence*, Ms. Toussaint has written articles for *Working Woman* and *Black Enterprise*.

Pamela Toussaint

Great Books for African-American Children

A PLUME BOOK

PLUME
Published by the Penguin Group
Penguin Putnam Inc., 375 Hudson Street, New York, New York 10014, U.S.A.
Penguin Books Ltd, 27 Wrights Lane, London W8 5TZ, England
Penguin Books Australia Ltd, Ringwood, Victoria, Australia
Penguin Books Canada Ltd, 10 Alcorn Avenue, Toronto, Ontario, Canada M4V 3B2
Penguin Books (N.Z.) Ltd, 182–190 Wairau Road, Auckland 10, New Zealand

Penguin Books Ltd, Registered Offices: Harmondsworth, Middlesex, England

First published by Plume, a member of Penguin Putnam Inc.

First Printing, February, 1999
10 9 8 7 6 5 4 3 2 1

 REGISTERED TRADEMARK — MARCA REGISTRADA

LIBRARY OF CONGRESS CATALOGING-IN-PUBLICATION DATA
Toussaint, Pamela.
    Great books for African-American children / Pamel Toussaint.
       p.   cm.
    ISBN 0-452-28044-3
    1. Afro-American children—Books and reading.   2. Children's literature,
English—Bibliography.   3. English literature—Black authors—Bibliography.
4. Afro-Americans—Juvenile literature—Bibliography.   5. Blacks—Juvenile
literature—Bibliography.   I. Title.
Z1039.B56T68   1999
028.1'62—dc21   98-31519
                                                                    CIP

Printed in the United States of America
Set in New Baskerville
Designed by Eve L. Kirch

BOOKS ARE AVAILABLE AT QUANTITY DISCOUNTS WHEN USED TO PROMOTE PRODUCTS
OR SERVICES. FOR INFORMATION PLEASE WRITE TO PREMIUM MARKETING DIVISION,
PENGUIN PUTNAM INC., 375 HUDSON STREET, NEW YORK, NY 10014.

CONTENTS

Acknowledgments   vii

Introduction: Books on the Black Experience:
    We've Come a Long Way, Brown Baby   1

1. Helping Any Child Love Reading   13

2. Great Books for Very Young Children   15

3. Great Books for Children Four to Eight   27

4. Great Books for Children Eight to Eleven   113

5. Great Books for Preteens and Young Adults   165

6. Oops List: Great Out-of-Print Books   229

7. Great Reading Resources: Magazines, TV Shows,
    Websites, Videos, Books, and Other Sources That
    Promote Reading   241

8. Bookstores in Your Area   257

Indexes   269

ACKNOWLEDGMENTS

It takes a village (and frequent visits from a loving God) to create a book like this in five months. I would like to thank the following people for their kind assistance during my research and writing industry experts: Henrietta Smith and K. T. Horning; Richlin, Weldon, Noni, and Xavier Ryan, Andrew and Stephen Burnett, and all of the children and teens in my focus group; Jerry, Brian and Andrea Pinkney, talented children's book pioneers; Deb Brody, who led me to Deborah Brodie; and Phyllis Fogelman at Penguin; librarian Farida Shapiro; Cheryl and Wade Hudson of Just Us Books; Ann Brown; Holly Favino; Lori Pilong; Bradley Toms; Beverly Cook; Joy Johnson; and my editor, Jennifer Moore.

Train up a child in the way he should go,
and when he is old he will not turn from it.

—PROVERBS 22:6

Introduction

Books on the Black Experience:
We've Come a Long Way, Brown Baby

If you went to the library in the early 1900s for a book for a black child (that is, if they'd let you through the door), you would be confronted with the following choices: *Little Pickanninies*, *New Nigger Nursery Rhymes for Little Folk*, *Black Sambo* and *Mammy's Li'l' Chilluns*. And let's not forget *Nursery Numbers*, the circa 1901 book starring characters named Puss, Polly, Jim Crow, and Lazy Jerry. The author apparently thought nothing of teaching addition using rhymes like these: "Ten little nigger boys went out to dine, one choke his little self and that left nine . . ." (No, I'm not making this up.) Sadly, a second edition of *Nursery Numbers*, published forty years later and retitled *Ten Little Colored Boys*, still featured clownish black characters with bulging eyes and big pink lips. And what about the verbiage in *The Sad End of Erica's Blackamoor*, published in England during that period? It is all about a little white girl named Erica and her black doll (called a blackamoor), which "seemed to be quite good and tame, but it wasn't really. It had a black skin outside and a wicked, bad black heart inside: it wanted to run away and be a wild blackamoor again . . . just as wild as all the other blackies!" The book proceeds to show a full-page spread of illustrations of the "wild blackamoors" prancing around the toy shop.

It goes without saying that these books were disgustingly racist. They were written to degrade and belittle us for the amusement of white children. Certainly, they had no intention of helping a black child's self-esteem with that nonsense, though some actually claim to have been "well-meaning."

Thankfully, there have been a lot of changes in black children's book publishing since the 1950s. The turbulent and triumphant 1960s brought renewed interest on the part of the media in portraying blacks fairly in books, in magazines, and on television. Moral obligations aside, most of these power brokers realized that marketing black products to black people had the potential to bring in green dollars. As prolific author Walter Dean Myers noted in a *New York Times* article he wrote in 1986, "We were news, and what is news is marketable."

Publishers scrambled to sign up authors to write about the black experience for children—but most of those hired to do so were still white. Thus, we now had books that were *intended* for our children and *intended* to portray blacks positively—and some did—but that still sometimes lacked the important benefit of the author's personal experience "in the skin," as it were. Of course, white publishers had the ever prevalent problem of being "unable to find any black authors" who wanted to write children's books. Then in 1966, a contest sponsored by the Council on Interracial Books for Children was designed to find and promote black authors, and *voilà!* It received a great response to its $500 offer for stories and launched the careers of Walter Dean Myers, Kristin Hunter, Mildred Taylor, and Sharon Bell Mathis, among others. Taylor and Myers alone have since published more than sixty books on the black experience, many of which are award-winners and monetary successes. Unfortunately, the Council lost its ability to fund the contest and stopped offering it in the early 1970s. Nonetheless, Tom Feelings, Virginia Hamilton, Jerry

Pinkney, Ashley Bryan, Julius Lester, Lucille Clifton, and Leo and Diane Dillon were among the most noted artists and writers to begin their careers in children's books during this "decade of hope."

Even without contests to help find new talent, the future seemed bright for black children's book authors in the 1970s as more publishers sought manuscripts that fulfilled their "social responsibilities." By then the Elementary and Secondary Educational Act required that there be books on black experience in every classroom after school integration became law. But again, though a few black artists were making their mark on the industry, most of the writers and illustrators hired to produce books about African Americans were still white. To be sure, some white authors and illustrators of this time period did portray our culture quite sensitively: Ann Grifalconi, Eric Berry, Molly Bang, and Ezra Jack Keats, for example. A handful of black artists, including Mildred Taylor, Donald Crews, Nikki Grimes and George Ford, were among those who broke through the tight-knit web and received acceptance into the elite circle of children's book authors and illustrators at this time.

By the 1980s the tide had shifted again. Angela Johnson, Patricia and Frederick McKissack, Floyd Cooper, Jan Spivey Gilchrist, Brian Pinkney, Rita Williams Garcia, and Jacqueline Woodson emerged on the scene and African-American talent had succeeded in becoming more of a dominant force in children's books about the black experience. Stories now featured more than just brown-skinned characters in ghetto settings. They were about African life, about the Caribbean and the black South; they featured black professionals as well as rural black families, reflected the stories of single mothers and two-parent homes with active, involved black fathers. These books offered insightful and creative portrayals that better demonstrated a broader understanding of what is called the "black experience."

But by the time one could say, "I am a black children's book author," the tide had turned yet again, seemingly along with publishers' interests in producing and selling black children's books. Sadly, by 1984 there were half the number of black books out that there were in 1974, and industry expert Henrietta Smith, editor of *The Coretta Scott King Awards Book* and member of the task force that selects books for the King award, recalls that for the first time she received regret letters from publishers in response to the committee's requests for book nominations: "I'm sorry that I don't have anything to send this year . . ."

What happened? Conservative political, economic and social shifts of the time may account for the laissez-faire attitude that prevailed until the early 1990s, some say. However, a new surge of interest surfaced again with the turning of this decade. Today, there are approximately 2,000 children's books currently in print that were created by black authors or illustrators or that feature black characters and story lines that explore the black experience. Books by black authors and illustrators still make up just one percent of all children's books published, though that figure is slowly climbing. For every 51 children's books published for the general market, only one is published on the black experience, but again, that's better than one for every 100, which was the ratio in 1986.

Our newer books are lavishly and stunningly illustrated, sensitively and creatively written, and offer captivating story lines that broaden our horizons still. Our children can enjoy Nigerian poetry written just for them, imagine life as a child in Trinidad at Christmas, read about their favorite black heroes and sheroes in sports, science, politics, literature, and the arts. They can even learn the alphabet using English, Swahili or Zulu words, and discover our history and folklore in any number of creative and compelling books. Teens can see themselves reflected in a number of excellent books about teen life—the good, the bad, and the ugly—though this category still needs more.

The New Guard of black illustrators has officially emerged, with the sons and daughters of noted artists making their own unique contributions. Nina Crews, Brian Pinkney, Javaka Steptoe, Myles Pinkney, and Christopher Myers are examples of this exciting trend. This is no simple thing—it is history in the making, and a reason for celebration and hope! Jerry Pinkney noted, "In the early sixties books for black children didn't exist. The idea of making a living as an illustrator was unheard of." Today, it is a reality.

The pool of black authors and illustrators is growing. Christopher Paul Curtis, Angela Shelf Medearis, Bernette Ford, Andrea Davis Pinkney, and James Ransome are some welcome 1990s faces in the industry. The newer illustrators utilize a number of ingenious techniques in their artwork. Brian Pinkney uses a sharp tool to scratch his illustrations out of a white board covered with black ink. Nina Crews makes collages by cutting and layering color photographs, and Christopher Myers uses a combination of collage, watercolors, and ink in his work. Javaka Steptoe, who won the 1998 Coretta Scott King Award for illustrations in his debut book, uses bold multimedia, layering paper, sand, and everyday objects to produce a three-dimensional effect, a fresh look in black children's books. Myles Pinkney's beautiful candid photographs of black children will no doubt adorn many books in the future.

Finally, the color of folks at the top in this industry is showing some slight evidence of change—yet it is moving at a snail's pace. As of this writing, there were only two black children's book editors in senior positions out of all 7,500 publishing companies in the United States, a shameful statistic to be sure. This means that there are few if any black minds evaluating the manuscripts that are submitted by black authors and illustrators for possible publication (though some are sent "outside" for black opinions). Just Us Books, founded by Cheryl and Wade Hudson, stands as the only black-owned company that exclusively publishes children's books on the black experience. They follow in the footsteps of Associated Publishers, a black-owned outfit that operated in the 1940s in Washington, D.C., and published books by black authors when no one else would. Hopefully, we will do better in the new millennium.

The future looks bright—but it will only stay that way as long as we continue to support our authors and illustrators by regularly buying books on the black experience for our children—and for *all* children. Promise you will?

Who needs a "black book"?

The answer is: all of us (non-blacks, too). Numerous psychologists, educators and researchers have confirmed the fact that children develop an awareness of racial differences at an early age. Helen Trager and Martin Yarrow noted way back in 1952 in their book *They Learn What They Live* that generally, white youngsters in kindergarten and the first and second grades already have negative attitudes and express hostility toward black Americans. A 1960 study reported that many of our children had poor "self-concepts." Psychologists Derek and Darlene Hopson, authors of *Different and Wonderful: Raising Black Children in a Race-Conscious Society* note, "Without help from a concerned adult, the danger is that Black children will identify with, or see themselves in, the negative images of Blacks mirrored back to them by society."

Books in which black children see themselves reflected *positively*, sensitively, and authentically in illustrations and story lines can have a trememdous impact on those negative self-images. "Growing up in Boston a few decades ago—and reading voraciously everything available in our branch library—I knew that books were about *other* people," recalled author and teacher Elizabeth Fitzgerald Howard in *Education Week*. "You could not become the characters you read about. . . ." Sound familiar? Many parents tell me how they routinely color in the faces of the characters in their children's books with a brown magic marker to make them ethnically correct for their children. For shame that we have to do that! And this is even more true in the Christian children's book publishing world, where it's hard to find a black face on a book for a child. (I know; I searched diligently and lamented with several churchgoing parents.)

Thankfully, most of today's progressive educators, white and black, agree that every child's reading list should be diverse, including a liberal dose of books in which a child can see himself reflected. Amos Wilson, author of *Awakening the Natural Genius of Black Children*, recommends that African-based content and materials be utilized whenever and wherever possible and suggests that black parents should demonstrate a love and enthusiasm for things African in front of children as early as preschool. "We need language to tell us who we are, how we feel, what we're capable of—to explain the pains and glory of our existence," noted Pulitzer prize–winning poet and author Dr. Maya Angelou in a HomeArts Network interview on America Online.

And we need more of it.

What makes a book "great"?

In 1944, noted black librarian Augusta Baker thought that a great book for a black child was one that was not written in heavy dialect too difficult for a child to understand and enjoy; one in which the illustrations showed a sensitivity to black beauty—dark skin, crinkly hair, a short or wide nose, and full lips should not be exaggerated to appear caricatured. And the black characters should not be described "in terms of derision," or be portrayed in a negative, debasing light.

Today, the recommendations are basically the same, but there are much sharper eyes out now as well as higher-quality, more authentic books for children on the black experience. Rudine Sims Bishop, national expert on African-American children's literature, notes that the long, sad history of U.S. race relations, coupled with the tradition of negative images of blacks presented in children's books, make African-American readers and other knowledgeable critics sensitive to even the most subtle manifestations of racism, negative attitudes and prejudices. One way to help ensure that you've chosen a gem is to ask yourself, "Who wrote this book?" and to take a good look at its story line and illustrations before you take it to the cash register.

Great books, in my opinion, reflect a wide range of the black experience and are both written and illustrated with sensitivity, creativity and authenticity. I believe that books should also teach, even better if they do so subtly and craftily, helping the child learn without him realizing it because he's having such a good time reading or being read to. As Henrietta Smith said, "If you just put a book down after you've read it, what difference did it make?" West African writer Wagué Diakité, author of *The Hunterman and the Crocodile* (page 65), notes that in Mali stories told to children were for "much more than just entertainment," but were an important way to encourage good morals. I hope you appreciate the format I've created to select books that will help "train up a child" while delighting them at the same time.

How to Best Use This Book

I believe you will find this book to be an easy-to-use guide to selecting great books on the black experience for your child. It is not divided by genre, but is sectioned as follows: Great Books for Very Young Children, Children Four to Eight, Children Eight to Eleven, Preteens and Young Adults. I felt that parents and educators would benefit from seeing reviews of a variety of appropriate books rather than books listed under "historical fiction," "adventure" or other such labels. This way of grouping basically follows the age categories that children's books fall into. The outer age overlaps into the next category. That means that a book in the four to eight chapter could also be fine, if slightly less interesting, for a nine-year-old; and a precocious three-year-old may enjoy attempting to read words from a book in the four to eight section, and so on.

You may find that your child's reading abilities are above the reading level recommended for certain books reviewed here, while others will find that their children are reading below grade—please don't be upset if you find that some books seem to be listed in the "wrong" age group. It's a bit tricky figuring out what books are appropriate for what age, since many publishers no longer put age recommendations on books. However, with the aid of longtime librarians, educators, children's book editors, parents and children, I have attempted to place the books according to their most appropriate age group. The best guide, though, is you. Know your child's reading abilities before you buy a book, and it's more likely to be a hit. Take them with you to the store as much as possible when buying. Often children enjoy books we would never think to buy for them. Ultimately, though, they read *what they like* and *what's made available* to them (as Richard Wright showed us by learning to read using the comics and scraps of old newspapers he found in the trash).

Most of the books included here are award-winners, "honor" books or notable books, meaning that expert panels of literary examiners found them to be outstanding. Some are yet unheralded books that I thought were excellent and capturing. The reviews summarize the story and offer insights into the value of the book for a child. These are reviews, not critiques. Books I felt the need to criticize too much, I decided to leave out. All of the books with full reviews are in print and are available for purchase in bookstores and through my website, **www.greatbooks4A-Akids.com**, with the exception of those on the OOPS list (Out of Print) at the back of the book. If your local bookstore or library doesn't have a book, just ask them to order it for you. For books that are part of a series, the word "series" appears in bold, and I may note some of the other titles at the end of the review. Here's how a sample review heading appears:

 BLACK IS BROWN IS TAN
By Arnold Adoff. Illustrator: Emily Arnold McCully.
Publisher: HarperTrophy, 1973. PB$4.95 US/$6.75
CAN. MVP: Appreciating multiracialness, Classic, Read
Aloud

Title; Author; Illustrator; Publisher; Year of publication; "PB" or "HC" for paperback or hardcover; U.S. or Canadian prices (when the latter was listed); MVP (main value points) or Theme; the word "Classic" if it's been in print for more than twenty years; Read Aloud; availability on Audiocassette, Video, or CD; Awards the book has won; and Explore These, which are thought-provoking questions to ask a child about the story.

BOOK AWARDS

Coretta Scott King Award or **Honor*** is for distinguished or outstanding children's books on the black experience (see next page for more details).

Newbery Medal or **Honor** is for distinguished or outstanding writing in a children's book.

Caldecott Medal or **Honor** is for distinguished or outstanding illustration in a children's book.

* "Honors" go to runners-up.

ALA Award or **Notable** is given to outstanding books chosen by the American Library Association.

Boston Globe/Horn Book Award is for outstanding fiction, nonfiction, and illustration in a children's book.

Reading Rainbow selects books based on literary merit, visual impact and artistic achievement, adaptability to television, and ability to interest children of various cultures, including African Americans.

What is the Coretta Scott King Award? It is an award that has been given to outstanding children's books on the black experience every year since 1970, selected by a special task force of the American Library Association's Social Responsibility Round Table. Books are chosen based on how well they "promote an understanding and appreciation of the culture and acknowledge the contribution of all people to the realization of the 'American Dream.' " Awards are given each June. The award also honors Dr. Martin Luther King's widow, Coretta, for continuing the work for peace and world brotherhood. A King award means it's a great book for our children! For more information on past winners and current books for children on the black experience, see Great Reading Resources.

WHAT THE NOTATIONS MEAN

MVP (main value points) were designed to give a parent or teacher a sense of the book's main theme or value as far as helping a child's character development. Some books have two or three.

Explore These offers questions that can open the door to a meaningful conversation between a parent/teacher and child, encourage a learning moment or spur an exciting future project you can do with a child. The "Explore These" section will usually offer a knowledge/comprehension question, to see if the child "got" the basic points of the story, usually followed by an application/analysis question, which encourages the child to think more deeply about the theme and put themselves in the dilemma. Sometimes, I suggest simple projects that can be done relating to the book's main value points (MVP). The questions are for you to ask the child, to help reading comprehension. (To be fair and inclusive, I alternate usage of "him" and "her" when I am referring to a child in this section.) Reviews of books of poetry that are not themed usually do not have these exploratory questions added. Always ask a child what he thought about the poem, how it made him feel. Feel free to throw out some good questions of your own that relate to your child specifically.

Read Aloud means it's a good book to read aloud.

Indexes at the back of the book should make it easy for you to find the review of a book whose title you may have forgotten but whose author's name you may remember, or vice versa. One index lists all books alphabetically by title and also by author, on the same list. In the second index, all the book titles are listed again alphabetically according to their MVP. So if you want to find a book for your child on Determination, you can look under that heading in the index and find great books that convey that quality.

The Oops List gives you titles, publisher's information and short reviews of great books that are unfortunately no longer in print. They all should be available on request through your local library. If you have access to the Internet, amazon.com will make an attempt to find an old book for you through their links with bookstores that specialize in used and out-of-print books.

Author's Note: Time did not permit me to read all of the books that have been written for our children, as great new ones were coming out even as we went to press. I'm sure I have omitted some good ones. (Please forgive me, it was not intentional.) These books were so delicious, enlightening, tear-jerking, compelling and simply amazing that I was sorry I couldn't just read them for pleasure and then go to bed. But nontheless, here they are, over 250 of what I believe are some of the best and most creative books out there for children and young adults on the black experience. Read on and enjoy!

1

Helping Any Child Love Reading

Reading is essential for building a child's vocabulary, confidence, imagination and self-esteem. Here are twenty-five simple things you can do at home with your child to help him learn to enjoy reading:

- Create a reading corner in your child's room; have a shelf for favorite books.
- Keep a drawing pad and writing materials handy to encourage spontaneous creativity.
- Treat your child to a new book frequently, borrowed from the library or purchased.
- Get your child subscriptions to children's magazines in his or her name (see listing in Great Reading Resources).
- Encourage your children to play board games—they often require reading.
- Collect books on a theme that's of interest to your child.

- Read books with your child *before* seeing the movie or renting the video.
- Do crossword puzzles together.
- Leave notes for your child if you're at work or away from home.
- Cook from a simple recipe together and read it as you go along.
- Always take books on trips so the whole family can read; listen to books on tape in the car on long drives.
- Enroll your children in free reading sessions at the local library; let your child choose his own books to borrow.
- Read to your child after dinner or at bedtime.
- Read aloud to children while they're babies—and commit to continuing the habit into junior high.
- Quote from books or newspaper articles when you talk to your child.
- Encourage pen pals.
- Get brochures or maps on the state or country you're planning to visit on your next vacation; have your child locate it on a map and trace the route.
- Always ask a child to tell you what happened in school that day.
- Let your child see you giving books to other children on birthdays and special occasions.
- Ask for books as gifts for your child.
- Have your child read to adult relatives when they visit (if they are agreeable).
- Keep reading material around the house (newspapers, wholesome magazines, books) and encourage children age ten and up to begin reading them *regularly* to get used to handling informational prose.
- Avoid comparing the reading progress of one child to that of another.
- Encourage but do not force your child to read—the pressure defeats the purpose.
- Last and most important, *read yourself!*

2

Great Books for Very Young Children

Babies and toddlers who are just learning how to recognize colors, shapes and words

Books they like have . . .

- About twenty-four pages or less
- Large pictures or illustrations on every page
- Short amounts of text
- Very simple concepts and stories, and are usually about things that exist at an adult's waist level or below, i.e. the grass, shoes, toys
- Zany, silly humor or funny language
- Short, rhythmic, or rhyming sentences that are easy to memorize
- Safe, relatively predictable endings

If it is true, as studies show, that children develop attitudes about race by the time they reach first grade, then it is imperative that we build up a black child's self-concept early on. Experts say that it is never too early to begin surrounding a child with positive cultural images, and our African ancestors seemed to agree. One South African ritual is to prepare for a baby's birth by hanging colored beads and carvings around the birthing room so the newborn looks at something special the moment it makes its entrance into the world. What's more special than seeing a small child wiggle with excitement as he realizes that images in a book look just like him?

Thanks to series such as Just Us Books by Scholastic, Inc., Essence Books for Children, published in conjunction with Golden Books, and a number of other great individual board books for infants and toddlers, we now have a variety of sweet and sturdy books that celebrate the joys of being a beautiful brown baby. In this section, "MVP" is replaced by "Theme."

AFRO-BETS BOOK OF COLORS
By Margery W. Brown. Illustrator: Culverson Blair.
Publisher: Just Us Books, 1991. PB$3.95. Theme:
Learning colors

This slim book is part of the Afro-Bets series of books for black children. It teaches them about colors by associating them with common items in a child's world. Brown is "the color of many people you know" and, in this book, "is the color of the basketball you throw." Nice illustrations of multihued children in the "Color Family" with skin tones that range from deep brown to yellow. **Afro-Bets ABC Book,** also published by Just Us Books, teaches the alphabet by using everyday words and words that are specific to black culture: "E is for egg *and* Egyptians; K is for keys *and* for Kente cloth." "Q is for queen" shows a nice image of a black woman in a gown wearing a crown. See also, *Afro-Bets 123 Book on Counting,* and the *Afro-Bets Book of Shapes.*

BABY SAYS
Written and Illustrated by John Steptoe. Publisher:
Lothrop, Lee & Shepard, 1988. HC$9.95/PB$3.95.
Theme: Learning to talk

This simple book reinforces the three words and meanings that a toddler probably hears most: "Uh-oh," "No, no," and "Okay." It shows a baby growing bored playing in his crib and trying to get his older brother to play with him by throwing his teddy bear closer and closer to big brother's house of blocks. You can guess what happens next—down goes the house. "Uh-oh." Now it's time for big brother to take a deep breath and say, "Okay, baby, okay." One industry expert noted that squeals of laughter come from babies as young as six months and children as old as five when this book is read to them. It is also great for even older children who are struggling with learning to read. Pronounce the words for a baby or toddler and allow time for him to imitate you.

 BIG FRIEND, LITTLE FRIEND
By Eloise Greenfield. Illustrator: Jan Spivey Gilchrist.
Publisher: Black Butterfly (Writers and Readers
Publishers), 1991. Board, $5.95. Theme: Growing up

This small boy has the best of both worlds—he has an older girl and a younger boy as his friends. What he learns from his big friend he teaches to his little friend, like saying "Bless you!" after someone sneezes and telling them to cover their mouths. This is a nice way to teach a toddler the important role of being a big brother or sister to a new baby. See *Sweet Baby's Coming*, also by this noted author/illustrator team.

Black Illustrators' Notebook: George Ford received the first Coretta Scott King Award for illustration in 1974 and has illustrated more than two dozen books for young readers, including *Bright Eyes, Brown Skin* (below) and *Jamal's Busy Day* (page 72).

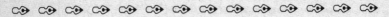

BRIGHT EYES, BROWN SKIN
By Cheryl Willis Hudson & Bernette G. Ford.
Illustrator: George Ford. Publisher: Just Us Books, 1990. HC$12.95/PB$6.95. Theme: Self-image/building self-esteem

This book of brown images reinforces to our children the fact that blond hair and blue eyes are not the only features worth celebrating—their bright eyes and brown skin are just as beautiful. Full-size illustrations of black children at play and at school, enjoying their braided heads, sweet noses and dimpled cheeks, plus simple, rhyming words make this an excellent first book. Have a child point to her appropriate features as you read. See also *Animal Sounds for Baby*, illustrated by George Ford, and *Let's Count Baby*, *Good Morning Baby*, and *Good Night Baby*.

THE CALYPSO ALPHABET
By John Agard. Illustrator: Jennifer Bent. Publisher: Henry Holt, 1989. HC$13.95. Theme: Learning new words

Another beautifully illustrated book that challenges the Eurocentric way most children learn the alphabet. Our children can now be assured that A is for apple, for Africa, or, in this book, for Anancy, the famous spider that appears in Afro-Caribbean folktales. With America becoming such a milieu of brown-skinned peoples, these Caribbean words will serve to broaden a child's vocabulary and expose him to the phrases used in other black nations. Those of us of West Indian descent will smile when we read that "E is for Eh-Eh!," a sound of surprise, "R is for roti" and "S is for sugarcane," and children should giggle at the sounds. A lively and culturally relevant way to teach preschoolers the alphabet.

 FINGERS, NOSE AND TOES
Photographs by John Pinderhughes. Publisher: Golden Books, 1997. Board, $3.50. Theme: Learning what body parts do

This is a book full of great shots of children, done by master photographer Pinderhughes, demonstrating what eyes, ears, noses, hands, legs, and other body parts can do: tongue is for tasting, eyes for peeking, hands for holding, and hair for braiding. A great double-page photo of children demonstrating "hands for holding" should be called "clothes for wearing"—they are all beautifully dressed in sharp kenté-patterned outfits, as on several other pages. See also *Ring! Bang! Boom!*, about the sounds children hear and make.

 I CAN COUNT
By Denise Lewis Patrick. Illustrator: Fred Wilingham. Publisher: Golden Books, 1997. Larger board, $4.50. Theme: Counting objects

This book depicts a sweet little brown boy standing in front of his refrigerator playing with number magnets. He is learning how to count using various toys. The illustrator creatively chose things like play-saxophones and trumpets for "Six horns to toot," and for "Ten animals to parade," we see giraffes, elephants, kangaroos, rhinos and tigers, all animals found in Africa; he even has "two maracas to shake." See also *Baby's Colors* (girl), *See What I Can Do!* (girl), *No Diapers for Baby!* and *Peekaboo, Baby!*

I CAN! GOD HELPS ME FROM A TO Z
By Debby Anderson. Publisher: Chariot Books, 1995.
Board, $10.99. Theme: Confidence in God

This book's most important value is the fact that it teaches children about God as an active force in their little lives. They can have confidence that God loves and cares for them as they grow. God helps them **B**uild, **O**bey and **S**hare, but He also knows their **F**eelings, good and bad, and is always available to **P**ray to—"even at the zoo." This unique board book can be used with both toddlers and preschoolers because it teaches the alphabet and also features verbs that begin with each letter. Sensitive illustrations of black children and parents are featured on almost every page, including the cover. You can help your children see God in their everyday lives by expanding and personalizing the statements on each page of the book.

I SMELL HONEY
By Andrea and Brian Pinkney. Publisher: Red Wagon
Books (Harcourt Brace Jovanovich), 1997. Board, $4.95
US/$6.95 CAN. Theme: Learning kitchen routines

This was one of my favorites. Most toddlers love to help out in the kitchen (too bad it doesn't last!). This book shows a small girl and her mom making a delicious down-home dinner together. The girl hands the utensils to Mom while she whips up a feast of sweet potato pie and fried catfish, and stirs a big ol' pot of red beans. She also gets to "feel wet leaves of collard greens" as she helps her mother wash the vegetables. See also *Shake Shake Shake.*

JAHA AND JAMIL WENT DOWN THE HILL, AN AFRICAN MOTHER GOOSE
**By Virginia Kroll. Illustrator: Katherine Roundtree.
Publisher: Charlesbridge Publishing, 1995.
HC$14.95/PB$6.95. Theme: African-inspired rhymes**

Forget Peter Peter Pumpkin Eater. This is an absolutely wonderful set of nursery rhymes for young children that follows the rhyme scheme of Mother Goose's famous poems, but instead of Jack and Jill it is Jaha and Jamil from Tanzania who go down the hill. Each page features themes about nature and the way of life in a different African country. From Rwandan culture, there is "Where, Oh Where?", a poem about a lost colobus bird. The illustrations are gorgeous, with deep, rich colors that correspond with the poems beautifully. From Botswana there is, "Taleh, Taleh . . . needed water/for her thirsty little daughter/Put it in an strich shell/And there she kept it very well," and from Malawi: "Little child, little child, Where are you from? Far off in Africa, under the sun. Little child, little child, What do you eat? Cassava and fishes, oh what a treat!" This offers a good opportunity to introduce the African foods and lifestyles depicted in the rhymes.

MAX
**Written and illustrated by Ken Wilson-Max. Publisher:
Hyperion Books for Children. Large board, pop-up,
$12.95 US/$17.95 CAN. Theme: Rooms in a house**

Young ones will love Max, especially since they can interact with him by pulling tabs and opening flaps throughout this sturdy book. Max lives in a bright orange house with his elephant and his pig. A child discovers them when they open the pop-out windows and doors, and take a tour of Max's house. Children can help him wiggle his Jell-O (Max and his friends' favorite food), play ball and shut the shade when it's time for bed. The last page, "Good night" features a unique interactive wheel that reveals a star shooting past the moon as you turn it.

MY AUNT CAME BACK
Written and illustrated by Pat Cummings. Publisher:
HarperCollins, 1998. Board book, $5.95. Theme:
Souvenirs from travels

   This delightfully colorful rhyming book centers around a little girl and her traveling aunt. Everywhere Auntie goes she brings back a souvenir for her niece. The souvenirs rhyme with the place they're from. By the end of this lively book, Auntie's off to Katmandu, "but this time she's taking me too!" Great for toddlers learning to talk; they'll love the singsongy, three-syllable words that rhyme. Ask the child to point out which colors he sees. Say the foreign words for good-bye provided at the end and wave bye-bye as you say them.

MY DADDY AND I
By Eloise Greenfield. Illustrator: Jan Spivey Gilchrist.
Black Butterfly (Writers and Readers Publishers), 1991.
Board, $5.95. Theme: Father/son relationship

   A black dad and his young son adorn the cover of this book. Inside, the boy tells about all the things he does with Dad, including household chores. They paint the kitchen, do wash, shop and dust. (Make sure you or your husband are willing to live up to this image once you present it!) The boy does the little parts, like turn the page when they read together and carries the basketball when they go to the park, and Dad does the real work. At the end of their exhausting day, they give each other a big hug.

ONE FALL DAY
Written and illustrated by Molly Bang. Publisher:
Greenwillow Books (William Morrow), 1994.
HC$15.00. Theme: The sweetness of childhood

Bang uses real photographs of dolls, toys, props and paintings
to tell the charming story of one child's day. A mother's words
put her child to bed, describing from dawn to dusk the happy
play the child will have the next day. (When you wake, your
friends wake with you.) The child's friends are a collection of her
favorite toys. Bang uses tiny everyday things to fashion the child's
toy playmates, like bottle caps for the toy car wheels, and so on.
Together, the child and the toys have breakfast, go outside to
play under the yellow leaves, and listen to the sounds of passing
trucks, trains, the whispering marsh reeds, the crashing waves, and
the rumble of thunder. In the afternoon the child and her toy
companions paint pictures. Later, the child prepares for bed and
the promise of another great day. Oh, if only adulthood were this
sweet! You could introduce a project in which you and your child
create a scene from a favorite part of your child's day using scraps
of fabric, small toys, Play-Doh, toothpicks, sand—any household
items you can spare—just as Bang did in her pictures.

PRETTY BROWN FACE
By Andrea and Brian Pinkney. Publisher: Red Wagon
Books (Harcourt Brace Jovanovich), 1997. Board, $4.95
US/$6.95 CAN. Theme: Positive self-image

Brian Pinkney's now-famous scratchboard illustrations jump
off the pages of this colorful—and powerful—little book depict-
ing tender moments shared by a boy toddler and his dad. The
beautiful cover shows a dad holding his baby son, each touching
the other's face, marveling. Dad shows the boy his image in the
hall mirror and points out his son's curly, soft hair, wide eyes,
proud nose and strong chin, much to his delight. At the end, the
baby uses his "lips to kiss" the reflection he's discovered in the

mirror. This book offers a great way to introduce the unique beauty of a black child.

THE SNOWY DAY
By Ezra Jack Keats. Publisher: Viking (Penguin Putnam), 1996. Thick board (also available in a larger-sized paperback version), $6.99 US/$8.99 CAN. Theme: Discovering snow. Classic, Audio

This simple story about a small boy's first experience with snow has been a favorite of millions since it was first printed in 1962. Little Peter, in his bright red hooded suit, can't wait to try out this thing called snow. He gazes at it from his bedroom window with amazement. Once outside, he looks back at his footprints and sees that he can make different shapes in the snow if he changes the way he walks. He's too small to be in a big boys' snowball fight, but just the right size to make a snowman and snow angels. Once back home, he wonders where that snowball he saved in his pocket went. He is sad about its disappearance, but is comforted when he realizes there will be new snow again tomorrow.

TEN, NINE, EIGHT
By Molly Bang. Publisher: Tupelo Books (William Morrow), 1996. Board, $6.95. Theme: Learning to count

On the opening pages of this learn-to-count book is a nice two-part illustration of a dad holding out his arms beckoning his little daughter to sit with him. It focuses on familiar items in a child's bedroom to teach counting: six seashells in the mobile over her crib, this many shoes and so on, then four sleepy eyes (Dad's and hers) and three kisses good night.

WHISTLE FOR WILLIE
By Ezra Jack Keats. Publisher: Puffin (Penguin Putnam), 1987. PB$4.50 US/$5.99 CAN. Theme: Learning to whistle. Classic

Another well-liked book for young preschoolers, this one is about a boy who wants to learn how to whistle for his dog, Willie, but can't. He tries everything: spinning around, sitting in a crate, drawing on the sidewalk, even wearing his father's hat, but when he puffs up his cheeks and blows, nothing comes out. Finally, he hides under a carton so Willie can't see him, blows as hard as he can, and the whistle comes out! He then whistles for Mom, Dad and for everyone to hear.

3

Great Books for Children Four to Eight

Children who are learning to read

Books children age four to eight like have:

- Lots of illustrations or pictures
- An element of fantasy
- More involved story lines than books for very young children
- Endings where good triumphs over evil

Most of these books are excellent stories to read aloud to a preschool child or with a first or second grader (even if they struggle along). If you are reading aloud, here are some tips that will help make this time together more fulfilling.

- Pick a regular reading time and a "reading corner" to give structure and importance to storytime.

- Choose books with dynamic, eye-catching illustrations; pick ones to show your child as you read.
- Choose stories with twists and turns; this keeps children thinking.
- Fool around with the language in the story: change your voice, roll your tongue, and feel free to skip over words or simplify concepts that may be too difficult for your child.
- Use household items as props to dramatize the story. Put the props in a special "story box" beforehand, not to be opened until storytime. The box could include something small a child can keep afterward as a reminder of the story's theme.
- Ask them questions about the book, but don't lead them too much. Encourage them—and allow them—to give you their honest answers, not just the ones they know you want to hear.
- When reading poems, simply ask children what they liked about it; there's no need for deep analysis until they are junior high school age.

In many libraries and bookstores, picture books, especially paperbacks, are thrown together on shelves in no particular order, often without their bindings showing. It's a job to sit and sift through that many books to find one that features a black child—but it is worth the effort. If you know book titles, ask a bookstore salesperson to look the book up for you on the computer, if they have one. They can tell you if they have copies in stock, where in the store it should be, and how it is shelved (i.e by author's last name, by title, etc.). This can save you about a half-hour of vain searching. If they do not stock the book you are looking for, they should offer to order it for you. If they don't, ask them to. Most bookstores can order books at a customer's request, and libraries can special-order from other branches.

ABBY
By Jeannette Caines. Illustrator: Steven Kellogg.
Publisher: Harper & Row, 1984. HC$4.95. MVP: Being
adopted, Being loved. Classic

Little Abby was adopted when she was almost a year old. Her family loves her very much and she enjoys looking at her baby book over and over again. She likes hearing what she wore the day her parents picked her up and what her first word was. Underlying her curiosity is the sense that she needs this constant confirmation of her existence for security, to make sure she's wanted. When her older brother says he doesn't like girls, Abby immediately says she's a boy and begins to cry. She wants and needs her older brother's love and acceptance, maybe more than a non-adopted child would. After Mom explains this to Kevin, he shows Abby how much he loves her by spending time with her and arranging to take her to school for show and tell. "I'm gonna say how we get to keep you forever and ever."

Explore These: Why did Abby like looking in her baby book so much? What did her brother do to hurt her feelings? Is it important to know where we were born, what we had on and how our parents felt about our arrival? Does your child have a baby book? If so, look through it with him and let him ask you questions like Abby did. If not, encourage him to ask the questions anyway and start one now. You can use a blank notebook, decorate it and pattern it after a baby keepsake book.

ABIYOYO
By Pete Seeger. Illustrator: Michael Hays. Publisher:
Macmillan, 1986. HC$16.00/PB$5.99. MVP:
Appreciating unique gifts. Read Aloud, Reading
Rainbow, Audio

The humorous illustrations and fanciful text of this fairy tale story will keep this book a children's favorite. No one in the town likes the little boy to play his noisy ukulele, nor do they like his father, who causes a commotion by making things disappear with his magic wand. So the two are sent to live on the edge of town where they won't bother anyone. But one day, as "the sun rose blood red over the hill," the ferocious monster Abiyoyo comes to terrorize the town. Seeger's vivid description of Abiyoyo will thrill small children and make them laugh: "He had slobbery teeth 'cause he didn't brush 'em, stinking feet 'cause he didn't wash 'em, matted hair 'cause he didn't comb it." Everyone cowers before Abiyoyo, except the small boy and his father. The father knows that if he could only make Abiyoyo lie down he could make him disappear. At this point, the little boy runs before Abiyoyo, playing his ukulele and singing with all his might, "A-BI-YO-YO!" The monster is so amused by the song that he begins to dance faster and faster to the music—so fast that he finally falls down. The father rids the town of the creature, and the two become heroes.

Explore These: How did the boy and his father outwit Abiyoyo? Explain that this story is taken from a folktale (a story that is timeless and placeless, and is passed on from generation to generation among a group of people). Folktales are told orally and thus are sometimes changed as they are told. Ask your child to make up a different ending to Abiyoyo, and let her retell it to you.

"As a student, I leaned heavily on the dream of being an artist because that was something I could do. I was the class artist so I could always do an art project for extra credit. I graduated from elementary school with honors!"

        —**Jerry Pinkney,** award-winning children's book illustrator

---

 THE AFRICAN DRAWING BOOK
Publisher: Heritage Collection, 1995. PB$2.95. Theme: Animals, Learning to draw

   This skinny little workbook teaches the mechanics of professional drawing using the animals of Africa. Characteristics of each animal are explained and a gridded page is provided to draw each animal on. Six sketching steps teach the use of circles, triangles, and rectangles as the basis of a drawing, then fleshing it out with lines and erasing sketch marks. A nice workbook to teach a child to draw proportionately or to encourage children with artistic talent.

Explore These: Once your child has drawn all the animals in the book correctly, purchase a gridded notebook and encourage her to use the sketching guidelines to draw other animals or people. They can use pictures of objects they want to draw to guide them.

ALWAYS MY DAD
By Sharon Dennis Wyeth. Illustrator: Raul Colon.
Publisher: Alfred A. Knopf, 1995. HC$17.00 US/$21.50
CAN. MVP: The importance of a dad, Coping with loss.
Reading Rainbow

In this thoughtful and courageous book, we feel the joy and pain of a young girl and her three brothers who miss their mostly absent dad. When the children visit their paternal grandparents' farm, Daddy makes a long-awaited trip home. When he arrives, everything livens up instantly—the children are allowed to run barefoot, chase fireflies, ride a horse and eat hot peppers. Even toothbrush time is made exciting—brushing at the outdoor water pump instead of in the bathroom because "Daddy said it was more fun." Still, when Daddy says he has to go, the children's pain is evident. He takes the time to assure his daughter that she will always be loved and that he will always be her dad. We never see Daddy's face in this story—he represents every father who, for one reason or another, can't be a full-time dad to his children. The book ends soberly with one of Colon's beautiful fall-colored etchings of the daughter looking wistfully down the road, hoping Daddy will return again soon.

Explore These: Why were the children so sad when their dad left? What were some reasons why the dad in this story couldn't live with his family? Ask your child: What do you think about that? What are some ways you can still have a good relationship with a dad or mom if you don't see them every day? What can you do when you feel sad because you miss a mom or dad?

 AMAZING GRACE
By Mary Hoffman. Illustrator: Caroline Binch.
Publisher: Dial Books (Penguin Putnam), 1995.
HC$16.95. MVP: Believe in yourself

Grace loves to hear stories, but more than that, she loves to become the characters in the stories she hears. In the middle of a story Grace is liable to jump up and act out the most exciting parts. She uses whatever is handy—dolls, empty boxes, old clothes and even her cat—to help her reenactments. One day she is Aladdin, the next Joan of Arc. If someone at home feels a little under the weather, Grace dresses as the family doctor, checking heartbeats with her wooden-spoon stethoscope. Pretending to be anything she wants to be is easy at home, but when Grace wants to be Peter in the school play, *Peter Pan,* her classmates mock her. "You can't—he's a boy," says one. "You can't, he's not black!" says another. Grace is stumped and hurt. Is what they say true? Her Ma says no, but Grace isn't totally convinced. When her smart-thinking Nana takes her to see *Romeo and Juliet*—featuring a beautiful black Juliet—Grace makes up her mind: she can and *will* be anything she wants.

Explore These: How did Grace act out the stories she heard? Encourage a child to play dress-up and act out one of her favorite stories using household items and clothes as props. Ask your child: Do you think that there are things you can't do or can't be because of your race or sex? What can you learn from this book about believing in yourself? Discuss and affirm. Outing: Take a child to a play where women or African Americans are playing "nontraditional" roles. Reinforce.

Black Writers' Notebook: Author **Angela Shelf Medearis** based her book *Annie's Gifts* on her own childhood. She is the author of several children's books, including *Dancing With the Indians,* page 122.

ANNIE'S GIFTS
By Angela Shelf Medearis. Illustrator: Anna Rich.
Publisher: Just Us Books, 1997. PB$6.95. MVP: Finding
your talents

When a child sees that she is talented, it boosts her self-esteem and self-confidence. In this book, a child tells the story of discovering her own special gift. Annie watches her brother and sister shine with musical talent—one plays the trumpet, one sings and plays piano and even her parents love to dance and sway to their favorite jazz tunes. But when she tries to do anything musical, it bombs. In Anna Rich's large, colorful, humorous illustrations, charging elephants, clucking chickens and croaking frogs appear from nowhere (you can imagine them yelling "Stop that noise!") whenever Annie tries out her musical wings. In one scene, an imaginary diesel truck careens right into the middle of the living room while she's playing the piano! After many moments of despair, Annie finally rediscovers her talent for writing and drawing, with the encouragement of her parents.

Explore These: After reading, discuss your child's talents with him. Is he a poet or an artist like Annie? Talk about the importance of knowing your talents and come up with simple ways to help nurture them.

ASHLEY BRYAN'S ABC'S OF AFRICAN AMERICAN POETRY
By Ashley Bryan. Publisher: Atheneum, 1997.
HC$16.00. MVP: African-American poetry

This is not an alphabet book, as you might think. Rather, Ashley Bryan uses each letter of the alphabet to offer excerpts from twenty-five poems and one spiritual. Excerpts offer a sampling of the greats: Langston Hughes, Countee Cullen, Rita Dove, Paul Lawrence Dunbar, Gwendolyn Brooks, and others, in a setting of bold, vibrant artwork created with tempera paints and gouache (a method of painting with opaque watercolors). Poems range from the dramatic to the whimsical to the intense—something for everyone here.

AT THE CROSSROADS
Written and illustrated by Rachel Isadora. Publisher:
Greenwillow Books (William Morrow), 1991.
HC$13.95/PB$4.95. MVP: Delayed gratification. Video

What's more difficult for a child than waiting for something he wants? Especially when that something is their father. This story, set in a South African township, paints a stirring picture of family loyalty and love. Everyone in the township is rejoicing because the men are coming home today, after working for many months in the faraway mines. The women cook and bathe the children (no small thing when water is scarce), and try out their home-made instruments to make music for the homecoming celebration. Even at school, the hymns that are sung speak of the fathers' return. But as the sun sets on the dimming festivities, there are no men in sight. Many turn back for home, but one group of children refuses to leave. They will not go home without their fathers. The illustration of the children, mostly boys, with their dejected expressions against the deep blue night sky, is heart-wrenching. Their mother comes with food for them and urges them to come home—but "she knows we will not." Finally, at dawn they hear a rooster crow, and the rumble of a truck.

"Wake up, our fathers are here! Our fathers are here!" Jubilant, they run into the arms of their tired but happy fathers.

Explore These: Why were the children waiting for their fathers? Ask your child to: Describe a time when he waited a long time for someone or for something he really wanted. How did it feel waiting? How did he feel when it finally came?

 AUNT FLOSSIE'S HATS (AND CRAB CAKES LATER)
By Elizabeth Fitzgerald Howard. Illustrator: James
Ransome. Publisher: Clarion, 1991. HC$14.95. MVP:
Learning from elders

Susan and Sarah can't wait for their visits to their great-great-aunt Flossie, who always has a new story to tell about the days of long ago. She serves them tea and cookies and lets them rummage through her memorabilia. Aunt Flossie has the best collection of storytelling hats there is! Every one the girls try on, from the furry red cap to the dark blue fedora, has a tale behind it. One green hat still smells of smoke from a fire in the neighborhood where Aunt Flossie lived. Everything for miles around caught the smoke smell, she remembers wistfully. But the best story of all is the one Susan and Sara know best, because they're in it. One afternoon Aunt Flossie was wearing her very best, most favorite yellow church hat when a gust of wind took it off her head and dropped it into a stream. Their mom and dad both tried in vain to grab it. But along came a big brown dog named Gretchen who saves the day—and rescues Aunt Flossie's most favorite yellow church hat.

Explore These: Why did the girls like going over to their aunt Flossie's house so much? Is there a relative or family friend that likes to tell stories about the old days? Arrange for your child to spend some time with them. Show your child something from your past and tell the story behind it. Start a memory box with your child so they can have a place to put away special things to share with others later, or look back at.

**AUNT HARRIET'S UNDERGROUND RAILROAD
IN THE SKY**
**Written and illustrated by Faith Ringgold. Publisher:
Crown, 1992. HC$15.00 US/$19.00 CAN. MVP: Using
your imagination**

Ringgold does a delightful job introducing very young readers
to the story of Harriet Tubman and the Underground Railroad,
using imagination, suspense, and a story that is easy to follow.
Once again the author introduces Cassie (see *Tar Beach* review)
and her younger brother Be Be, who has now grown out of babyhood. Cassie has taught Be Be to fly, and together they find a
train flying through the air—with Harriet Tubman herself as conductor. Be Be promptly jumps on and is whisked away, leaving
Cassie with "Aunt" Harriet who briefly explains slavery to her and
sends her on a ride on the Railroad herself, following Be Be's
trail. Cassie finds herself knocking on strange doors using coded
words, or hiding out in cemeteries wearing a disguise, the same
way our ancestors did on their way North. At the end of the book
the author provides a brief biography of Harriet Tubman and the
Underground Railroad, as well as a reading list.

Explore These: Why did people have to hide and use coded
language when they "rode" the Underground Railroad? Have
your child check out a book on Harriet Tubman from the library
(see *Minty* by Julius Lester). Ask your child: If you could fly, where
would you go? Who would you take with you? What would you do
when you got there?

BABY JESUS LIKE MY BROTHER
**By Margery Wheeler Brown. Illustrator: George Ford.
Publisher: Just Us Books, 1995. PB$7.95. MVP:
Keeping Christ in Christmas**

It's always gratifying for me to see faith brought to life in a contemporary setting. In this sweet book, a sister teaches her little
brother about the real meaning of Christmas as they take a trip

downtown. His sister uses everything they see—bright lights, decorations, gifts and giving—to remind him of the real story of Jesus's birth. He learns about Jesus and Mary as he thinks about his mother, at home cradling his new baby brother. He asks kid questions such as, "Why's Jesus in that funny little house?" when he sees a manger. And she provides sage answers. It's touching when she tells him that there was no room in the inn for the baby Jesus and his parents—she likens it to the time their family was evicted and couldn't find a place to stay.

Explore These: Use this book to expand on the biblical story of Jesus's birth found in the book of Matthew. Explain why his birth is considered so significant by many. Visit a manger at Christmas or attend a Nativity play and remind the child about the biblical story.

Black Illustrators' Notebook: Ashley Bryan has had a long and distinguished career as the illustrator of more than 30 books for children. His *Beat the Story-Drum, Pum, Pum* was awarded the 1981 Coretta Scott King Award for Illustration. He also illustrated the hilarious story *The Dancing Granny* (see "Oops" List) and *The Cat's Purr* (see page 43).

 BEAT THE STORY-DRUM, PUM-PUM
Written and illustrated by Ashley Bryan. Publisher:
Atheneum, 1980. HC$10.95. MVP: Learning
about life

Children are introduced to life's little challenges in these five humorous tales, most of which feature animals as the main protagonists. The use of cultural expressions like "Aie-yaie!" "pitti-pong, pitti-pong," "choops" (sucking your teeth) and other such colloquialisms adds flavor and fun to the text. In one story, Hen is concerned about protecting herself during a storm, while the carefree frog decides to wing it with no preparation, only to take advantage of Hen's good planning later when he almost drowns. True friendship is illustrated in another story by a young snake and another frog who meet and become best buddies, that is, until they realize that they are supposed to be enemies. Coached by their "parents," both of them begin plotting how to outsmart the other. And then there is Rabbit, who is so lazy he misses the day that God is handing out tails to all the animals. He sends his friend the fox to pick his tail up and of course gets the short end of the stick, so to speak. The stories are humorous and well told. They also introduce lots of verbs and adjectives that will help build a child's vocabulary: "jostled," "bounded," "drowsy," "tingling," "croaking" and "soaring."

Explore These: Ask your child to: Pick one or two of the animals and tell what their problem was. What could they have done differently to have things turn out better for them? Do any of the animals in the story remind him of people he knows? If yes, ask him to explain how.

 BEN'S TRUMPET
Written and illustrated by Rachel Isadora. Publisher:
Greenwillow Books (William Morrow), 1991.
HC$16.00/PB$5.95. MVP: Dream becoming reality.
Classic, Audio

There's nothing little Ben likes to do more than listen to the musicians at the neighborhood Zig Zag Jazz Club practice. As he blasts away on his own imaginary trumpet while sitting on the fire escape, he dreams of owning a real one someday and becoming a fine musician like the men he studies. His friends make fun of his invisible instrument, which makes Ben sad. One day, the trumpeter from the club walks down Ben's street while on his break. He invites a sad-looking Ben to the club with him. He is finally learning to play a real live trumpet! Ben gets his chance.

Explore These: Why was Ben playing an imaginary trumpet?

Was it smart of Ben to do that? Why? Ask your child: What would you do if your friends made fun of you the way they teased Ben?

BIGMAMA'S
Written and illustrated by Donald Crews. Publisher:
Greenwillow Books (William Morrow), 1991.
HC$16.00/PB$4.95. MVP: City children appreciating
country life. Read Aloud

Through the eyes of four children, Donald Crews offers endearing glimpses of the summers he spent in Florida with his grandparents. He depicts everything from the exciting train ride from the city, to searching for worms to go fishing with, to drinking well water and talking so much around the table that there was hardly enough time to eat. Large, vivid illustrations will show children who don't leave the city much what life on a farm looks like. Others who are used to their annual summer trek "down South" or who live in a rural setting can read the story and talk about what's different or the same as what they know.

Explore These: What are some of the things the children did when they arrived at Bigmama's? Ask your child: Did you learn anything new about what happens on a farm? If you live on a farm or visit one frequently, ask your child to tell you about some other things that go on there that weren't mentioned in the story. If your child has ever taken an overnight train trip, ask him to describe the things he noticed, liked or disliked about it.

BITTER BANANAS
By Issac Olaleye. Illustrator: Ed Young. Publisher:
Boyds Mills Press, 1994. HC$14.95 US/$21.00 CAN/
PB$5.99 US. MVP: Problem-solving, Appreciating
African culture

Yusuf lives in a rain forest in Africa. His job in the family is to gather the sweet sap from the palm trees and sell it in the market, only the baboons like the sap as much as Yusuf and his family do. They sneak in and drink it all up before he can get there. Through trial and error, Yusuf finds a way to outsmart the baboons. The stunning illustrations of the lush rain forest and the use of different-colored text and typestyle variations bring this story to life.

Explore These: Where did Yusef live? What is a rain forest? What was Yusef's biggest problem? How many ways did he try to solve it? What were they? Ask your child: Did you ever have a problem at school that was hard to solve? What was it? What did you do about it?

 BLACK IS BROWN IS TAN
By Arnold Adoff. Illustrator: Emily Arnold McCully.
Publisher: HarperTrophy, 1992. PB$4.95 US/$6.75
CAN. MVP: Appreciating multiracialness. Classic, Read
Aloud

This powerful award-winning little story depicts a multiracial family just being a family—kissing good night, having relatives over, reading a book, taking a bath—but taking note of the different colors everyone and everything brings to the world. Mom is black—but not *black black*—she's really the color of chocolate milk. Dad is white, but he's not *white white* either, not like snow or milk—he's more like light brown—except when he's upset, then he gets red. "This is the way it is for us. This is the way we are." The easy rhyming words, "red" and "bed," "man" and "tan," "light" and "night," and child-friendly construction of the poems make this book entertaining and enlightening.

Explore These: What color is your skin? How would you describe it? Describe the skin colors of your mother, father, sisters, and brothers individually. Talk to your child about the beauty of each skin shade.

Black Writers' Notebook: Gwendolyn Brooks is the first black American to be awarded a Pulitzer Prize, for her second volume of poetry, *Annie Allen*. She was inducted into the Women's Hall of Fame in 1988 and given a Lifetime Achievement Award from the National Endowment for the Arts in 1989.

 BRONZEVILLE BOYS AND GIRLS
By Gwendolyn Brooks. Illustrator: Ronni Solbert.
Publisher: Harper & Row, 1956. $15.98, Library
edition. MVP: Growing up in the city. Classic

Pulitzer prize–winner Gwendolyn Brooks has a knack for writing poems that meet children right where they live. This timeless book of poems is set in "Bronzeville," or Any Black Town USA. Some express the happiness and carefreeness of being a child, like pretending to be a knight in a street-corner duel, trying to watch a flower grow, having a tea party with a girlfriend, or sneaking a listen to grownups' conversation. Others express dissatisfaction or fear: wanting to live on a big farm instead of in a small apartment, being sad about the Christmas gifts you never got, or the scolding you did get, or admitting your fear of lightning. And still others simply express wonder: wondering who you really are, wondering if you're pretty, wondering if you'll make new friends, or just wondering.

 BROWN ANGELS
By Walter Dean Myers. Photographs. Publisher:
HarperCollins, 1993. HC$16.00. MVP: Appreciating
family history

At first, you wonder if this delightful book is too precious for young children, who might not appreciate and cherish it the way an adult 'would. However, there are such wonderful old photographs of black children in this "album book" that they beg to be shared with this generation. Most memorable is a photo of a small boy in his best Sunday suit, clutching his rooster. Myers adds a poem for each set of photos. One poem children will love is called "Jeannie Had a Giggle." All told, each one is a celebration of our children—"dark and precious with sweet wondrous lives to live."

Explore These: Read this book to your child lovingly. These poems are great for wind-down time just before bed. Compare how children dressed in the old days to how they dress today. Give your child a disposable camera and tell her to take portraits of other children. Eventually, you can help her put together a photo album or portfolio of her best work.

CAROUSEL
Written and illustrated by Pat Cummings. Publisher: Bradbury Press (Macmillan), 1994. HC$14.95 US/$19.50 CAN. MVP: Handling disappointment

Alex's mother, aunts and father have gone to a lot of trouble and expense to make her birthday special. There's a frilly party dress, colorful balloons and party hats, lots of food, cake and presents—but Alex isn't impressed. Her dad is not home from his business trip yet. Dad leaves Alex a beautiful carousel as a gift, in case he doesn't make it home in time, but Alex tosses it in the corner. She knows she's being rude but she can't help it—where is her father?! As she drifts off into a deep sleep, Alex dreams about the carousel animals coming to life. She goes after them, riding on the very zebra that broke off when she threw the carousel down (she tells him she's sorry). Alex has a wonderful time with the animals and forgets her troubles for a while. When she wakes up, guess whose smile is there to greet her—Daddy's! The book depicts Alex's father explaining why he was late and how angry he felt when his plane was delayed. The fact that he cared enough to share his own hurt feelings reassures her that he was happy to be home.

Explore These: Why was Alex so angry? Could she have had a nice birthday anyway, without her dad? Why or why not? Ask your child to: Describe a time when he was disappointed recently. How did he react? What made him feel better?

THE CAT'S PURR
Written and illustrated by Ashley Bryan. Publisher: Atheneum, 1985. HC$14.00. Theme: The result of jealousy. Classic

What do you do when your friend has something that you want but can't have? Cat and Rat, the protagonists in this book, deal with the issue of jealousy in a way children will grasp in this charming West Indian tale. The hand-sized format and simple illustrations make it easy to read to or with a child. Cat's uncle gives him a special miniature drum as a gift, but he is cautioned not to let anyone else play it. His friend Rat sees the drum and immediately covets it. Rat cannot understand why he too can't play the drum, but Cat is firm about enforcing his uncle's warning. Still, the churning desire to have what is forbidden gets the best of Rat—he decides to feign sickness so he can stay home and play the drum when Cat is at work. One day, Cat hides near the house and catches Rat with drum in hand. Rat runs away but is cornered by Cat and his large fangs. Thinking quickly, Rat throws the drum into Cat's waiting jaws. Cat swallows the drum instead of the rat and Rat runs for his life. As the story goes, this is the reason why cats make that deep purring noise—and it's also why cats hate rats to this day.

Explore These: Why did Rat pretend to be sick? Have you ever really wanted something someone else had? What did you do about it?

THE CHALK DOLL
By Charlotte Pomerantz. Illustrator: Frané Lessac.
Publisher: J.B. Lippincott, 1989. HC$12.95. MVP:
Making do with less

There's nothing like one of mom or dad's hard-time-growing-up stories to make a child appreciate what they have. They may even realize that the little their parents had was actually more. Rosy is home in bed with a cold, being cared for by her mother. She wants her old teddy bear for comfort and also wants to hear stories of her mother's childhood in Jamaica, West Indies. Mom didn't have a closet full of frilly dresses, big birthday parties or even a store-bought "chalk" doll when she was growing up, but her endearing stories of how she enjoyed the little she had are a good lesson for Rosy—and for all children. Along the way we see colorful portraits of a rich but simple childhood on a tropical island—going to school barefoot, drinking tea mixed with sweet condensed milk for breakfast and making high heels out of mango seeds. When her mom tells her about how she made her own rag doll as a girl, Rosy decides to make one, too.

Explore These: Why did Rosy end up wanting a rag doll when she already had lots of "chalk" dolls? Ask your child: How much do you think you could buy with three pennies today? Explain how expensive new toys are and think of some toys, games and snacks that can be made at home inexpensively; have fun making a few with your child. You can make a rag doll by following the instructions in the book.

CHERRIES AND CHERRY PITS
Written and illustrated by Vera B. Williams. Publisher:
Greenwillow Books (William Morrow), 1986.
HC$11.75. MVP: Using your imagination, Creativity

Young Bidemmi is a creative girl who loves to draw with her colored markers. A thoughtful artist, she tells the story of what she is drawing as she creates. She is careful to include all the little details in her drawings, like the man's striped shirt and the fat wrinkle he has across his forehead (her mother says those come from worrying); another of her stories has a character with "long, long legs and purple and white running shoes." She draws four stories, three about other people and the last one about herself. The theme of each of the stories is that someone brings home a bag of delicious red cherries for someone else to enjoy. Her wonderful magic marker drawings will serve as an inspiration to any child who loves to color. She gives each drawing a pretty border of triangles, stars, circles or diamonds. In Bidemmi's own story, she eats all her cherries but saves the pits. She plants the pits, and they grow into trees that produce—of course—more cherries. Soon there is a whole forest of cherry trees right on her New York City block. I particularly like the illustration of Bidemmi drawing at her makeshift easel, with her pictures tacked up on the wall behind her.

Explore These: What is the main focus of Bidemmi's stories? What do you notice about her drawings? Encourage a child to think creatively by having him think up a story theme, like the cherries, and build characters and a storyline around that theme. Have him draw the story, using one piece of paper for each "scene." Remind him to include little details and decorative touches in his drawings.

"A story can have impact on your music. It can give you ideas for music or help you organize your music . . . But the book I still dig the most, in terms of high literature, is the Bible."
    —**Wynton Marsalis,** recipient of the first
        Pulitzer Prize for music awarded to a jazz artist

CHILDREN OF COLOR STORYBOOK BIBLE
Contemporary English Version. Publisher: Children of
Color, Thomas Nelson, 1997. Suggested price:
HC$15.00. MVP: Biblical wisdom

Our children must understand that brown-skinned people also played key roles in biblical history, especially as both Christianity and the Bible have been grossly misused to condone racial superiority. This beautiful child's book of Bible stories is one of the first that features ethnically sensitive, full-color illustrations of scenes from both the Old and New Testaments, and is written in the Contemporary English Version, which simplifies biblical language for easier comprehension. Helpful transitional paragraphs are set in slightly lighter type to distinguish them as commentary. The 61 well-known stories, some humorously depicted, also offer scripture references for further examination. Five smiling brown children appear on the cover and each page has a kenté cloth border—a beautiful gift. See also *Holy Bible, Illustrated Especially for Children of Color* (World Publishing), the complete Bible with no commentary, available in King James and New International versions. Song lyrics included.

Explore These: Explain to your child that the stories in the Bible are part of our heritage too, occurring way before civil rights and slavery. Explain that these stories took place in North Africa, the continent where our people originated. Read the stories with your child often and use them as the basis for instilling moral values.

 CHINYE, A WEST AFRICAN FOLK TALE
By Obi Onyefulu. Illustrator: Evie Safarewicz.
Publisher: Puffin (Penguin Putnam), 1996. PB$5.99.
MVP: Obedience

This is a West African Cinderella story, minus the prince. Chinye must cook, clean and fetch everything for her mean stepmother, Nkechi, and stepsister, Adanma, while they loaf about. But when they send her into the foreboding woods at night for water, they can never imagine the grief they will bring on themselves. Chinye encounters magical characters in the woods: a talking antelope and hyena, and a wise old woman who directs her to a hut full of beautiful gourds of every size and shape, one of which will bring her treasures beyond her wildest dreams. When her evil guardians get wind of this, they rush off to the woods to get a gourd for themselves. But Adanma's greed overwhelms any good sense and she chooses the wrong one, against the advice of the woman in the forest. That gourd proves to be more like a vacuum than a treasure chest—Nkechi and Adanma look on with horror as all of their worldly goods are magically swooped out of the window and are gone forever. They leave the town in shame. Chinye lives happily ever after, sharing her newfound wealth with the rest of the village.

Explore These: What did the old woman tell Chinye to do? Ask your child to: Describe a time that you went ahead and did the opposite of what you were told to do. Why do you think adults tell children what is right to do? Discuss.

CLIMBING JACOB'S LADDER, HEROES OF THE BIBLE IN AFRICAN-AMERICAN SPIRITUALS
Selected and edited by John Langstaff. Illustrator: Ashley Bryan. Publisher: Margaret K. McElderry Books (Macmillan), 1991. HC$13.95. MVP: Learning about biblical heroes through song

This book of African-American spirituals comes complete with ethnically sensitive paintings of biblical heroes, a synopsis of each person's accomplishment and the music for piano and guitar. Spirituals include favorites like "Rock-a My Soul," "Go Down, Moses," and "Didn't My Lord Deliver Daniel," which sing-tell the stories of Abraham, Moses, and Daniel, respectively. Beneath the meaningful words lies the continual hope of freedom and deliverance for our people. It can be used by families and groups of all faiths to introduce the Bible to children in a fun way. The only thing missing is the heroines of the Bible, such as Ruth and Queen Esther but which can be incorporated by a parent or teacher. See also, *All Night, All Day: A Child's First Book of African American Spirituals* by Ashley Bryan..

Explore These: Ask your child: Which is your favorite story-song? Tell why. Which hero do you think you'd like to imitate? Help your child look in the Bible for more about his favorite hero and his or her life story. Extract the qualities that hero possessed and encourage him to develop them in his own character.

COLORS COME FROM GOD . . . JUST LIKE ME!
By Carolyn A. Forché. Illustrator: Charles Cox.
Publisher: Abington Press, 1995. HC$11.99. MVP:
Self-worth

It will be comforting for any black child to have the constant reinforcement that God made them just the way they are, "beautiful brown," as this book declares on almost every page. The child in this book is examining all the things of beauty that God made—the birds, the sun, goldfish, fruit—and she ends with how He made us all in a rainbow of colors. Positive references to our skin color and cultural heritage appear in each rhyme and, besides the young black girl who is the narrator, all of the other children are tan or brown-skinned. We learn that God watered the Garden of Eden with the four African rivers (the Bible reference for this is noted on the page). Cleverly, we read that God painted the fruit we eat an array of marvelous colors, but "made berries sweetest when they are dark and mellow." At the end of her day of discovery, the child prays that those who "misbehave and say hurtful things" will see their shame in light of God's love for us all. Overall, this book offers sound, fundamental tools to help a child build their sense of self-worth, and which can be used to refute negative comments from others about their race.

Explore These: Explain to the child that the Bible backs up what this book proclaims; use a child's Bible to explore some of the scripture references together. Talk about how much God loves us and how He created us each uniquely. Tell the child what's special about him or her.

COME SUNDAY
By Nikki Grimes. Illustrator: Michael Bryant.
Publisher: W.B. Eerdmans, 1996. HC$10.00. MVP:
Honesty, Faith

Nikki Grimes's simple prose finds a home in this down-to-earth book about a young girl discovering her faith in God. LaTasha has accompanied her parents to the big brick church every Sunday since she was a tot, mostly "itchin to go the other way . . . to escape the blue-haired ladies aching to pinch my cheek every week." When she decides on her own to get baptized ("Mommy let me make the choice"), LaTasha experiences a "joy, joy, joy" she's never known before. Now she can sing and clap to "Rock-a-My-Soul" along with all the blue-haired ladies she used to run away from. Bryant's bright, full-page, watercolor illustrations of traditional black church scenes (most notably, "The Hats") will delight most young children—and parents. A great way to teach a child about church and about personal faith.

Explore These: What are some of the things LaTasha does at church? If you attend church as a family, ask the child to recall all the things he does to get ready. What does he enjoy most about church or Sunday school? Least? If the child doesn't go to church, ask him if he would like to visit one.

CORNROWS
By Camille Yarbrough. Illustrator: Carole Byard.
Publisher: Sandcastle (Penguin Putnam), 1997.
PB$5.99. MVP: Loving our hair. Classic, Coretta Scott
King Award

One ritual that's universally reflective of black home life is sitting between your mother's knees getting your hair combed. In this classic book, two generations of black women pass history down to the next generation through song and storytelling. Mama and Great-Grammaw's braided hairstyles have a history—the cornrows were patterned after the aisles of corn that slaves worked in the fields, and before that, originated in the Motherland. What begins as a hair-fixing session grows into the older women telling the youngsters about "how it was." They talk about the courage, honor, wisdom, love and strength of our African ancestors, of their creativity as sculptors and dancers, and of their unique braided hair. You could tell a princess from a bride, and one clan from another, just by the pattern in which they wore their hair. Though slavers tried to strip this heritage from us, ". . . the spirit of the symbol [of cornrows] is not changed by time, place, class or fame, and not even by hate or shame." The book ends with a celebration of black hair and black heroes.

Explore These: What were cornrows patterned after? In Africa, what was significant about the style in which you braided your hair? Ask your child: Do you know how to braid? Help a child learn on her own hair or on yours. You can also use three pieces of rope or ribbon knotted at the top to practice.

Black Illustrators' Notebook: Illustrator **James Ransome** won a Coretta Scott King award for his illustration of *The Creation*. His work appears in more than a dozen books for children.

THE CREATION
By James Weldon Johnson. Illustrator: James Ransome.
Publisher: Holiday House, 1994. HC$15.95. MVP: How
God made the world. Read Aloud, Coretta Scott King
Award

   Renowned poet James Weldon Johnson wrote this poetic sermon way back in 1919—but it is still a wonderful tool for teaching children today. Illustrator James Ransome placed the poem
in the setting of a Southern elder telling the story of the Creation
to children while they sit under a big ol' country oak tree. His
colorful, expressive paintings bring out the passion of this amazing story, as evidenced by the riveted looks on the faces of the
children gathered 'round listening. The story builds in intensity
as the elder describes how God made the stars, moon, sun, flowers and animals of every type. It is wonderfully refreshing to
see a beautiful, brown-skinned Adam sitting in the Garden when
Johnson crescendoes to the description of God's most awesome creation—us—"shaped in His own Image." An excellent
book to give children a foundation for positive identity.
   Explore These: Gather a group of children around and read
this story to them just as the elder in the book does; outdoors is a
great setting. Point to clouds, flowers, trees, and insects as examples of how creative God is. Ask children to point out other
things of beauty in nature. Emphasize the care God put into making our beautiful world (multicolored flowers, fish, animals) and
making all of us in His own image, no matter what color we are.

**DADDY AND ME: A PHOTO STORY OF ARTHUR
ASHE AND HIS DAUGHTER CAMERA**
Photographs and text by Jeanne Moutoussamy-Ashe.
Publisher: Alfred A. Knopf, 1993. HC$13.00 US/
$16.00 CAN MVP: Father-daughter love, Coping with
serious illness

   It's hard to find books that appeal to children yet deal with difficult subjects such as sickness and death from a child's point of

view. This book accomplishes that task, but it mostly depicts the wonderful love between a father and a child. There are many hugs, kisses and evocative, loving looks between Camera and her dad, Arthur Ashe. To Camera, the symptoms of her father's advancing disease (AIDS) were "like when you have a stomach ache/you just don't feel very good." Beautiful, heart-wrenching photos of her taking her dad's temperature ("I make him wait for the thermometer to beep, just like he does for me"), feeding him his pills and holding up his breathing tube abound. And we see an ailing Arthur Ashe taking care of his daughter: washing and combing her hair, dressing her, reading to her, playing with her—and praying with her before bed. A wonderful book to "humanize" the AIDS virus for a child who is unfamiliar with it, and an excellent tool to show a child what father-daughter love should *really* look like.

Explore These: Ask a child, Who was Arthur Ashe? What are some of the things Camera did with her dad? What were some of the things Arthur had to do to treat his AIDS? Is anyone close to you really sick? How do you feel about it? Do you act differently around them because they're sick? If so, why?

DAVE AND THE TOOTH FAIRY
By Verna Allette Wilkings. Illustrator: Paul Hunt.
Publisher: Gareth Stevens, 1998. HC$18.95/PB$5.99.
MVP: Determination

David Alexander Curtis wants a new kite. How's he going to get it? Well, there's always the tooth fairy. Endearing, real-life illustrations (particularly his granddad's magnified false teeth in a glass) move young readers from page to page as David makes his dream happen. His creativity proves that when you want something bad enough, you'll fight for it. The book's secondary theme demonstrates that in life, sometimes change is necessary. Even Afiya, the beautiful black tooth fairy, gets burned out and makes a job change. You'll read this book again and again to your children as they anticipate each tooth fairy visit. Wilkings unwittingly instills the concept of saving toward an important goal.

Explore These: What is it that Dave really wanted? How did he get it? Ask your child to: Think of something she'd like to achieve. What are some creative ways she can work toward that goal?

Is poetry important? Yes! So much of the joy, pain and hope of our people are expressed in verse that it is essential that poetry be a part of a black child's literary diet. It will also be helpful for them to be familiar with the genre well before they begin studying it, usually in high school. Most children and teenagers enjoy poetry when it is read to them. The trick is not to analyze poems too much at first. Let them "feel it" themselves, in their own way. Read them a few times so children can take in the sounds. That's mostly what they'll enjoy well before they understand the deeper meanings behind the words. Ask them what they felt about the poem after you've read it a few times. With older children, you can point out the structure or parameters of a few of the poems and encourage them to try writing their own.

 THE DISTANT TALKING DRUM
Poems from Nigeria by Isaac Olaleye. Illustrator:
Frané Lessac. Publisher: Wordsong (Boyds Mills Press),
1995. HC$14.95 US/$21.00 CAN. MVP: Appreciating
African life

This colorful book of poems offers little glimpses into everyday life in a Nigerian farming village. Each poem focuses on an activity that children will find familiar yet different: doing laundry (by a stream), playing hide-and-seek (in the dark), watching the rain outside your classroom window (falling so hard you cannot go home), going food shopping with your mom (at an outdoor marketplace). The poems are manageable, each about three to four stanzas long and are accompanied by child-friendly paintings framed with eye-catching African-inspired borders.

Explore These: What are some things about the way the African children in these poems live that are different from the way you live? What's the same?

DOWN THE ROAD
By Alice Schertle. Illustrator: E. B. Lewis. Publisher:
Browndeer Press (Harcourt Brace), 1995. HC$16.00
US/$22.00 CAN. MVP: Handling responsibility,
Dealing with disappointment

Learning how to cope with minor disappointments in life is an important and inevitable lesson for young children. This sunny tale charmingly shows that good things can come from seemingly bad situations. Hetty lives on a country road outside of town, but she's never been allowed to walk down the dusty road by herself. One day, Mama gives Hetty an important job: to go into town and buy a dozen fresh eggs. Hetty is elated, and relishes her walk into town, singing, running, and practicing walking so carefully to bring those eggs home intact. When she reaches the store she greets Mr. Birdie, the store owner, just like Mama does, and roams the aisles as if she is considering other things to purchase. On the way home a tree filled with "sweet, juicy, crackly-crisp apples" catches Hetty's eye. As she stretches to reach for one, suddenly all her eggs spill out and are broken. Hetty is so disappointed she just wants to hide, and climbs the apple tree to sit and think. Her father comes after her and joins her in the tree branches. ("Everyone should spend some time in an apple tree, Papa agreed, good-naturedly"), and the family eats apple pie for breakfast instead of eggs the next morning. The watercolor illustrations by E. B. Lewis are cheery and delightful, perfectly capturing Hetty's expressions and drawing the reader into the bright, whitewashed jumble of the dry goods store and the sun-drenched warmth of the country road.
Explore These: What did Hetty do when her father asked what happened? Ask your child: What is the best way to deal with a mistake you've made? What did Hetty's parents do about her disappointment? Explain to the child the meaning behind the adage,

"When life gives you lemons, make lemonade" (or apple pie, in this case).

THE DREAM KEEPER
By Langston Hughes. Illustrator: Brian Pinkney.
Publisher: Alfred A. Knopf, 1994. PB$7.99 US/$10.50
CAN. MVP: The importance of dreams

Reach, dream, rise, soar, sing—this is what Langston beseeches us to do in this compilation of his poems illustrated by Brian Pinkney. There is something for every age in this book—some poems are as short as five lines, some as long as two pages. Pinkney, known for his swirling, scratchboard illustrations (he covers a white board with black ink and then uses a sharp, scratching tool), gives us one or two images on every page which keep the book moving nicely.

Black Writers' Notebook: Langston Hughes's mother was a teacher, his father a lawyer. Unfortunately, his father left the family shortly after Langston's birth, and he went on to live in many different cities during his childhood. Langston had been a waiter and a mess boy on a ship before he had his first book published at age twenty-four. He died in 1967 in his beloved Harlem and left behind an important exhortation for us today—"hold fast to dreams." (From "Dreams")

EAT UP, GEMMA
By Sarah Hayes. Illustrator: Jan Oremerod. Publisher:
Lothrop, Lee, & Shephard, 1988. HC$16.00/PB$4.95.
MVP: Learning what babies do

This is an adorable book about a baby named Gemma. Everyone wants her to "eat up," but she just wants to play. It's a great book to help an older child understand the funny-but-normal things babies do, and will be especially useful if there is a new sibling in the house. Gemma will push her food around, smash it, feed it to the dog—anything but put it in her mouth. Then one day at church, Gemma spies a woman with a wide-brimmed hat. She just keeps staring and staring at the cluster of fake fruit attached to the woman's hat ribbon. In one swoop, Gemma grabs for the fruit with her little hand and declares, "Eat up, Gemma!" pulling off the entire hat in the process. The family laughs about it later and decides that there may be some method to the madness—maybe this will help Gemma eat. Her older brother sets up an overturned bowl on a plate and surrounds it with grapes and bananas to resemble the lady's hat. It works! Gemma eats to her heart's content. She even tries to eat the banana skins, after which she proudly announces, "Gemma eat up." Big brother saved the day.

Explore These: Why wouldn't Gemma eat? Ask your child: What did you learn about babies by reading about Gemma? If you have a baby in your home, ask: What does the baby like and respond well to? How can you make things more fun for him or her by using your creative talents?

EMERALD BLUE
By Anne Marie Linden. Illustrator: Katherine Doyle.
Publisher: Atheneum, 1994. HC$15.95. MVP: Holding
on to good memories

Emerald Blue is a poetically written, sensory experience of the author's blissful childhood memories in Barbados and her migration to the U.S. The story is appropriately illustrated with chalk in the lush, warm tones of the Caribbean, with purple and gold clouds casting long shadows on the porch at sunset, with children dressed in bright orange and yellow playing on the beach, and lightning cutting across a purply-black sky as a storm approaches. To the girl in this story, called Chile by her grandmother, the memory of Barbados is not just the scenery but the tastes. Everything on that island tasted sweet: guava jam, mango cheese, banana bread, soup with breadfruit, pumpkin and callaloo, and much more. Even the air is scented with cinnamon and nutmeg. One night a hurricane threatens the family, and Grandma awakes the children in the night as they hear the rain beat on their tin roof like a hundred steel drums. They hurry through the driving winds to the brick schoolhouse at the top of the hill—but the next morning the storm is gone, leaving the island smelling fresh and clean. To the children it was all just another adventure with a happy ending. But one day the children's mother returns ("I did not remember her, though Em did") from the new country with tales of snow and a different life, ready to take her children with her. They go willingly, thinking the trip is just a visit, saying good-bye to the grandma, who cries when they leave. The girl takes with her the memories of her sweet Barbados.

Explore These: Why do you think the girl's mom went away for so long? Find Barbados on a globe or map. Look in an encyclopedia or cookbook and show the children what mango, guava, and callaloo are, or let them smell the cinnamon and nutmeg from your spice rack. Fry some thin slices of plantain (available in many grocery stores) and make a plantain chip snack (if your children are not already familiar with it).

 EVAN'S CORNER
By Elizabeth Starr Hill. Illustrator: Sandra Speidel.
Publisher: Viking Books (Penguin Putnam), 1991.
HC$13.99/PB$4.99. MVP: The importance of family relationships

Young Evan shares his two-room apartment with his parents, three sisters, and two brothers. His greatest wish is to have a space of his own so he can have "a chance to be lonely." His mother understands his need and helps him decorate a special corner of the apartment that will be all his. Evan is excited. He brings home more and more things for his little corner until it has a makeshift stool and desk, a flowerpot, a picture, and a pet turtle he saved for weeks to buy. Evan often sits in his corner and enjoys the peace and quiet; he even gets permission to eat his dinner there. Every-one agrees that Evan's corner is beautiful. But something isn't right; only Evan doesn't know what it is. He has everything he could want, why isn't he happy? Evan learns that even solitude gets dull sometimes. What he needs is to give himself away, like by help-ing his little brother Adam decorate his own corner. *Inter*depen-dence versus independence as the key to true satisfaction and joy in life is a valuable lesson for a child to learn.

Explore These: Why did Evan want a space of his own? How come he wasn't happy when he got it? Ask your child: Are you happier when you are alone or with family or friends? Do you like to be with one special friend or relative, or prefer being part of a big group? Explore answers. (This can give you good clues as to your child's personality type.)

"My mother—who usually worked two or three jobs—would create a reading club for us and the neighborhood kids each summer. She would set a goal of ten books to be read by the end of summer vaca-tion and charted our progress on a board with stars. The competition made us strive. I think I read more books then than during the whole school year."

—**Vanessa Bell Calloway,** actress and mother of two

 EVERETT ANDERSON'S GOODBYE
By Lucille Clifton. Illustrator: Ann Grifalconi.
Publisher: Henry Holt, 1983. HC$9.95. MVP:
Overcoming loss. Coretta Scott King Award, Reading
Rainbow

Everett Anderson just lost his daddy, and he is having a hard time coping. As the book progresses, we see him going through the five stages of grief: denial, anger, bargaining, depression and, finally, acceptance. At first he hates everyone, including his baby sister, Santa Claus, and candy. He just cries and cries. Most heart-wrenching are his pleas to God to bring his daddy back in exchange for his promised good behavior. But through his grief, little Everett realizes that his dad's love will never die—it is forever. This is the last book in the acclaimed series about little Everett Anderson. The illustration opposite the title page of the book is captivating—it is a beautifully rendered close-up of a little boy's sweet round face, with a tear ready to roll down his cheek. An excellent book to give a child who has lost someone they love.

Explore These: Why was Everett so sad? What did he go through before he felt better? Ask your child: What emotions do they see on Everett's face in the various illustrations? Have you ever felt like that? Ask a child to share their own feelings about a loved one who passed away. May be a perfect opportunity to talk frankly to your child about death.

FATHER AND SON
By Denizé Lauture. Illustrator: Jonathan Green.
Publisher: PaperStar (Penguin Putnam), 1992. PB$5.95
US/$7.95 CAN. MVP: Being just like Dad. Horn
Book Award

It is often in the preschool years that a boy begins to develop a strong identity with his father or the male father figure in his life. This is a great book to encourage and validate that important identification. Its full-page, bright, oil-on-canvas paintings tell the story of the bond between father and son that develops as they go about everyday life. They are basically "just chillin" together. Few words are needed (and there are very few in this book) to convey the warm relationship as a son walks next to his dad: "They swing together, the same arm, land together, the same foot . . . the shadow of one touching the shadow of the other. . . ." The story is set in the South Carolina low country, home of the Gullah people. Green's peaceful beach, meadow and country road scenes provide a lovely framework.

Explore These: What are some of the things the boy and his dad do together? Talk about the importance of just being together (versus going to a special event), as illustrated in their relationship. Ask a child to talk about what he admires most about his father or father figure and what he enjoys doing (or imagines doing) with him most. Encourage children to draw pictures that convey their feelings about their fathers, positive or negative, and to give or send them to him along with a simple note.

FIRST PINK LIGHT
By Eloise Greenfield. Illustrator: Jan Spivey Gilchrist.
Publisher: Black Butterfly, 1991. HC$13.95/PB$6.95.
MVP: Love for Dad

There is something extra special about a child's bond with his or her dad. It is from his role model—good or bad—that children get their sense of what a man is supposed to be. In this story, Tyree is angry that his dad isn't home yet (though he's not due back until early morning) and is angry at his mother, who won't let him stay up all night and wait. It's nice to see that Mom understands her son's frustration and urgency to see his dad, who's been gone for a whole month, the moment he walks in the door. She allows Tyree to sleep in an armchair in the living room and tells him to wake up at the first pink light before sunrise to see his dad come home. Of course, the chair begins to feel mighty cozy, especially with the pillow and blanket Mom brought out, and Tyree's resolve wanes into zzz's. All he knows is that at the first pink light, he is being held in his dad's strong arms and carried to bed.

Explore These: Why was Tyree so angry at his mother? Ask your child to: Describe a time when you tried to stay up really late for something special. How did you do? Have you ever been up in time to see the "first pink light"? If not, try it one morning and take note of other predawn sights and sounds.

FIVE GREAT EXPLORERS
By Wade Hudson. Publisher: Scholastic, 1995. PB$3.50
U.S./$4.50 CAN. MVP: Appreciating our history

In this very readable book children learn about such notables as Esteban, the Moroccan explorer, and Matthew Henson, who discovered the North Pole. The stories are set in large type with illustrations on every page. Jean DuSable, James Beckwourth, and astronaut Mae Jemison are also profiled. See also *Five Notable Inventors.*

Explore These: Ask a child: Relate the details of one of the stories. Is there anyplace you've wanted to explore? Tell about it and why. How would you go about it? What would you need?

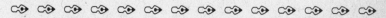

Black Writers' Notebook: Phillis Wheatley was one of America's first black poets. She was taught to read by her slave master and started writing poems at age fourteen. Her first book was published in London when Phyllis was in her twenties—but she had to first prove to a group of disbelieving white men that she actually wrote them!

FROM A CHILD'S HEART
Poems by Nikki Grimes. Illustrator: Brenda Joysmith. Just Us Books, 1993. $7.95. MVP: Conversations with God

Though this book is a compilation of prayers from the hearts of children, I think adults will recognize some of these petitions from their own prayer lists—I did! Children pray about making friends in a new neighborhood, missing Mommy and doing well on tests. But Grimes goes further, touching on the harsher realities of life that affect children deeply. Children also pray that Mom and Dad will stop arguing, that their dreams will not be crushed by racism, that Daddy will get another job and that Grandma won't die. These are real issues that are on children's minds, even though they often do not share those thoughts with adults. Joysmith's careful pastel drawings capture the emotions on the faces of the children well. This comforting book can free children to pray in their own words, anytime, anywhere.

Explore These: If you have not already taught your children to pray, this is a good book to use to do so. Let them use their own words. Reassure them that God is always available to hear them.

Black Illustrators' Notebook: Floyd Cooper has lent his talents to more than 15 children's books, including *Brown Honey in Broomwheat Tea*, which won a Coretta Scott King Honor for illustration.

GRANDPA'S FACE
By Eloise Greenfield. Illustrator: Floyd Cooper.
Publisher: Philomel Books (Penguin Putnam), 1988.
HC$14.95 US/$19.50 CAN. MVP: Love for
grandparent. Read Aloud

Tamika loves the talk-walks she takes with her Grandpa. She feels very close to him when they spend time together. She knows he loves her and she's very comforted by that fact. He is very expressive—without saying a word Grandpa can ask a question or show that he's upset or amused. Tamika has seen all the faces and loves them all. So she is totally unprepared when Grandpa, rehearsing in his room for a part in a play, has his face all angry and snarled up while staring into the mirror. Tamika peeps in and sees this horrific face, and her emotions go berserk. She doesn't want to eat or behave, for that matter, because "her stomach was filled with scared places that made her want to cry." Grandpa making that cold, angry actor-face scares her; she thinks maybe it might be directed at her "for real" someday and she will lose Grandpa's special love. Picking up on her feelings, Grandpa takes

Tamika for an overdue talk-walk to straighten things out. How nice when grown-ups treat children like their feelings matter!

Explore These: Why did Tamika get scared? Ask your child: What are some other ways Tamika's parents and even her grandpa could have handled her problem? When you are angry or hurt, do you hold it in or let it out? Describe a situation. What are some good ways to let out our bad feelings when there's no one around to tell?

"My mother was an English teacher, a voracious reader, and I did what she did, so I read a lot too. One book that impacted me was The Contender *by Robert Lipsyte, which I read in eighth-grade English class. I was excited because it had a black character in it. Also, my father was a master storyteller who could make very mundane things—like finding a parking space—sound interesting. Now that recognizing good stories is my profession, I see the value of his gift."*
—**Andrea Davis Pinkney,**
senior editor, Jump at the Sun, Hyperion Books

HALALA MEANS WELCOME!
A Book of Zulu Words. Written and illustrated by Ken Wilson-Max. Publisher: Hyperion Books 1998, HC$11.95 US/$15.95CAN. MVP: Learning African words

In this brightly illustrated, tall book, Chidi and Michael are friends who live in South Africa. Michael comes over to Chidi's house to play and in the course of their visit the children are taught the Zulu words for the toys and other everyday things. Since most African words are pronounced the way they are spelled, children shouldn't have a hard time with this. Some words, like *Umama*, which means *mother*, are easier than others, like *Isikhukhukazi*, which means *hen*. All of the Zulu words in the story are listed in a glossary in the back along with help on how to say them. For instance, we learn that I-si-khu-khu-ka-zi isn't that hard to pronounce after all, and children should enjoy the singsong-y way the new words sound.

Explore These: Where does this story take place? What is the name of the language they speak there? Use the map in the front of the book to teach a child that Africa is made up of more than fifty countries, similar to the United States. Show him where South Africa is. Practice saying a few Zulu words and their meanings.

HOW SWEET THE SOUND: AFRICAN-AMERICAN SONGS FOR CHILDREN.
Selected by Wade and Cheryl Hudson. Illustrator: Floyd Cooper. Publisher: Just Us Books, 1995. Book with audiotape, $9.95 US/$12.99 CAN; PB book alone, $3.50 US. MVP: Learning traditional African-American songs

Music has always been such an important part of our lives. In all its forms it comforts us, encourages us, warns us, teaches us, commiserates with us, moves our bodies, and makes us laugh. This beautifully illustrated book offers traditional and contemporary music to share with our children. Girls will see favorites they already know like "Miss Mary Mack," the hand-clapping song, and both boys and girls will enjoy singing, "This Little Light of Mine." The familiar is mixed with new songs and new versions of old songs in this great collection, which includes musical chords for playing along on guitar or piano (or just with your voice) and a brief introduction to the history behind each song. The accompanying one-hour cassette features nine foot-stomping songs, first with voices, then without. Try some out!
Explore These: What's your favorite song? If not one of these, can you make up a hand-clap game or step to go along with your favorite?

HUE BOY.
By Rita Phillips Mitchell. Illustrator: Caroline Binch. Publisher: Dial Books for Young Readers (Penguin Putnam), 1993. HC$13.99. MVP: Self-confidence

This book will particularly speak to any child who has ever been the smallest in their class, or to anyone who has been labeled "different" for whatever reason. Set in the Caribbean, this book tells the tale of Hue Boy, who, spurred by the return and love of his father, learns to put aside the worries about his height. His mother is concerned about her son being teased at school, so she measures him every morning and tries to feed him extra helpings of fruit and vegetables to make him grow. Though Hue Boy's neighbor teaches him stretching exercises and his mother takes him to the wisest man in the village, the doctor, *and* the local healer, all of it is useless. But one day the biggest ship Hue Boy has ever seen docks in the harbor. A very tall man walks off with the rest of the passengers—it is his father, who had been away working on the ship. His father hugs him tight, takes his hand and walks home with him in view of all who teased him. Hue Boy finally "walked tall."

Explore These: How do you think Hue Boy felt when he was teased by the other children? Ask your child: What is the right way to behave when someone is being teased? Can you feel tall on the inside even if you are not on the outside?

 HUNTERMAN AND THE CROCODILE
Written and illustrated by Baba Wagué Diakité.
Publisher: Scholastic, 1997. HC$15.95. MVP: Respect for nature

The next time you see a bunch of crocodiles making a pilgrimage to Mecca, think twice when they ask you for directions. In this whimsical South African tale by the author whose name is pronounced, "Wa-gay," it is the animals that rule. The goal is to teach children to respect nature by showing them how we have disrespected it and our environment for sport and wealth. The four lost crocodiles ask the hunterman, Bamba, to help carry them back home. He's skeptical—he doesn't want to get chomped for his good deed—but they promise to behave. One hilarious illustration, done on painted ceramic tiles, shows the hunterman stacking the crocodiles one on top of the other and carrying them on his head. Once in the water, the now-hungry crocodiles think the man would make a nice evening meal.

Bamba argues with the crocodiles about right and wrong and enlists the support of cows, horses, chickens, and even a talking mango tree, to no avail. Each have good reasons why they won't help him—after all, man has taken the cows' milk, beaten the horses, killed so many chickens and cut down so many trees that none of them care what happens to him. Only the rabbit offers Bamba a clever plan that outwits the crocodiles—for a while. In the end, we see how both man and beast need each other to survive.

Explore These: Why wouldn't any of the animals or the mango tree help Bamba? What foods do we get from cows and chickens? Who needed whom more in the story? Ask your child: What can we do to show more respect for nature? Project: Go on a little nature trip and catch some butterflies, fireflies, ladybugs or caterpillars (or whatever's around). Admire their beauty for a while and then set them free.

I LIKE ME!
By Deborah Connor Coker. Illustrator: Keaf Holliday.
Publisher: Golden Books, 1995. HC$6.00/PB$5.95.
MVP: Positive self-image

Who better to launch a line of books that build positive self-images in our children than the creators of *Essence* magazine? This book features a young girl (no doubt a soon-to-be *Essence* reader) who is reveling in her self-esteem, built up by the positive things people say about her and what she is learning about herself. Nia Natasha's skin is the "color of all the leaves in fall" and she can do anything: with her long legs she can run, turn cartwheels or dance ballet; she can hug you with her strong arms and create a clay masterpiece with the gentle touch of her fingers. One particularly nice image is of Nia and her dad seated at a piano. She looks so absolutely thrilled to be learning to play—her enthusiasm may just serve as inspiration for your children.

Explore These: What are some of the positive things Nia Natasha discovers about herself? Ask your child to name five things that are positive about you.

I LOVE MY HAIR
By Natasha Anastasia Tarpley. Illustrator: E. B. Lewis.
Publisher: Little Brown, 1998.
HC$14.95US/$19.95CAN. MVP: Loving our hair

Many African-American women have struggled with loving their hair since they were teenagers. This book teaches young girls to celebrate the way they were made, to love their hair just the way it is, with all its tight coils, kinks, and curls, and most important, for all its possibilities. Taken from the author's childhood memories of sitting between her mother's knees as she combed her hair, the story follows young Keyana as she goes through the nightly ritual. As the comb catches her tangles and she shouts for her mother to stop, her mother puts down the comb and explains that Keyana is lucky to have her head of hair, "because it's beautiful and you can wear it in any style you choose." Using the vibrant and sunny watercolor illustrations of E. B. Lewis, Keyana is shown imagining herself with favorite styles: cornrow braids that merge into the green planted rows of a farmer's field, or her straight-up Afro that surrounds her head like a globe, "with stars and planets behind." The author notes that she went though every hair phase possible—including mohawks—until she got comfortable with her own beautiful African hair.

Explore These: Why didn't Keyana like her hair? Ask your daughter: What's your favorite way to wear your hair? Explain the beauty and versatility of her hair. Have her draw pictures of herself in different hairstyles; help her try some of the styles out.

I NEED A LUNCH BOX
By Jeannette Caines. Illustrator: Pat Cummings.
Publisher: Harper and Row, 1988. HC$12.89. MVP:
Patience

This enjoyable book for small children will reinforce a few basic colors and introduce them to the days of the school week, while they listen to a simple, child-friendly tale. Every child with older siblings knows the frustration of watching big sisters or brothers get privileges first. In this story, a little boy's big sister, Doris, is starting first grade, and their parents buy her a multitude of supplies for the first day: a raincoat, book covers, a pencil case, an umbrella, and more. But the item the little boy covets most of all is her beautiful lunch box. He imagines all the toys he could tote if he just had a lunch box. At night he dreams of a lunch box for each day of the school week, each one with a different color all fancifully illustrated by Cummings. He dreams he is under the sea, while a lunch box shaped like a whale floats above him and schools of fish swim by. Only his dreams help him make it through each day—but when he wakes up he is rewarded with a big surprise.

Explore These: Show your child a calendar and explain what a week is and how it is composed of different days. Let him color each row of a particular day a new color, perhaps identifying them as the story did (i.e., blue for Monday, green for Tuesday, etc.).

Black Writers' Notebook: Poet, photographer and award-winning children's book author **Nikki Grimes** has been praised for her "lively and delicious poetry."

IT'S RAINING LAUGHTER
By Nikki Grimes. Photographer: Myles C. Pinkney.
Publisher: Dial Books (Penguin Putnam), 1997.
HC$14.99 US/$21.75 CAN. MVP: Loving life. Horn
Book Award, Reading Rainbow

This book will make children who don't like poems, like poems. They are bursting with the simple pleasures of childhood and made even more vibrant by wonderful photographs of black children doin' their thang: running through a garden hose in the backyard on a hot summer day; blowing bubbles from a plastic jar; playing piano; getting lost in a book in the library; running, laughing, swinging and Rollerblading—living. Myles Pinkney (son of award-winning illustrator Jerry and brother of award-winning illustrator Brian) makes a stunning debut with these lively and adorable photographs. Happy brown children talk about being "goofy gigglers, sadness chasers and good-mood makers." A young piano player tells us proudly, "I have a symphony in me." And a confident, climbing boy declares that "someday there'll be poems about me blazing new trails just because I could."

JAFTA AND THE WEDDING
By Hugh Lewin. Illustrator: Lisa Kopper. Publisher:
Carolrhoda Books, 1983. SC$4.95 US/$6.95 CAN.
MVP: The joy of a wedding/African traditions.
Reading Rainbow

Jafta's older sister, Nomsa, is getting married and each member of the extended family is doing their part to help prepare for the big wedding. This book's value to children is the importance it places on the wedding itself, and the fact that it introduces some African wedding traditions; it is part of a series of books centering around Jafta and his family. Too many of our children don't even understand what a wedding is really about; to some, "boyfriend and girlfriend" is the same as "husband and wife." This book can be used to explain the importance of the union between a man and a woman. We see many special rituals illustrated here: Nomsa is bathed with scented oils by the elder women and her hair is braided with beads; Mama prepares the best foods and drinks days in advance; musicians from other villages arrive early and practice the special songs they will play at the wedding; the elder men of the family take Dan, Nomsa's intended, aside to talk seriously with him about becoming a husband; the elders are all present at the ceremony to offer their blessing to the couple and present them before God. Afterwards, a great party begins. Jafta enjoys the festivities, but deep down, he is sad to lose his sister. But when Nomsa's new husband addresses him as "brother," Jafta knows everything will be all right.

Explore These: Why did the family make so much fuss over Nomsa's wedding? Ask your child to: Describe a wedding they've been to. What does it mean when a couple decide to get married? How might your relationship change when a brother or sister gets married? See the other Jafta books, especially *Jafta and the Homecoming*, in which Jafta's father returns after long months away working in the mines.

JAMAICA'S FIND
By Juanita Havill. Illustrator: Anne Sibley O'Brien.
Publisher: Houghton Mifflin, 1986. HC$12.95. MVP:
Honesty

At some point, every child finds something that belongs to someone else and wants to keep it. This book (part of a delightful series featuring a little girl named Jamaica) is a small treasure that can help parents enjoyably explain the importance of honesty. Jamaica goes to the playground one evening before dinner and finds a red hat and a worn but cuddly stuffed dog. She takes the hat to the park's lost and found but rides home with the dog in her bicycle basket. The author artfully details the way her mother shows her disapproval, gently but firmly dropping hints, never telling her outright what to do, but guiding her to the right decision. In the end, Jamaica decides to return the dog, too. She is rewarded when she returns to the park and finds the "girl that belongs to that dog."

Explore These: Why did Jamaica return the hat and not the dog? How do you think the other little girl felt when she realized she had lost her dog? Ask your child to: Remember a time when she lost a favorite toy. How did she feel? See if she can guess how Jamaica felt when she showed the little girl where to find her dog.

✚ **JAMAICA TAG-ALONG**
By Juanita Havill. Illustrator: Anne Sibley O'Brien.
Publisher: Houghton Mifflin, 1989. PB$4.95. MVP:
Compassion

No child likes to feel left out. Jamaica's big brother Ossie
makes plans with his friends and doesn't want her tagging along.
When she sneaks over to the basketball court where he and his
friends are playing, she wants to play so badly, she runs onto the
court and shoots a basket just to show them she can. She misses.
Ossie is furious and orders her to play in the kiddie park. There,
a scorned Jamaica learns a lesson about giving and receiving
compassion. When she tries to swing, a small child runs in front
of her. She wishes his mother would keep him away from the big
kids' playground. Then she tries to build a sand castle and a little
boy starts to help. Jamaica quickly says, "No, you'll only mess it
up," and turns her back to him. When little Berto tries to step
over her castle and his foot smashes one of the walls, Jamaica is
mad. Don't little kids know that big kids want to play alone? she
wonders, exasperated. Then she realizes—that's just what her
brother always says to her and it hurts her feelings. Jamaica
changes her attitude and extends friendship to little Berto. In the
end, even a remorseful Ossie joins in.

Explore These: Why didn't Ossie want Jamaica to "tag along?"
Why did Jamaica decide to let Berto play with her even though
he was a baby? Ask your child to: Describe a time when someone
left him out. How did it feel? Did he start to treat other people
the same way he was treated, or did he do something different?

---

*"As a youngster, I read both to learn about the world in which I lived
and to escape my rural, small-town setting. Most of the people around
me did not read very well, or that often. I dreamt about a life that offered
more, and I learned about different opportunities, people and cultures
through books. Two that influenced me profoundly were biographies of
George Washington Carver and Booker T. Washington. I was inspired
to 'make a difference' and leave my mark as those two men had done."*
—**Wade Hudson**, co-founder, president & CEO, Just Us Books

JAMAL'S BUSY DAY
By Wade Hudson. Illustrator: George Ford. Publisher:
Just Us Books, 1991. HC$12.95/PB$6.95 MVP: New
responsibilities

Sometimes as adults we get so caught up in our world of work,
bills and social activities that we forget that our children lead busy
lives, too. This book reminds us that growing up is hard work by
paralleling young Jamal's day with that of his two working parents. He too gets up early, gets ready for school, rides a crowded
bus, works with numbers in his math class (like his mom the accountant does at her job), settles disputes between "co-workers"
(friends at school) and even brings work home like Mom and
Dad. At the end of his tiring day, Jamal is ready to relax, unwind
and eat dinner just like an adult. Only in his case, when Jamal finally hits the bed, he "can't wait until tomorrow!"

Explore These: Go over the "order of things" in your child's
day. Tell him what you're doing at work or at home while he's
working hard in math class or having recess; foster appreciation
on both ends.

**JAMBO MEANS HELLO: SWAHILI ALPHABET
BOOK**
By Muriel Feelings. Illustrator: Tom Feelings.
Publisher: Dial Books (Penguin Putnam), 1974.
PB$5.99 US. Theme: Learning African words.
Classic, Caldecott Honor, Horn Book Award

This book has long been considered a must-have, classic book
for black children—and rightly so. It combines the essential elements for brown-skinned children this age: learning the alphabet
and new words, and learning in the context of black culture.
Compared to the many full-color alphabet books out now, Tom
Feelings's beautiful, gray-scale illustrations may seem pale, but are
no less effective, especially as each one sprawls across two wide
pages. Children learn the alphabet, corresponding Swahili words,

their pronunciation, and a brief description of what the words mean. None of the words are more than eight letters and they are also spelled phonetically, with the syllable of emphasis highlighted in green. Contrary to popular belief, African words are actually very easy to pronounce, as most are spelled just as they sound. Example: *ngoma* (n-go'-mah) means *drum* and *dance*; *rafiki* (rah-fee-key) means *friend.* The corresponding illustration depicts the word in action. Along the way, children learn about respecting elders (*heshima*), helping out with younger siblings and household chores.

Explore These: Develop a short word list for the Swahili words and encourage the child to use them. Add English words to the list too, so the child can see the correlation. Show the child where Africa is using a globe or world map. Use the information in the book's Introduction to point out where Swahili is spoken.

 JASMINE'S PARLOUR DAY
By Lynn Joseph. Illustrator: Ann Grifalconi. Publisher: Lothrop, Lee & Shepard, 1994. HC$15.00 US. MVP: Community spirit

If you know anything about the Caribbean, you know that delicious food and drinks along with long stretches of beach are key tourist attractions of the region. Jasmine, her mom and many other "parlour" operators prepare their best wares to sell on the Trinidadian beachfront as people come out to soak up the sun. Jasmine helps sell sugar cakes while her mother displays fresh fish. Everyone shares some of what they sell with the children, who juggle dented pommeracs (fruits) and generally have a good time before the rush begins. But once the cars with surfboards begin to announce their arrival on the beach (you can hear the calypso music shouting from the car radios), everyone is about business. Still, kind-spirited Jasmine finds the time to share her last piece of sugar cake with a stodgy old vendor who never smiles.

Explore These: What happens on Parlour Day? Ask your child:

Have you ever tasted any of the fruits or drinks mentioned in the book? What do they taste like? If you owned a booth at the beach, what would you sell? Why? Think about what would be involved in setting up a stand in your neighborhood to sell something. Help your child write down everything they would need to set it up.

Black Illustrators' Notebook: Anna Rich says her art career began in kindergarten, where she preferred coloring and drawing to her other classwork. She received her Bachelor of Fine Arts degree from Rhode Island School of Design. Her work appears in *Annie's Gifts* (see page 33), *Joshua's Masai Mask* and several other children's books.

JOSHUA'S MASAI MASK
By Dakari Hru. Illustrator: Anna Rich. Publisher: Lee & Low, 1993. HC$14.95. MVP: Loving yourself

Joshua has to do something in the school talent show, but what? Everyone wants to hear rappers and see dancers, not him playing the Africa kalimba, a musical instrument his Uncle Zambezi plays. But that's all he has. Then Uncle Z gives him a huge, feathered African mask to go with it. Now he's really sunk. What are the kids at school going to think of *this* getup? He'd give anything to be Kareem Cooper, the rapper everyone likes. As Joshua tries on the mask, something strange happens. He begins to change into Kareem Cooper, his cool rapper friend, just as he wished. Ten minutes into Kareem's life, with his angry sister, disillusioned father and empty refrigerator, the grass on the other side doesn't look so green to Joshua anymore. He tries turning into a rap star, but gets mauled by teenagers as he walks down the street. When cool Kareem's act flops on talent night, Joshua must make a quick exit and turn back into his funky, kalimba-playin' self again, much to the delight of the audience, and Kareem, too.

Explore These: Why didn't Joshua want to dress up and play the kalimba in the talent show? Ask your child: Have you ever wanted to be just like someone else? Why? Think realistically about what their lives could be like behind closed doors.

 JULIUS
By Angela Johnson. Illustrator: Dav Pilkey. Publisher: Orchard Books, 1993. HC$14.95. MVP: Friendship

This colorfully illustrated book teaches children to appreciate friendships, and the reciprocal way that friends learn from each other. When Maya's grandfather brings her a pig named Julius back from Alaska, he seems like nothing but trouble. He eats too much food, makes too much noise, makes too many messes, and leaves crumbs on the sheets. But Maya loves Julius because he actually teaches her things that even "all the older brothers in the world could have taught her." He plays with her, protects her from scary things, and teaches her how to dance to jazz records. Even old Julius "realized" that Maya taught him some things too—like the fact that though he was a pig, he didn't always have to act like one. Parents will also find that the illustrations are unique, reminiscent of Caribbean-style artwork.
Explore These: What did Maya learn from her friendship with Julius? Ask your child to: Think of things you have learned from your friends. Help them to make up a story about an imaginary friend.

 JUST US WOMEN
By Jeannette Caines. Illustrator: Pat Cummings. Publisher: Harper and Row, 1982. HC$9.89. MVP: Adventurous spirit

What girl doesn't love time spent with "just us women," especially when it means going on a nice, long road trip with a favorite aunt? In this delightful story, a young girl and her aunt set out on their annual summer trip to North Carolina, with lunches packed in shoe boxes and a full measure of anticipation. With no one to tell them they can't stop or that they have to hurry, the girl knows the trip holds the promise of impromptu adventure minus nervous parents or kid brothers. The two will take advantage of a wealth of simple summertime indulgences. They will stop at roadside markets "and buy all the junk we like," or walk in the rain, or ". . . mosey down the back roads and talk to the farmers and buy their fruit." Through these simple examples, the story helps teach children how a sense of adventure and an eager attitude can transform mundane activities into exciting pastimes.

Explore These: Why did the little girl enjoy the trip with her aunt so much? Take a child on a road trip or even a short afternoon excursion with "just us women" (or "just us men" if the child is a boy). Enjoy fun, impromptu activities: have a roadside or pond-side picnic, go fishing, visit yard sales, stop and go fruit picking or park the car and wander into town for ice cream.

KNOXVILLE, TENNESSEE
By Nikki Giovanni. Illustrator: Larry Johnson.
Publisher: Scholastic, 1994. HC$14.95. MVP: Loving your family and friends

This book is the kind that small children long to climb into the pages of, reveling in the innocence, security, and beauty that those early childhood years should ideally be filled with. It depicts a series of verses about a young girl's favorite summertime impressions, all revolving around good times spent with family, neighbors and members of her church. She always likes summer best because of the fresh corn and other vegetables she can eat from her daddy's garden, the big barbecue, the church picnics, and sitting outside the church in the evening listening to gospel music. The Impressionist-style illustrations are flooded with the green of the rich Tennessee grass and the hot blue of the summer sky. The warmth and love the little girl feels carry through to the end of the day, when her grandmother tenderly leans over her as she says her prayers. The words are taken from a poem in crisp verse written by Giovanni.

Explore These: Explain to your child what a poem is, and read a few more simple examples. Ask a child: What are her favorite summertime activities? Why does she like them so much? Using some pastel paints, have your child create a painting in the Impressionist style. Explain that this was a style that made the ordinary look extraordinary by using dots of paint. Visit a museum where Impressionists are exhibited.

MA DEAR'S APRONS
By Patricia C. McKissack. Illustrator: Floyd Cooper.
Publisher: Simon & Schuster, 1997. HC$16.00
US/$21.50 CAN. MVP: Mother-child love

Set in the early 1900s, this story focuses on Jonelle, called Ma Dear by her little son, David Earl Jr. Ma Dear must work hard to raise her son alone after David Earl Sr. is killed at war. Like many preschoolers, David has trouble remembering the days of the week, so he uses the colors of his mom's aprons to remember which day is which. She wears her yellow apron on ironing day, "because yellow is the color of the sun, and sunshine makes me feel good, even when I have to iron all day!"

Explore These: Explain that this story took place about a hundred years ago when there were no washing machines and lawn mowers like we have today. Most black men and women did farm or domestic work at that time. How does David Earl remember what day of the week it is? Ask your child: Do you know why your parent(s) have to work? Think of the things the money they earn pays for. What machines do we have now that help us with our chores? What would you do if you didn't have them?

MANY THOUSAND GONE: AFRICAN AMERICANS FROM SLAVERY TO FREEDOM
By Virginia Hamilton. Illustrator: Leo and Diane Dillon.
Publisher: Alfred A. Knopf, 1993. HC$18.00 US. MVP:
Determination. Read Aloud, Coretta Scott King Honor

This book delivers everything you would expect when three award-winners get together to tell our history to children. Virginia Hamilton and the Dillons marry a conversational tone with dark and powerful illustrations that draw us into the lives of thirty of our ancestors, the famous and the unknown, one gripping story at a time. A great book to read to or with children because the stories are concise (2–3 pages each) and riveting. Children and parents will be amazed as they follow "The Running-Aways" during their ingenious escapes from hellish plantation life. Another nice element is the personal notes about our heroes and sheroes. Who knew that as a teenager Frederick Douglass ran a Sunday school and made his escape from slavery by disguising himself as a sailor? Or that Isabella Baumfree, whom we know as Sojourner Truth, was inspired to begin her anti-slavery crusade at age forty-six after becoming "born again?" The book includes stories of how white abolitionists often played key roles assisting black slaves in their escapes.

Explore These: It will be best if you read a book about African heritage with your children before introducing the concept of U.S. slavery. Ask your child: Which was your favorite story? Tell why. What is determination? Look it up in the dictionary and talk about some things you feel determined to do. What might your determination cost you? (Hard work, sacrifice, being unpopular, etc.) What would be some of the benefits?

"It's a real danger making children's books too easy, presenting lessons in them instantly and effortlessly. . . . Nothing in life that is worth anything is presented instantly to us. . . . Our fear that they are not going to read at all if we give them something challenging is just crazy. We're shooting ourselves in the foot."

—Poet Laureate **Rita Dove**

ME & NEESIE
By Eloise Greenfield. Illustrator: Moneta Barnett.
Publisher: Harper Trophy (HarperCollins), 1975.
PB$4.95 US/$6.75 CAN. MVP: Imaginary friends.
Classic, Reading Rainbow

As many parents have discovered, preschool-age children often create imaginary friends. Psychologists say that these harmless pretend playmates provide comfort and companionship to a child as they transition out of babyhood into school age. In this book, Janell's imaginary friend Neesie is her alter ego. Neesie says and does the things Janell knows better than to say or do—like grabbing a chair that a visiting aunt was just about to sit in or wanting to play when Mom needs help fixing lunch. Neesie is a source of humor for Janell, whose perplexed mother doesn't know how to react when they are "talking," like most parents who are unfamiliar with this common preschool behavior. One hilarious illustration shows Aunt Bea trying to swat Neesie away, thinking she's a ghost. However, as soon as Janell turns her mind to the first day of school, Neesie's role diminishes—she knows that the days of imaginary friends are numbered, for there is no place for them in a classroom. (A child's pretend friend usually disappears once real school friends present themselves.) Sure enough, when school starts, Janell must leave Neesie at home, but she will always remember her first "best friend."

Explore These: How is Janell different from her imaginary friend? Why didn't Neesie go to school with Janell? Use this opportunity to talk to your child if she has an imaginary friend. Listen to what she says. You can actually learn a lot about what's going on in your child's mind by watching her "play" with the imaginary friend. Reassure her that it's okay for now.

MEET DANITRA BROWN
By Nikki Grimes. Illustrator: Floyd Cooper. Publisher: Lee & Low, 1994. HC$16.00/PB$4.95 MVP: Positive self-image, True friendship

Danitra Brown is the most splendiferous girl in town (and we know it's true because her best friend is telling us the story). Nikki Grimes's poetry for children works wonderfully here, giving us a different glimpse of Danitra's life on each page. Just by the look illustrator Floyd Cooper puts on Danitra's face in each large picture, we can tell that she is no ordinary girl. She believes she can do or be anything she wants to—stare down bullies, ride a bike with no hands, keep house, and even comfort a friend with a problem. Though she wears thick glasses and a boy named Freddy teases her about it, she pays it no mind—Danitra Brown has no time for idle chatter because she's "got books to read and hills to climb that Freddy's never seen." What makes her have such a high opinion of herself? She knows something about her identity. Her mother tells her about the great kings and queens that she descended from, so Danitra wears *only* the royal color purple—just in case she's a princess. Her friend, our narrator, is so encouraged by the way Danitra carries herself, we can feel her own self-image being built up just by being around Danitra. And that's what real friendship is about, isn't it?

Explore These: Talk to a child about how she sees herself. Is she confident like Danitra Brown? If not, discuss why. Reassure her about our rich heritage in God and in our African ancestors. Ask a child: Do you have any friends who are like Danitra, and encourage you when you're sad? What would it take for you to become a friend like that to another child?

MINTY, A STORY OF YOUNG HARRIET TUBMAN
By Alan Schroeder. Illustrator: Jerry Pinkney. Publisher:
Dial Books (Penguin Putnam), 1996. HC$16.99. MVP:
Single-mindedness, Selflessness. Coretta Scott King
Award, ALA Notable

No one living knows the exact details of Harriet Tubman's growing up, but we do know that her birth name was Araminta and that she was a slave on the Brodas plantation on Maryland's Eastern Shore, the author attests. This lovely book features large, splendid illustrations and well-done text that makes us laugh (as when Harriet secretly sticks her tongue out at her mistress) and cry (as when she is stripped and beaten as a child for attempting to escape). Young readers will feel pain when Minty's only little rag doll is thrown into the fire by a raving mistress, upset over a spill at the table. But if Minty is the heroine in this book, her dad is definitely the hero. It was his belief in her (or so the story depicts) that compelled him to teach his daughter how to survive in the woods, catch fish, skin squirrels, and swim the river. How dangerous it was for him to teach her these important things! He could have easily been caught and beaten, or even lynched. As a result, Minty was later responsible for saving the lives of hundreds of slaves and thousands of their free offspring.

Explore These: What did Minty's dad teach her about surviving in the woods? Why do you think Minty was so determined to escape and help others escape, too? Ask your child: Would you risk your life to save someone else's? If someone wrote about your life, what are some of the things they would say about your personality?

MIRANDY AND BROTHER WIND
By Patricia C. McKissack. Illustrator: Jerry Pinkney.
Publisher: Dragonfly Books, 1988. HC$18.00 US. MVP:
Confidence, Determination. Coretta Scott King Honor,
Caldecott Honor, ALA, Audio

In this masterfully illustrated book, author Patricia McKissack tells a story based on her grandparents winning a cakewalk (or dance contest) in the early 1900s. The dance was called the cake-walk because whoever won received a triple-decker cake as their prize. In this story, little Mirandy wants to win the junior cake-walk contest, but she doesn't have a partner. She enlists the help of her grandmother, the corner grocer, and even a conjure woman to help her catch Brother Wind to ensure her win—but he is elusive. When she finally captures the Wind, she gets one wish—to dance with her friend Ezel in the contest. The book culminates with a heartwarming illustration of the two with their heads held high, backs arched, strutting to victory—just the way McKissack imagined it. (This book is also available as a puzzle.)

Explore These: Point out the fact that parts of this book are written in dialect, the way people spoke at the time. Note that sentences beginning, "He be . . ." or "Can't nobody . . ." is not proper grammar. Help your child to have her own "cakewalk" dance contest with her friends (see the back panel of the book for other tips on this).

MISS TIZZY
By Libba Moore Gray. Illustrator: Jada Rowland.
Publisher: Simon and Schuster, 1993. HC$14.00 MVP:
Friendship with elders, Kindness

Miss Tizzy is the kind of neighbor any child would love, but through her friendship and love for children, she becomes a role model who teaches them the beauty of giving back what they have learned. In the tradition of the popular Amelia Bedelia, Miss Tizzy—who always wears green hightops and a purple hat with a flower in it—may seem peculiar to some of her neighbors, but she dearly loves the neighborhood children. Each day of the week they come to her house and pick flowers from her yard, bake cookies, hold puppet shows, make music out of pots and pans, draw pictures and deliver them to "people who had stopped smiling." One week, Miss Tizzy becomes sick and must stay in bed. The children are sad and miss their friend, until they realize that the fun and kindness she gave them will be the perfect get-well gift for her. Gray's prose is clear and descriptive: Miss Tizzy's house "sat like a fat blossom in the middle of a street . . ." and her cat sometimes "climbed on her shoulders like a tired old fur piece." Rowland's watercolor illustrations are soft and inviting.

Explore These: Why do the children love Miss Tizzy so much? Is it okay to like older people who are considered peculiar, like Miss Tizzy? Ask a child to: Think of "Miss Tizzy" things he can do: Put on a puppet show for a live audience, bake cookies for someone else, or draw a picture for an elderly person in your neighborhood.

"We need to take on the responsibility to give children black books— it's not a privilege, it's a responsibility. If you can pay $60 for a pair of sneakers, you can buy a $5 book for a child."
> —**Henrietta M. Smith,** librarian, historian, editor

 MOLLY THE BRAVE AND ME
By Jane O'Connor. Illustrator: Sheila Hamanaka.
Publisher: Random House, 1990. PB$3.99. MVP:
Bravery

This is one of those rare little books in which a black child is the heroine who is looked up to by a white child. Molly, the black girl, has "guts . . . more guts than anybody in the second grade. I wish I was like her," says her admiring white friend, Beth. Molly isn't afraid of bugs or mean older kids or anybody. Her family has a big country home on a farm (and why not?), where she invites Beth to visit. When the two friends get lost romping through cornfields taller than they are, Molly shows fear for the first time. Beth, who is scared too, is instrumental in getting the two out of their jam. In the process, Molly helps her realize that she has "guts" too.

Explore These: Why does Beth admire Molly so much? Ask your child: Do you think you're brave? If so, tell why. Or would you like to be brave like someone else? If so, tell why. Describe a time when you were lost and scared. How did you get over your fear?

MY FIRST KWANZAA BOOK
By Deborah M. Newton Chocolate. Illustrator: Cal
Massey. Publisher: Scholastic, 1992. PB$10.95 MVP:
Appreciating African family values

This book teaches children about Kwanzaa by showing them
the simple, special things one family does during the celebration:
wear African garb, read about Africa, tell stories, and do crafts. A
helpful glossary of terms and explanation of the seven principles
of Kwanzaa appear at the book's end. See also, *Seven Days of
Kwanzaa:* A Holiday Step Book by Ella Grier.

MY MAMA NEEDS ME
By Mildred Pitts Walter. Illustrator: Pat Cummings.
Publisher: Lee & Low, 1983. HC$9.50. MVP: Feeling
needed. Classic, Coretta Scott King Award

Jason has a new baby sister and a good attitude. He wants to
help out, but it seems as if he is always in the way. Both the baby
and his mom sleep a lot, and it never seems like the right time for
Jason to hold his new sister. He can't help feed her because she's
breast-fed. He can't do much of anything, yet Jason longs to be
needed. Like many children adapting to a new little sibling, he
feels useless, abandoned, and displaced—he's not the baby anymore. He can't even enjoy playing with his friends because he's
afraid his mama might need him, so he stays close to home. Finally, Jason's mom *does* need him. He rushes home excitedly and
helps to give his sister her first bath. When Mama stops just to
give him a big hug and tell him he's always needed, especially for
hugging, he feels loved again. A great book to help encourage an
older child struggling with a new baby in the house.
Explore These: Why doesn't Jason want to go out and play like
he used to? Use the book to help explain to a child that he is (or
will be) no less loved than before the new baby.

Black Writers' Notebook: Did you know that Presidential Poet Laureate and critically acclaimed author **Maya Angelou** has written several books for children? Her award-winning autobiography, *I Know Why The Caged Bird Sings* (page 186), has become an American classic, and she has been hailed as one of the great voices of contemporary literature.

 MY PAINTED HOUSE, MY FRIENDLY CHICKEN, AND ME
By Maya Angelou. Photographs by Margaret Courtney-Clarke. Publisher: Clarkson Potter, 1994. HC$16.00 US/$21.50 CAN. MVP: Appreciating other cultures

Through the eyes of Thandi, our eight-year-old South African tour guide in this colorful book, we see intimate portrayals of everyday life in that country. Thandi's best confidante is her chicken, who keeps all of her secrets safe. Her tribe, the Ndebele, has a tradition of painting intricate geometric designs on the outside of their houses. Thandi has just learned how to make these beautiful painstaking designs from her mother. "Your hand must be steady to make the patterns sharp and your legs must be strong, because sometimes the walls are high," Thandi tells us. We also learn about making beaded aprons called *amaphotho* and loincloths called *ghabi*. Thandi's name means "hope," and she hopes we will become real friends instead of "stranger-friends" by the end of the book. See also *Kofi and His Magic*.

Explore These: What is one of the traditions of Thandi's tribe? Show a child where South Africa is on a globe or world map, in relation to where you live. Point out that Africa is made up of many countries with different names, like the states. Project: Have a painting day where children try to imitate the Ndebele designs or create their own; for something different, they could try painting on bricks or large stones; they could also make items with beads and shells.

> *"The girl in* Nappy Hair *got sad sometimes 'cause she couldn't really brush her hair down. But it doesn't matter what people tell you if you know who you really are."*
>
> —**Lydia,** age 10

 NAPPY HAIR
By Carolivia Herron. Illustrator: Joe Cepeda. Publisher: Alfred A. Knopf, 1997. HC$17.00 US/$22.00 CAN.
MVP: Loving our hair

Restrain yourself from saying, "Hey, those folks are breakin' on the poor girl's hair!" when you pick up this book. Read on and you'll see that they are doing quite the opposite. *Nappy Hair* combines hilarious, vibrant illustrations by Cepeda with a great story that introduces us to Brenda and her wonderful head of thick, coiled, African hair. Using the black church tradition of call and response as its format, Brenda's Uncle Mordecai begins by poking friendly fun at her hair and, by the book's end, he rises into a celebration of its strength and wonderousness in God's sight. Brenda's family members respond to Mordecai's singsongy lines as if they were in church, egging the preacher on. Uncle Mordecai says, "This nap come riding express, coming on across the ocean from Africa, wouldn't stop for nothing. Danced right on through all the wimp hair. Wouldn't mix, wouldn't slow down for nobody!" And everyone said, "Sure enough!" A very creative way to address the important issue of maintaining a black child's self-image in a straight-haired country.

Explore These: Read this book in two different voices, one for the "call," one for the "response," to help a child understand the concept; use an exuberant, preacher-like tone of voice. Explain how this style is used in many black churches today. Emphasize how God made our hair uniquely beautiful, coiled in "five, six, seven, maybe eight complete circles per inch!"

NOT SO FAST SONGOLOLO
Written and illustrated by Niki Daly. Publisher:
Atheneum, 1986. HC$11.95. MVP: Gratitude, Affection
for grandparents

Every child who has a close relationship with a grandparent will relate to this South African story, which demonstrates the bond that can be shared between generations despite age differences and distance. Malusi's grandmother, Gogo, needs his help to walk into town. He likes to be slow, but she is slower. In the soft watercolor illustrations, Gogo is heavy, with hands that "were hard and used to hard work," but shown beside Malusi she is small and spry. When Malusi delights in the sights, noises, people, and cars downtown, Gogo gasps for breath at the exertion of her walk, clicks her tongue in disapproval, and worries over the fast-changing traffic lights. Malusi is patient as he helps his grandmother. As they walk between the crowds, Malusi turns and sees, as if for the first time, how aged his grandmother is: "She looked older in the city, he thought." In a store window Malusi looks longingly at a pair of red "tackies" (tennis shoes), especially since his hand-me-down sneakers are filled with holes. Before they leave town, Gogo shows her love for Songololo (her pet name for him) by rewarding him with a special gift.

Explore These: Why did Gogo buy the shoes for Malusi after all? Ask your child to: Make a list of all the things you like about one of your grandparents or another elderly person you know. Make a homemade card with the list written inside and give the card to the person when it is finished.

ONE HOT SUMMER DAY
Written and designed by Nina Crews. Publisher:
Greenwillow Books (William Morrow), 1995.
HC$15.00. MVP: Appreciating simple things

You can tell that author Nina Crews knows firsthand what it's like to be a child growing up in a big city. There is no quiet, air-conditioned beach house to escape to on summer weekends in this story. It's summer in the city, and everyone is feelin' hot, hot hot. A little girl finds relief from the heat—and a good deal of fun—right on her city block. She forgoes the too-hot playground and instead finds a shady place to draw, teases her shadow, eats not one but two grape Popsicles and even tries to fry an egg on the sidewalk. Authentic "inner" city scenes of open fire hydrants and women shading themselves under umbrellas in front of the corner store (in this case a bodega) are heartwarming. Relief from the heat finally comes in the form of a big rainstorm that cools everything—and everyone—off again. A New York native, Crews patterned the story after her own childhood, which was full of "concrete summers" like these. Her funky photo collages give her characters a fun, three-dimensional quality that matches the book's lighthearted theme. This book was a favorite in our focus group.

Explore These: What did the little girl do to keep cool? Why did she try to fry an egg on the sidewalk? What happened after it rained? Ask your child: What are some things you do to cool off when it's really hot?

THE PATCHWORK QUILT
By Valerie Flournoy. Illustrator: Jerry Pinkney.
Publisher: Dial Books (Penguin Putnam), 1985.
HC$15.99. MVP: Sensitivity, Honoring elders.
Read Aloud, Coretta Scott King Award, ALA Notable,
Reading Rainbow, Audio, Audio CD

Sometimes tradition gets lost in the business of modern life. In this case, the tradition of quilting—patching together squares of material taken from family members' favorite clothing—is destined to die in one family without a child's help. Tanya loves her grandmother's quilt idea and spends many hours helping her make it. But before it is finished, Grandma takes ill. The half-done masterpiece sits alone on the big chair until Tanya decides to continue it herself, with the help of her mother. Even her two rough-and-tumble brothers help out by cutting squares of fabric for Tanya to sew. Little do they know that Grandma has been watching them with pride. When she feels better she asks to be brought near the window. "I needs the Lord's light," so she can finish where Tanya and the boys left off. The result is a deepened appreciation of a black family tradition and a beautiful quilt for Tanya to hand down to her own children someday.

Explore These: Tanya's mother didn't think much of Grandma's quilt at first. Why not? What's special about the material that makes up a patchwork quilt? Encourage your child to begin collecting pieces of material from family members to begin sewing a collage, placemat or even a whole quilt.

Black Writers' Notebook: Author extraordinare **Virginia Hamilton** was awarded the 1995 Laura Ingalls Wilder Medal for her "substantial and lasting contribution to literature for children." She lives in the same Ohio town where her grandfather settled after escaping from slavery.

 THE PEOPLE COULD FLY: AMERICAN BLACK FOLKTALES By Virginia Hamilton. Illustrators: Leo and Diane Dillon. Publisher: Alfred A. Knopf, 1985. PB$13.00 US/$17.00 CAN. MVP: Tales of freedom. Coretta Scott King Award, ALA Notable, Horn Book Award

Slave tales, animal tales, fantasy and legend are all included in this captivating collection of stories for children. The Dillons' wonderful wraparound cover art is only surpassed by their compelling use of light and dark shading in the book's interior. The stories will surely delight children, and there is lots to learn from the Introduction and afternotes about how our folktales came to be and what the characters symbolize. Like the fact that rabbits appear in so many of our tales because the enslaved storytellers identified with the small, helpless creature, but gave him a cunning wit and a quick mind so he could outsmart his larger opponents (the same way many of our folks did in battles with ruthless slave owners). The book gets its title from the final story. In this tale of emancipation, beaten-down field slaves utter magic words remembered from Africa and are able to rise up and fly away from the plantation—right in front of the dreaded Overseer. This could have been a metaphor for slaves who successfully ran away to freedom in the North.

Explore These: Use the excellent notes that follow each story to give children an understanding of the characters and the setting.

Parent Note: With the exception of the supernatural tales, these make fine bedtime stories for children this age. When reading the more chilling tales, be sure to explain ahead of time that these are made-up stories, not reality. Think twice before reading them if you suspect your child will become fearful. See also *Her Stories.*

"I liked Psalm 23 *because the kids weren't afraid of anything because God was with them."*

—**Noni,** age 6

PSALM 23
Illustrator: Tom Ladwig, Publisher: Eerdmans, 1997.
HC$16.00/PB$8.00. MVP: God's protection

Retired minister Tom Ladwig has sensitively taken the Twenty-Third Psalm and set it in the middle of a struggling urban community. Using the actual verses of the famous psalm as his text, he brings the words many of us know by heart to life in a relevant and exciting way with his full-page, vibrant watercolor illustrations of life in the 'hood. It is compelling to read these powerful words and see them lived out in contemporary scenes from a black family's life in the city. Grandma preparing a good breakfast for her two grandchildren before school illustrates the verse, "I shall not be in want." "Though I walk through the valley of the shadow of death, I will fear no evil, for you are with me," is illustrated by the four children cautiously walking home from school as they pass unsavory-looking characters hangin' out. "You anoint my head with oil; my cup overflows," shows a grandmother lovingly bathing her grandkids and preparing to comb some hair. All of the illustrations are done in wonderful detail. It is a great tool to use to teach children this important psalm and to remind them of God's provision and protection, wherever they are.

Explore These: Not every child will relate to the scenes in this book as their own experience of everyday life. If you live in a suburban or rural neighborhood, make the story relevant to *your* child's life. Ask the child to recall times when he feels protected, provided for or comforted, and to recognize that as God's love. Have children memorize the psalm two verses at time until they know it by heart.

 RAIN, RAIN GO AWAY
By Teresa Reed. Illustrator: Stacey Schuett. Publisher:
Aladdin Paperbacks (Simon & Schuster), 1996. PB$3.25
US/$4.50 CAN. MVP: Respect for nature

If your children enjoy the Nickelodeon television series *Gullah Gullah Island*, they will love this simple little book that features two of the children from the show, James and Shaina. The two live on the Georgia Sea Island where sudden rainstorms are a common occurrence. The children run home to avoid getting caught in the rain, but they become bored sitting home with nothing to do and wish the rain would stop. Their parents (conveniently home lounging on the sofa in the middle of the day) teach them to enjoy the rain and point out how it makes "the same old things look and sound different." The children discover that rain isn't that bad after all.

Explore These: What did James and Shaina do while it rained? How many animals can you find hidden in the rain scene at the middle of the book? Why do we need rain? What does it do? What can you listen and look for the next time it rains and you have to stay inside? See also, *Case of the Missing Cookies, Happy Birthday,* and *Daddy and Shaina's Garden,* which also feature members of the *Gullah Gullah Island* cast.

RED DANCING SHOES
By Denise Lewis Patrick. Illustrator: James E. Ransome.
Publisher: Tambourine (William Morrow), 1993.
HC$16.00/PB$4.95 MVP: Valuing gifts

Wasn't it great when relatives would visit you and bring you little things from wherever they came from? In this simple story a visiting grandmama brings her granddaughter a pair of shiny red shoes as a gift. Grandmama called them "dancing shoes" and so they were. The little girl whirled and twirled all over the place when she wore those red shoes. She wanted to show them off to everyone in the neighborhood—and she did. But just as she got to her Nen's house (her grandmother's sister), she slipped and fell into a pile of dirt, dropping her sticky snow cone all over herself—and her shoes. Now the shoes that were her pride and joy were dirty and scuffed. She feared they would never be the same. Of course, Nen knew that she could bring them back to life. With a little wiping and polishing, the red dancing shoes were as good as new. James Ransome's oil paintings of the little girl dancing and sitting with her older relatives are lovely and authentic.

Explore These: Who gave the little girl her new red shoes? Why did she want to show them off so much? Ask your child: Did anyone ever give you a gift that you loved so much you wanted to show it to the whole world? What was it? Why was it so important to you? Where is it now?

Black Writers' Notebook: Author/illustrator **Julius Lester** has collaborated with Jerry Pinkney on six award-winning children's books. He is the author of the groundbreaking *To Be a Slave* (see page 220), a Newbery Honor Book and ALA Notable classic just reissued in a thirtieth anniversary edition. His book *Long Journey Home: Stories from Black History* (see page 194) was a National Book Award finalist.

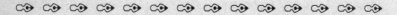

SAM AND THE TIGERS
By Julius Lester. Illustrator: Jerry Pinkney. Publisher:
Dial Books (Penguin Putnam), 1996. HC$15.99
US/$22.99 CAN. MVP: The perils of envy. Read Aloud

Courageously, award-winning writer–artist team Lester and
Pinkney preserved the fondness of this story about a boy and his
encounter with tigers, while eliminating the offensive racial
stereotyping that appears in the Little Black Sambo by Helen
Bannnerman. They succeeded in producing a beautifully illustrated large-format book whose story is as captivating as its pictures. (After all, a story is about who's tellin' it, no?) In the
fictitious town of Sam-sam-sa-mara, animals and humans live and
work together "like they didn't know they weren't supposed to,"
and everyone's name is Sam. Young Sam lives with his parents,
whose names, of course, are also Sam. This makes for some fun
dialogue between the boy and his mother and father, as you
could imagine. The Sams go shopping for clothes with their boy
and every merchant is an animal smartly dressed in coat and
hat—elephants, alligators, giraffes and more—all selling their
wares. Sam insists on choosing the gaudiest, loudest-colored
clothes to purchase, which his mother and father allow, with
some reservations. Sporting his ultra-bright outfit, complete with
silver shoes and lime green umbrella, Sam thinks he is the finest
thing since Denzel Washington, and so do the yellow tigers who
follow him on his way to school. They each threaten to eat him
if he doesn't hand over a piece of his new clothing. Soon, Sam
is left crying in his undies. However, the tigers get so caught up
in showing off their new duds to one another and fighting over
who looks the best that they run themselves into the ground—
literally—and dissolve into a big yellow whirl. Sam gets his clothes
back, and everyone eats their fill of yellow-and-black-striped
"tiger" pancakes.

Explore These: What made the tigers want to eat Sam? What
caused the fight between the tigers? How did Sam get his clothes
back? Ask a child: Have you ever been envious like the tigers
were? Describe what happened. Describe some things that might
happen if people and animals really lived, ate, worked, and
talked together.

**SHE COME BRINGING ME THAT LITTLE
BABY GIRL**
By Eloise Greenfield. Illustrator: John Steptoe.
Publisher: J.B. Lippincott, 1993. HC$11.95/PB$6.00
MVP: Adapting to change. Classic

When there's a new baby in the house, older children experience a range of emotions, usually feeling a heavy dose of jealousy and frustration. This book allows children to relate to Kevin and his disappointment with the new baby, but see their fears dispelled as he is reassured by his mother's love and the importance of being a big brother. Kevin is disappointed with his sister from day one. He was hoping for a baby brother, and he didn't like the way his parents looked at her, "Like she was the only baby in the world." On top of that, the baby cries too much, and no one seemed to be paying attention to him like they used to. It isn't until Mama comes over and puts the baby in his lap and explains that she'll need his help that he really looks at her and begins to like her. He feels even more like a big brother after Uncle Roy explains how he looked after Mama when they were little and "wouldn't let nobody bother my little sister." Surprise! Kevin laughs at the idea of Uncle Roy as a boy and Mama as a baby— he'd never thought of *that* before.

Explore These: Why was Kevin so frustrated? Ask a child, have you ever felt that way? Describe. Explain to the child or children how they received just as much love, tenderness and attention when they were born (this is a good time to turn some attention back to them and tell them the story of their birth). Explain the role of a big brother or big sister, stressing the advantages and importance of being older (i.e., helping Mommy and Daddy, teaching the baby new things, getting to go places, or do things that the baby can't do yet, etc.).

SHORTCUT
Written and illustrated by Donald Crews. Publisher:
Mulberry Books (William Morrow), 1992. PB$4.95
US/$6.75 CAN. MVP: Being alert to danger

This book is great for every child who's ever wanted to break their parents' safety warnings "just this once" (and who hasn't?). Donald Crews's dusky, double-page illustrations add wonderfully to the suspense of this story about a group of children walking home just before dark. They are late and want to take the short-cut home—only that means they must walk along the train tracks. There is no place to run if a train comes while they are on the tracks; deep slopes filled with thorny bushes, water and snakes are on either side. The children play and fool around as they walk the tracks, nearing their path home. Barely noticeable, the words *"whoo-whoo"* appear in the upper left-hand corner of the page. As each page turns, the *"whoo-whoo"* gets larger and larger. A train is spotted and is heading their way! The panicked children, now halfway home, can't decide whether to run back to the cutoff or ahead to the path. Either choice could get them killed. They begin to run back, but there isn't enough time. The *"WHOO"* of the train is large now, and its headlights approach the children at lightning speed. The screaming children decide to jump down into the side slope. Crews's twelve-page illustration of the huge freight train passing as the children hide is haunting. They get home safely, but they'll never speak about their brush with death—and they'll never take the shortcut again.

Explore These: Why didn't the children hear the first *"Whoo's"* of the train? Ask your child: Recall a situation where you disobeyed a safety rule. What happened or what could have happened?

SOMETHING ON MY MIND
By Nikki Grimes. Illustrator: Tom Feelings. Publisher:
Dial Books (Penguin Putnam), 1995. HC$18.25/
PB$7.50 Theme: Explores children's unspoken
thoughts. Read Aloud, Coretta Scott King Award

Tom Feelings's masterful artwork and Nikki Grimes's tell-it-like-it-is prose come together in this book, which offers fifteen short poems for children. The best way to describe these poems is to say that they deal with how some black children feel deep down inside, and capture the way they express themselves when adults aren't around. They gather to talk on the front steps about going somewhere, someday, where they can just be themselves. Others are all dressed, anxiously awaiting their Daddy's visit, while another revels in the new dress her father brought home just for her. One is tired of being sent outside to play when he just wants someone to talk to, and another struggles with writing a paper on her summer vacation—she's afraid there isn't much to tell that her teacher will appreciate. The book ends with a somber poem about an older girl who just broke up with her boyfriend. "No more walks home from school, no more holding hands for me . . . he doesn't even care if he broke my heart."

Explore These: After reading to them, ask children what their favorite poem was and have them explain why. Encourage children to write their own poem about something they think about a lot, maybe something they're confused or sad about. Remind them that it doesn't have to rhyme. Point out the way Tom Feelings shows detail in his artwork. This can inspire a drawing session in which children focus on bringing out that element in their own work.

STEVIE
Written and illustrated by John Steptoe. Publisher:
Harper & Row, 1969. PB$5.95 US/$7.95 CAN. MVP:
Valuing friendship. Classic, ALA Notable

Robert's mother decides to take in a little boy while his parents
sort things out and Robert doesn't like it one bit. He even thinks
the boy's name, Stevie, is dumb. "My momma don't call me
Robert-ie," he chides. He has to take little Stevie (alias "ol' stupid") everywhere and it's really cramping his style. As far as
Robert's concerned, Stevie doesn't do anything right, and he
gets away with murder. Just when Robert can't stand it anymore,
Stevie's parents come to take him home for good. Suddenly,
there is no one to play cops and robbers with on the stoop, and
soon Robert misses even the annoying things Stevie did. Like
Robert, often we don't value someone until after they're gone.

Explore These: Ask children with younger siblings what they
like and dislike about being older brothers or sisters. Would they
miss them if they were gone? What might Stevie have been feeling, having to live away from his own parents and calling Robert's
mother "Mommy"? Do they know anyone like Stevie? Ask them to
discuss ways they can be more sensitive to the difficult situations
some children live with.

 THE STORY OF THE THREE KINGDOMS
By Walter Dean Myers. Illustrator: Ashley Bryan.
Publisher: HarperCollins, 1995. PB$5.95 US/$7.95
CAN. MVP: Resourcefulness

Illustrated in bold, geometric drawings and designs, this story
celebrates the gift of storytelling and the power it has to transform our lives. According to this tale, in the beginning of the
world when "the earth had not settled in its turning and the stars
had not found their places in the night sky," there existed three
kingdoms, each ruled by a particular animal: the Elephant ruled
the forest, the Shark ruled the sea, and the Hawk ruled the air.
Each animal boasted of the greatness of his respective kingdom,

and each believed he was invincible. Then People entered the Earth, and since they were neither strong nor fierce, nor could they fly, all the creatures laughed at them and made them walk in fear. But as the people gather around to tell stories, they discover clever ways to subdue the animals. In the process they lose their fear and gain new wisdom about sharing the Earth with their fellow creatures.

Explore These: Why were the people afraid of the animals? Make up a fourth kingdom ruled by a particular animal. Write a little story or draw a picture of what it would look like if the people managed to outwit that animal as well.

A STREET CALLED HOME
By Amindah Brenda Lynn Robinson. Publisher:
Harcourt Brace, 1997. HC$18.00 US/$25.00 CAN.
MVP: Ingenuity

Color collages using paint, buttons, beads, stitches, and bits of fabric create this interactive multimedia book which describes the people you'd meet and things you'd see if you took a walk down bustling Mt. Vernon Avenue in Ohio, where the author's parents once lived. There are "doors" to flip open on every page, introducing you to the street merchants who sell whatever they have to folks on the avenue. Everyone had to use their entrepreneurial skills to survive on Mt. Vernon Avenue in the 1940s. The Brownyskin man sells fried pork rinds for snacking, the Chicken Foot woman offers crispy fried chicken feet ("Not much meat on them, but Oh! They taste so good!"), and the Ragman takes old cloths off your hands and trades you for new ones. Fold out the entire, twenty-two-panel book, and it will spread half across the room! This way you and your child can enjoy scanning all of the colorful images on this busy thoroughfare at once. When you're done, the accordion-style book ties closed with a silk ribbon.

Explore These: Ask a child: Who were some of the people you met along the street in this book? What did they sell? If you were a street merchant, what would you sell? Discuss the buying/selling process.

SWEET CLARA AND THE FREEDOM QUILT
By Deborah Hopkinson. Illustrator: James Ransome.
Publisher: Alfred A. Knopf, 1993. PB$6.99 US/$9.50
CAN. MVP: Determination, Thoughtfulness. Reading
Rainbow.

A book like this reminds us that we are an ingenious people. Clara is an enslaved girl who was torn from her mother and sold to another plantation. She is mothered by "Aunt" Rachel, who helps her learn to stitch and get a job sewing in the slaveowners' big house. While Clara's hands perform the work faithfully, the wheels of her mind are ever turning, planning her escape from this no-life. But how? Many a slave has been caught and beaten trying to escape. An inquisitive Clara learns about maps, or "pictures of the land." She embarks on drawing an escape map in the sand but realizes that it will only wash away. One day it hits her— she'll make a quilt-map. She uses blue scraps of material for water, green for fields, white for roads and pink for houses ("Missus liked to wear pink a lot"). Clara receives undercover help from the black coach drivers who pass the time at the big house waiting for their passengers. "By the way, Clara, I heard the master sayin' that he didn't want to travel to Mr. Morse's place 'cause *it's over twenty miles north o' here*," one would say. Clara's determination and steadfastness are admirable—it takes her many months of working in secret to complete the quilt. Finally, Clara makes her escape, leaving the quilt behind for others to use because she "had the memory of it in her head." Clara and her friend Jack risk returning to get Clara's mother and sister before they make their escape across the Ohio River. As a result of her hard work and unselfishness, many others use the same quilt to make their own successful escapes.

Explore These: What steps did Clara take to prepare for her escape? Why do you think Clara is called "Sweet" in the book's title? Explain the various aspects of slave life as you read this book; make them teachable moments. Help your children to do the activity at the back of the book, "Make A Map," using scraps, buttons, string and other household items to create a map of their neighborhood; then encourage them to put their maps to the test.

THE TALKING EGGS
By Robert San Souci. Illustrator: Jerry Pinkney.
Publisher: Dial Books (Penguin Putnam), 1989.
HC$12.95. MVP: The rewards of obedience. Caldecott
Honor, ALA Notable

This Southern tale is told wonderfully, and points out the value of listening to your elders and not being greedy. Blanche is the equivalent of Cinderella, treated poorly by her mother and older sister. That is, until she stumbles upon a treasure in the woods and brings all the spoils home. Now her greedy relatives want to find the secret to the treasure, rob Blanche of hers while she sleeps, and run her off the property. But the secret to the wealth is in being obedient, even-tempered, and content, not planning deceptive strategies. The former qualities are things the mother and sister just don't have. Guess who comes out on top in the end?

Explore These: Ask a child: What were some of the poor qualities Blanche's mother and sister had? What were some of Blanche's good qualities? How did they serve her well a number of times in the story? What would you have done if you were Blanche?

TAR BEACH
Written and Illustrated by Faith Ringgold. Publisher:
Crown, 1991. HC$18.00 US/$23.00 CAN. MVP: Faith.
Read Aloud, Caldecott Honor

If the passion and hope in the R. Kelly song "I Believe I Can Fly" could be embodied in a book, renowned Harlem-based painter, quilter, and author Faith Ringgold, has done it in *Tar Beach*. It is perfect for young children because of its simple language, concise sentences, brilliantly colored canvas paintings and oversized format. Cassie Louise Lightfoot and her little brother Be Be have big hopes—big *plans*—for themselves and their construction worker father. In Cassie's dreams she is catapulted from the mattress on the roof of her Harlem apartment up and over the George Washington Bridge into the stars. She looks down and claims what she wants—to someday own the bridge, the ice cream factory, and the union building that won't let her father join. These are indeed big dreams for a black girl to have in 1939, when the story is set. Cassie's high-flung hopes are reminiscent of our slave ancestors' longing for spiritual and physical emancipation. Ms. Cassie seems to want both, and she convinces you that she can have it here and now—and so can we. "Now I have claimed it," she exclaims as she flies over the Bridge, which was completed the day she was born. "All I had to do was fly over it for it to be mine forever . . . That means I am free to go wherever I want for the rest of my life." The borders of Ms. Ringgold's original story quilt, *Tar Beach,* are used to frame the exuberant paintings in this inspirational book.

Explore These: What do Cassie and her family do on the roof? What bridge does she fly over? What are some of the things she dreams about? Ask a child: Do you have a special place to go when you just want to dream? If not, can you find one? What do you dream about achieving or changing?

TELL ME A STORY, MAMA
By Angela Johnson. Illustrator: David Soman.
Publisher: Orchard Books, 1989. HC$16.00/PB$6.95
MVP: Parent-child bond

Children love bedtime stories, particularly when they are about their own family. In this gentle book, a mother and her daughter share a nighttime ritual: the child asks her mother to tell her stories of her childhood, and stories of when the girl was younger. Particularly well written is the mother's voice, whose words are interjected into her daughter's conversation in a way that's personal, sympathetic, and intimate. The story reads as if you were sitting in the room, witnessing the bedtime ritual live. "Remember the time when you were little and you found that puppy with no tail by the side of the road?" says the girl. "Poor little thing . . ." answers the mother. The book continues with them remembering tales of childhood fun (keeping the puppy) and fears (when the mother and her younger sister were sent on the train to live with their great-aunt for a few months). But as the story is told, the book reminds us that it is in these quiet times spent together that the private, pressing questions children have can be asked and answered ("Would you cry if I moved away, Mama?" asks the child). The watercolor illustrations by Soman depict the mother helping her daughter get ready for bed, interspersed with scenes of the memories of the tales they share.

Explore These: Why did the girl like her mama's bedtime stories? Make a point of sharing family stories with your child, or have the child write down a favorite memory or story of their own that they could pass on to their children someday.

THE TRAIN TO LULU'S
By Elizabeth Fitzgerald Howard. Illustrator: Robert Casilla. Publisher: Bradbury Press (Macmillan), 1988. HC$13.95/PB$4.95 MVP: Independence

A child's first trip apart from her parents can be both a frightening journey and an exciting, life-changing adventure. So it is in this memorable book for Beppy and Babs, who make their first trip alone on the train to spend the summer with Great-Aunt Lulu in Baltimore. Coming from Boston, the trip is nine hours, and Mommy has packed lunch and supper for them. Little Babs's initial sadness at leaving disappears as the scenery out the train window unfolds. The story is told from Beppy's first-person perspective, and we can see her boldness grow as she savors her newfound independence. Simple pleasures fill them with delight: walking unsteadily down the aisle of the shaking train sets them laughing, buying milk by themselves with the dollar Daddy gave them feels important, and opening the meals their Mommy packed for them is a sweet reminder of home and love ("We open our lunch boxes. Surprise! A Hershey bar for each of us. And chicken sandwiches."). Howard knowingly picks up on the fact that independence is new and exciting for children only when they get it in small doses. As the train trip progresses, the children exhaust their games and stories, and begin to tire and feel anxious. Finally, the trip ends and they are welcomed off the train with the hugs and kisses of their aunts, uncles, and best of all, great-aunt Lulu.

Explore These: Do you think the girls liked their train trip? Ask your child to: Write a story about a trip they took and describe their favorite parts. Or, write a story about a trip they would like to take, if they could go anywhere, alone.

 THE TREASURE HUNT
By Bill Cosby. Illustrator: Varnette Honeywood.
Publisher: Scholastic, 1997. PB$3.99 US/$4.99 CAN.
MVP: Finding your special talent

It's hard to lose with the combination of Bill Cosby's wry wit and Varnette Honeywood's knockout color paintings. This book is about how children find their true talents by exploring a variety of activities. One rainy day a bored Little Bill is introduced to jazz greats by his dad, antiques by his mom, and baseball card collecting by his big brother, but nothing excites him. He doesn't see what's so great about "some scratchy old records," "players I never even heard of," or a silver platter ("all I thought about was the turkey that went on it"). But Bill's great-grandmother takes a different turn, encouraging him to find his own unique talent. She urges him to tell her a story, and when he does, Bill discovers his gift—making people laugh. The hunt for his treasure is over.

Explore This: Why was Little Bill so bored? What were his father's, mother's, and brother's hobbies? Ask your child: Do you know what your treasure is? Help them discover it by telling them what you think they're good at.

"I liked The Twins Strike Back *because it shows that even though you look the same, you can still be your own person."*

—**Lydia,** age 10

THE TWINS STRIKE BACK
By Valerie Flournoy. Illustrator: Melodye Rosales.
Publisher: Just Us Books, 1994. PB$5.00. MVP:
Uniqueness

Perfect for twins and a great story for any child, this book's story line emphasizes the importance of treating people as individuals. Natalie and Nicole are best friends and identical twins, but Natalie is great at math and Nicole excels at reading. That's fine with them, but nobody else, including their mom, seems to understand that they are different people, with different likes, dislikes and talents. Everyone seems to want them to dress the same, act the same and *be* the same. When this "twins-itis" finally sends them over the edge, the girls decide to play a joke that will teach everyone a good lesson.

Explore These: Why didn't the twins like to be seen as the same even though they looked alike? Talk about any twins you know and discuss what's the same and what's different about them.

TY'S ONE-MAN BAND
By Mildred Pitts Walter. Illustrator: Margot Tomes.
Publisher: Scholastic, 1984. PB$5.99. MVP:
Resourcefulness

Using the character of Andro, this book illustrates how to make delicious lemonade out of sour lemons. Andro is a gifted musician who has only one leg. He is a poor man, a kind of nomad who roams from town to town making music and merriment. He is a one-man band, only he has no real instruments. And how can he dance with one leg? Ty stumbles upon Andro at the pond near his house and they develop an instant rapport. But nobody Ty talks to about Andro believes in a one-legged man with no instruments making music and dancing. Nonetheless, Ty gathers the washboard, wooden spoons, tin pan and comb that Andro needs. Through sheer ingenuity, the two create an orchestra that people enjoy for miles around.

Explore These: Why didn't Ty's relatives and friends believe that Andro could make music? Ask a child: What are some things you believe in even though other people don't? Project: Take three ordinary or household objects and use them to invent a useful item or a musical instrument.

 UNCLE JED'S BARBERSHOP
By Margaree King Mitchell. Illustrator: James Ransome.
Publisher: Simon & Schuster Books for Young Readers,
1993. HC$15.00/PB$5.99. MVP: Perseverance,
Planning. Read Aloud

Uncle Jed has a dream—to own his very own barbership in town. But in the segregated South in the 1920s, that would seem like an impossible dream for a black man to have. Uncle Jed isn't daunted, he's patient. When his granddaughter needs a life-saving operation, the family asks him to help with the costs. Of course, he could not, would not, allow his baby girl to die. But there goes his barbershop nest egg. After years of rebuilding his savings, the Great Depression hits and his bank goes under—along with all his money. At no time do we see Uncle Jed in despair or without hope. There is a faith and a singlemindedness that seems to spur him on no matter what. Even when his regular customers can only afford to pay him in groceries for their haircuts, he remains faithful to them and to his goal. Finally, on his seventy-ninth birthday, Uncle Jed opens his gleaming new barbershop and half the town comes out to celebrate, including his grand-daughter, whose life he saved long ago with his sacrifice. Shortly after the opening, Uncle Jed passes away a happy man. He leaves a legacy of strength and honor that will last much longer than the shop.

Explore These: What kept Uncle Jed from opening his barbershop sooner? Ask a child: Would you have given the money you'd saved for a relative's operation? Is there something big that you've wanted for a long time? How did/do you handle waiting for it? What principles can you take from Uncle Jed to apply to goals in your own life?

WAGON WHEELS
By Barbara Brenner. Illustrator: Don Bolognese.
Publisher: HarperCollins, 1978. PB$3.75. MVP:
Brotherly love, Resourcefulness. Classic, Reading
Rainbow, Audio

After a long, painful journey West, Ed Muldie finally spied free land where he and his three boys could settle down. The boys' mama didn't survive the arduous trip; she died on the way. The Muldies didn't expect to have to live in a cold dugout until spring, but the weather in Kansas wouldn't permit building until then. Things were not turning out as planned. Just as their food supply had run out, a strange and wonderful thing happened. A group of Indians on horses galloped through the area and dropped packages of meat, fish, beans, vegetables, and dry wood for the new settlers! Ed Muldie gathered his boys around and said, "Remember this day. When someone says bad things about Indians, tell them the Osage Indians saved our lives in Nicodemus." By spring, Mr. Muldie decided to find a more lush land on which to build a house for him and his boys. But he had to make his journey alone first, leaving his boys behind. They were scared but they listened to the instructions their father gave them and cared for one another admirably, even surviving a prairie fire. Finally, they got word that it was safe to come, along with a map. Ed Muldie had great confidence that his "big boys" could make the journey successfully, and the boys were determined to live up to their father's trust. They encountered snakes, wolves, panthers, and coyotes for three weeks, remembering what their father taught them about survival in the woods. At the end of their trip, they were elated to find a small wooden house, a patch of corn stalks, and their dad standing in front with outstretched arms.

Explore These: What were some of the hard things the Muldies endured when they moved out West? How do you think Mr. Muldie must have felt leaving his boys alone? Ask your child: Describe a time when a parent or teacher trusted you to do something without their supervision. How did you do? Have you ever had to take care of younger children? What were some of the ways you cared for them? Think about a time when someone of another race did something nice for you. How did that make you feel about them?

WHAT IS LOVE?
By Sara Eberle. Illustrator: Angela Jarecki. Publisher: Standard Publishing, 1996. PB$1.99. MVP: How to show love

Sometimes children this age think love is just hugs, kisses and toys. This simple book emphasizes that love is active and self-sacrificing, and offers children ways they can show it. It is great for preschoolers who are starting to interact with other children and learn about sharing and empathy. Love is not only going over to Grandma's and baking cookies, it is bringing her a cold drink even before she asks for one. Love is waiting for your little brother to catch up, or comforting your little sister when she hurts herself. Love is doing things for others to let them know you care.

Explore These: What are some of the loving things the children in this book did for their family? Ask your child: What makes you feel loved? What are some new ways you can show love to a sibling, parent or friend?

WHEN I AM OLD WITH YOU
By Angela A. Johnson. Illustrator: David Soman. Publisher: Orchard Books, 1990. HC$14.95/PB$5.95. MVP: Spending time together

For this sweet-faced, dreadlocked little boy there is nothing better than fishing, talking, playing, eating, walking, or even just sitting with his granddaddy. In his innocence, the boy tells his grandfather a story about all the things they will do when they are both old . . . together. The image of the older black man and his grandson is rich and heartwarming, as is the obvious love between them, illustrated in the expressive watercolor paintings that accompany the story. It also resonates with our sometimes-forgotten tradition where respect and appreciation for elders is cherished. In the special world the boy and his grandfather share, there is no yardstick to measure success or failure, as the boy describes: "We can fish beside the pond . . . we won't catch any fish . . . but that's all right, Granddaddy." They eat a breakfast of bacon and orange juice outside on the porch, play cards under a tree, look at old family pictures, take a trip to the ocean and throw rocks at the waves. The reward is simply enjoying each other's company. Children will enjoy this book for the unconditional love, security, and warmth it depicts. You might also use this book as a gentle way to introduce the fact that we will some-day lose people we love.

Explore These: What are some of the things the boy did with his granddaddy? What do you think was the most important thing they did together? Think of a wonderful way for your child to spend a day with someone older he enjoys being with (Hint: Try to pick something quiet and intimate, where the focus is on the relationship rather than the activity). Make these special times a regular part of your child's life.

 WHEN I WAS LITTLE
By Toyomi Igus. Illustrator: Higgins Bond. Publisher: Just Us Books, 1992. PB$6.95. MVP: Valuing our elders, The simple life

Some of you will remember dancing "the Smurf" to vinyl records played on a turntable (I do). The world our kids live in today is full of great technological advances like CDs, cordless phones and the Internet. But sometimes with progress, there is loss. We forget the simple things, like spending all day in a little boat with your grandfather learning how to fish, which is the set-ting for this heartwarming book. Little Noel can't imagine the life his grandfather describes: growing up with no washing ma-chines, no indoor toilet, no refrigerator and, worst of all, no air conditioning! But as Grandfather Will talks about the pleasures of his simple childhood—diving into the river and crunching ice chips to cool off on hot summer days, helping his mother hang the laundry on the clothesline, and being the first one to ride in his pastor's new Model A Ford—Noel begins to appreciate what his grandfather had. Finally, he is elated when he catches his first fish—even if he can't picture life without video games.

Explore These: What are some of the things Grandfather Will did when he was young? Talk to your child about everyday life when you were growing up, and contrast it with his life today; be sure to include things you did for fun. Teach your child an activity or game that you enjoyed as a child. Take an actual trip down memory lane the next time you visit your hometown. Show your child your old school, the park you played in, your secret place, etc.

Black Illustrators' Notebook: Leo and Diane Dillon have illustrated more than two dozen books for young people, two of which have won Caldecott Honor medals.

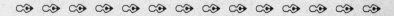

 WHY MOSQUITOES BUZZ IN PEOPLE'S EARS
By Verna Aardema. Illustrators: Leo and Diane Dillon.
Publisher: Puffin (Penguin Putnam), 1975.
HC$15.99/PB$5.99 US/$7.99 CAN. MVP: Avoid
assumptions and blame shifting. Read Aloud, Caldecott
Medal, ALA Notable

This charming West African tale is about a mosquito who unwittingly starts an uproar among an entire forest of animals. He tells a story to his friend the iguana, who doesn't believe him, who then puts sticks in his ears to avoid hearing anything more, which causes him not to hear when his friend the snake calls out to him, which causes the snake to feel snubbed. Snake decides the iguana is plotting to kill him and hides in a rabbit hole, which makes the rabbit flee, and runs to warn others of the danger. One set of assumptions leads to many others and everyone is now afraid. Mother Owl has lost one of her baby owls in the process of all the hubbub. When the mourning Owl refuses to give the signal for daylight, as she normally does every day, the animals are even more upset. They trace and trace the story until they get right back to the mosquito—only he is nowhere to be found. According to the story, this is why mosquitoes buzz in people's ears today—they are forever asking whether everyone is still angry at them. (The swat we give them in reply always answers their question.) The enjoyable story with its cutout watercolor illustrations offers a springboard for talking with a child about the consequences of making assumptions and shifting blame.

Explore These: Why didn't any of the animals want to take the blame for what happened? Explain what assuming is, then ask your child to: Describe a time when they assumed something and it was incorrect. What happened as a result? How could it have been handled better? Explain that shifting blame is just as bad as lying.

WORKING COTTON
By Sherley Anne Williams. Illustrator: Carole Byard.
Publisher: Harcourt Brace Jovanovich, 1992.
HC$14.95/PB$6.00. MVP: Hard work

Many children this age want to help wash the dishes, vacuum the floor or have their own paper route, but what if they really had to work for survival, like the family in this exquisitely illustrated story who pick cotton for a living? Based on the childhood memories of the author, and tenderly depicted by an award-winning illustrator, this story follows small Shelan and her family from the dark, "cold, cold, cold" predawn hours as they arrive at the field early for work, to sunset when the tired family packs up and heads home. Shelan is too small to carry her own sack, but she helps pile the fluffy white bolls in the middle of the row for Mamma. She sees many children in the field, and ". . . sometimes they be your friend. But you hardly ever see the same kids twice, especially after we moves to a new field." At lunch the family rests together in the field and eats cornbread and greens, sometimes a piece of meat. The acrylic illustrations transport the viewer into Shelan's world, where the rows of white cotton grow higher than a small child's head, where her sisters vie for a swig from a big jug of water, and sweat drips off the children's dark brows, framed against the deep blue summer sky. Even amidst the back-breaking work, Shelan's mom can still sing as she picks, and her dad can still hum along and admire the beauty of a late-blooming cotton blossom, "bound to bring us luck."

Explore These: What was Shelan's job in the cotton fields? Explain how slaves were used to pick cotton on Southern plantations, and the work remained common to many migrant laborers long after the Civil War. Describe how hard it was to pick cotton all day long (heat, thorns, dust, insects). Explain to the child where cotton is grown and how it is made into fabric. Ask your child: What if you couldn't go to school, but had to go to work instead? What would that be like?

 YO! YES?
Written and illustrated by Chris Raschka. Publisher: Orchard Books, 1993. HC$15.95/PB$6.95. MVP: Communication

Children will certainly have fun with this one- and two-word conversation book between boys, one black, one white. They meet each other, chat, and eventually become buddies in the book after an exchange of only about ten words. It reminds me of how many teenage boys communicate today: "Whas up?" says one. "I'm cool," says the other and so on, and before you know it, someone says, "Peace out" and the "talk" is over, yet they feel they've communicated. This cute book is vividly illustrated with large pictures of both boys, one on each side of the page, and huge words on each page. It can help a child learn that a word can convey an entire sentence if it's said right. You should find as much success reading it with your child as with John Steptoe's popular *Baby Says*, though this may appeal more to boys.

Explore These: What were the boys really saying to each other? Ask your child to: Try to say something using the least words possible and see if you can get your point across.

4

Great Books for Children Eight to Eleven

Children who can read, and those who enjoy reading aloud and reading independently

Books children eight to eleven like have:

- A little mystery or scariness
- Some rebellious character
- Less predictable storylines with more unexpected twists
- Some moral lesson
- An unpleasant or evil character who gets a second chance to improve (redemption theme)
- Wonderful, noble characters who endure hardship before they "win"
- Some dialect
- Satisfying or surprise endings, but that still conclude with good triumphing over evil

Continue reading books to your children, even though they are old enough to enjoy books independently. Reading together is excellent quality time, and will help children this age understand more complex words and sentences because they are hearing them spoken. Many children will *read* books on their grade level but will *enjoy* books written for a younger audience more. This is okay. When they improve their reading comprehension they will graduate to the books written for their age group, especially as the themes of those younger books become boring to them. If your children are reading lengthier books, be sure to skim through them in order to get a sense of the content. Be enthusiastic and ask them more casual questions about what they're reading, such as: You really seem to like that book. Tell me a little something about the story. Who is your favorite character? Why?

 ADVENTURES OF SPARROW BOY
Written and illustrated by Brian Pinkney. Publisher:
Simon & Schuster, 1997. HC$16.00. MVP: Imagination.
Caldecott Honor, Horn Book Award

What if you could be a newspaper delivery boy who rides his bicycle on the ground and in the air? That's what the main character in this book does (in his imagination), along with rescuing a little sparrow from the dangers of animals and humans. This book's fanciful theme and comic strip format will certainly appeal to middle readers and should catch the eye of reluctant readers.

Explore These: Why was the character called Sparrow Boy? What do you imagine yourself doing if you had no limits? Describe in detail.

AFRO-BETS FIRST BOOK ABOUT AFRICA
By Veronica Freeman Ellis. Illustrator: George Ford.
Publisher: Just Us Books, 1989 PB$6.95. MVP:
Learning African culture

This book introduces the history, flora and fauna of Africa to children via the Afro-Bets Kids, six children that make up the Afro-Bets Kids Club. They are all getting a history lesson on Africa together from Mr. Amegashie, their professor. He goes from introducing the people of Kush, dark-skinned Egyptians who existed back in 1300 B.C., and continues from there to briefly cover sculpture, music, animals and dance. Colorful illustrations and photographs make it an enjoyable lesson for a child at the older end of this age group.

Explore These: What happened to the great kingdoms of Africa? Trace the map of the continent of Africa onto a large piece of paper. Every few weeks fill in a different country and learn a few facts about it.

AIDA
Told by Leontyne Price. Illustrators: Leo and Diane
Dillon. Publisher: Gulliver Books (Harcourt Brace
Jovanovich), 1990. HC$16.95/PB$7.00. MVP: Love,
The result of being covetous

This delicious tale of love, power and sacrifice takes place in Ethiopia and Egypt. Marvelously illustrated by the Dillons and published on marbleized paper, it tells the story of the great operatic piece of the same name. And it is told by one of the greatest opera divas of our time, Leontyne Price. The beautiful dark Ethiopian princess Aida is captured by Egyptian soldiers and forced into slavery. While enslaved, she falls in love with Radames, the captain of the Egyptian army, and he with her. They must keep their love a secret lest the jealous Egyptian princess Amneris gets wind of it. She, too, is in love with Radames. It's wonderful just to see a love story depicted with African princesses and a dark, handsome prince decked out in the fine garments and elaborate decorative headgear of the day. When the two countries must wage war, Aida is torn between the man she loves and the memories of her family back home in Ethiopia. The Egyptians win the war, and eventually take her father, the king, as a prisoner. In addition, her beloved Radames must marry Princess Amneris, on the king's orders. Just when all seems lost, Aida and her father devise a plan of escape—only Radames must agree to forsake Amneris and his country and flee with her back home to Ethiopia. Radames agrees but is caught and accused of treason. Even on pain of a gruesome death, Radames does not forsake his love for Aida.

Explore These: How did Aida get captured? Why was Amneris upset about Radames's love for Aida? Explain what covetousness is and ask, Have you ever been covetous of another person's relationship with someone? Ask a child to: Describe a time when you had to make a hard choice between two things. What did you choose and why? On which continent are Ethiopia and Egypt located?

 ALVIN AILEY
By Andrea Davis Pinkney. Illustrator: Brian Pinkney. Publisher: Hyperion Books, 1995. PB$4.95 US/$6.95 CAN. MVP: Inspiration. Reading Rainbow, Horn Book Award

This book about Alvin Ailey's life is a wonderful combination of innovative illustration and captivating text. By the book's end we really understand what inspired Alvin Ailey to make his unique contribution to the arts. We read about Alvin's life as a child in Texas, singing and stomping to spirited gospel songs every Sunday in church, on to his adult life in Los Angeles, where he discovered that black people had an awesome style of dance and expression all their own. You can just imagine how Alvin felt when he saw his first black modern dance performance— Katherine Dunham and the Tropical Revue. Seeing his own people dance and move so beautifully and rhythmically gave him the courage and inspiration to dance and choreograph in that style—*our* style. But taking dance lessons was no easy accomplishment for a black man in 1949. Alvin found the only school who would accept him, and he thrived there. He experienced a new freedom in his dance classes that propelled him into his own world, dancing in a way that baffled and impressed even his classmates and teacher. Alvin is a testimony to the power of hard work and inspiration. He came to New York in 1958 and began his own dance company, the Alvin Ailey American Dance Theater, which still mesmerizes audiences of all races wherever they perform.

Explore These: How was Alvin able to follow his dream even though he had little money or opportunity? Ask a child: Do you have a dream that you would pursue no matter what? If not, think about it. If so, describe it.

 THE BABY GRAND, THE MOON IN JULY & ME
By Joyce Annette Barnes. Publisher: Dial Books
(Penguin Putnam), 1994. HC: $15.99/PB: $4.99. MVP:
Dreams

It is July 1969 and the most important thing to almost-eleven Annie Armstrong is that she catch the launching of the first manned flight to the moon on TV. You can bet on the fact that she's going to be an astronaut someday. It is July 1969 and the most important thing to her brother Matty Armstrong is that he find a way to buy a baby grand piano so he can play his beloved jazz. What his fingers do for those ivory keys is nothing short of genius. Both talented, both determined, the two use different methods to achieve their goals. Annie must carefully conquer her fears one by one, while fearless Matty is ready to risk striking out on his own, sink or swim. Will they actually make it? Who will get there faster and who will stay intact in the process? This book is inspiring because these kids believe they can do and be anything. Their cautious parents, while encouraging their children, aren't so sure; and the grandparents are just in awe. But Annie has a plan that will put everyone on the same page—she hopes.

Explore These: Were Annie and Matty's parents unsupportive of their childrens' big dreams? Why were they so mad when Matty bought the grand piano? Ask a child: Did you ever want something so bad you just went out and got it? Describe it. Do you think you are more practical or more of a risk-taker? Why or why not? Meet Annie and Matty a few years down the road in Barnes's sequel, *Promise Me the Moon* and find out how they did.

 BLACK COWBOY, WILD HORSES, A TRUE STORY By Julius Lester. Illustrator: Jerry Pinkney. Publisher: Dial Books (Penguin Putnam), 1998. HC$16.99 US/$24.50 CAN. MVP: Respect, Love for animals

Cowboy Bob Lemmons may not have ever learned to read, but he can tell you what a horse is thinking, where it's been and where it's about to go. This is the true story of a black Texas cowboy who was known for his innate tracking abilities when it came to horses. His self-appointed task was to singlehandedly corral the wildest horses on the plains—mustangs. To do this successfully, he has to observe them very carefully: examining their hoofprints, estimating their size and weight, and waiting. One beautifully illustrated picture is of Bob sitting on his horse Warrior, in the middle of a dark, torrential rainstorm—waiting. The mustangs can't be rushed or feel threatened; you must become "one of them" if you are to gain their trust and lead them home. When Bob comes within eyeshot of the horses, he lays flat on Warrior's back and blends in so he won't be noticed as a man among animals. Finally, the showdown between Warrior and the lead stallion begins. Warrior and the stallion snort, kick and bite each other, rearing up on their hind legs, with Bob holding on. Bob and Warrior charge and rush to victory in a fierce, dangerous battle (this is no scene from *Bonanza*!) and win the obedience of the entire pack. This book offers a bit of history, some of the adventure and excitement of a good Western.

Explore These: Who was Bob Lemmons? What are some of the things he did to get the horses to follow him? Ask your child: Put yourself in the mind of a horse, cat, dog or bird. What kinds of things might they think and feel?

THE BLACK SNOWMAN
By Phil Mendez. Illustrator: Carole Byard. Publisher:
Scholastic, 1989. HC$13.95/PB$5.99. MVP: Loving our
blackness

What do you say when your child comes home and announces, "I hate being black . . . everything black is bad." One thing's for sure, any old explanation won't do for most children, especially when they're hurt and angry. Jacob not only hates being black, he hates being poor, too. In his world, being poor and being black are synonymous. His mother tries her best to encourage him, but it takes an experience with an extraordinary snowman to turn Jacob around. Even the fact that he and his brother have only the dirty snow to play with angers Jacob. The boys are forced to make a grayish-black snowman instead of a white one. As soon as they decide to spruce him up by throwing an old piece of kente cloth around his neck, a wonderful thing happens—he comes alive! But this is no Frosty story. The black snowman is empowered with the wisdom of our ancestors to heal Jacob's hurt. It is no easy task, even for a magic snowman, and it is sobering to realize how deep the young boy's pain really is. When the snowman risks his "life" to rescue the boys from a perilous situation, Jacob realizes that he has a lot to live for after all.

Explore These: Why was Jacob so angry? Have you ever felt bad about being black? Talk about those feelings. From now on, when you make drawings or do artwork, remember to color the skin so it looks like yours.

BOOK OF BLACK HEROES: FROM A TO Z,
VOLUME ONE
By Wade Hudson and Valerie Wilson Wesley. Publisher:
Just Us Books, 1988. PB$7.95 US. MVP: Inspiration
from great achievers

From Ali, Muhammed, to Zulu, Shaka, this short book gives us page-length stories about fifty important black figures in American history. Each story is accompanied by a large black-and-white photo of the hero or heroine, their date and place of birth, and a brief phrase that describes them. A useful book for introducing young readers to our heritage.

Explore These: Which hero was your favorite? Why? Talk about what it must have been like in the time the hero lived. Project: Have a child pick one hero and do a report including other aspects of his or her life not discussed in the book.

BOUNDLESS GRACE
By Mary Hoffman. Illustrator: Caroline Binch.
Publisher: Dial Books (Penguin Putnam), 1995.
HC$14.99. MVP: Coping with separation, Longing for father

This is the equally excellent sequel to **Amazing Grace,** which features an older, wiser title character. Her dilemma this time is the fact that every family she reads about in her schoolbooks has a mother, a father, a boy, a girl, a dog, and a cat in it. "Our family's not right," Grace tells her Nana one day. "We need a father and a brother and a dog." She is still confused about what happened between her mother and father, though her mother told her the story of their divorce, his remarriage and his move to Africa a thousand times. But a father who was only visible through an occasional letter and a photo isn't much of a father in Grace's eyes—so she makes up better father stories instead. In fact, she makes up so many fantasy fathers that when her Dad writes and sends two tickets for her to visit him in Africa, she's all nerves. What would her real daddy be like? Would she like her dad's new wife and children? Would he love her as much as his new family? When Grace gets off the plane in Africa with her Nana, her dad is there to greet her with open arms. Though everyone treats her well, Grace can't help resenting the fact that her dad went on and created the storybook family without her, her mom and her Nana. Caroline Binch's carefully rendered illustrations of Grace in Africa are a treat. Eventually, Grace discovers that all families are as good as you make them.

Explore These: Why do you think Grace needed to create imaginary dads? Ask a child: What special qualities do a mother and a father bring to a family, individually? Do you think a family needs both? Why or why not?

THE CASE OF THE ELEVATOR DUCK
By Polly Berrien Berends. Illustrator: Diane Allison.
Publisher: Random House, 1989. PB$3.99 US/$5.50
CAN. MVP: Practice makes perfect

Gilbert is determined to be a detective when he grows up, and refuses to let life in a housing project stop him from practicing his craft. When a duck (of all things) unwittingly follows him onto the elevator one day, he is amazed and fascinated at the same time. He must find the duck's owner before the Housing Police get hold of him. As Gilbert races against time, he decides to allow the duck, now called Easter, to find its home by riding the elevator and letting him out on each floor. Gilbert hides and watches as the duck is scooped up by his overjoyed little owner. Job well done, end of story? Not quite. Hold out for a fun twist at the end—Easter escapes again! Find out how Gilbert handles this second caper. Nice pencil drawings appear about every two pages to help keep a young reader's interest.

Explore These: What does Gilbert want to be when he grows up? How did Gilbert sharpen his detective skills in his caper with the duck? Discuss what a real detective's job involves (following clues, being exposed to danger, thinking quickly, noting small details, expecting the unexpected, etc.).

CHRISTMAS IN THE BIG HOUSE, CHRISTMAS IN THE QUARTERS
By Patricia C. McKissack and Fredrick L. McKissack.
Illustrator: John Thompson. Publisher: Scholastic,
1995. HC$15.95. MVP: Appreciating our forebears,
Resourcefulness

The cover of this book depicts a happy mixture of white slave-owners and enslaved black people gathered 'round the Christmas tree, but things were rarely so cordial on Southern plantations. The book contrasts how the holidays were spent in the Big House and in the slave quarters. Some plantation owners allowed their slaves passes to visit relatives for the day, always a source of both joy and sorrow for those visiting and being visited. Despite the horrendous conditions, folks in the quarters did their best to enjoy the celebration of Christ's birth. There were small presents to make and special meals to prepare—Christmas was one of the few times when slaves knew the feeling of a full stomach. But first they had to scrub the Big House from top to bottom, decorate it, and prepare and serve multicourse meals for the many visiting relatives. The comparison format of this book works well to give children a real understanding of how hard it was for black families during slavery, and how relatively carefree life was for the white families they served. Though small gifts were exchanged between master and slave, as soon as Christmas ended, so did the festive atmosphere. The master announces which children of slaves will be sold away first thing on New Year's Day. Through the sadness, there is the underlying hope that runs throughout the book, which is set in 1859, several years before the Emancipation Proclamation was signed. "I got a feeling, we aine gon' need to run away," says a brown-skinned mother hugging her visiting son. "One day, soon, we gon' celebrate the Big Times in freedom." Indeed, many a Christmas prayer was answered.

Explore These: How were Christmas celebrations different for the enslaved black families versus those of the white families? As suggested in the Author Note, encourage children to be time travelers, maybe even to close their eyes during certain parts and envision themselves in the story. Have children tell their own stories of how their family gets ready for Christmas (and/or Kwanzaa). Let them understand how much better things are, at Christmas and all the time, thanks to the sacrifices of our enslaved elders. If it's near Christmas, you could host a gift-making afternoon where children must use their resourcefulness to make creative gifts from odds and ends.

 DANCING WITH THE INDIANS
By Angela Shelf Medearis. Illustrator: Samuel Byrd.
Publisher: Holiday House, 1991. HC$14.95. MVP:
Appreciating our Native American roots

There seem to be few books that creatively explain to children the important role Native Americans played in the lives of black people during slavery. This book does an exceptional job because it is the true story of the author's own great-grandfather, who was accepted into the tribe of the Seminole Indians in Oklahoma when he ran away from slavery. Since then, it has been a tradition in her family to participate in a powwow each year. The book, which is all in rhyme, describes the rhythmic circle dances done at a powwow, and the large, colorful illustrations capture their excitement—"Warriors' moccasined feet make rumbling, thundering sounds, wheeling, whooping, whirling, stomping on the ground."

Explore These: Why did the family go back to the Indian powwow? (It will be helpful to have gathered any other interesting stories or facts about the relationship between Native Americans and African Americans.) Get in a circle, join hands, and do your own version of the "rattlesnake dance." Use any slow drumbeat to keep you on pace.

 DITCH-DIGGER'S DAUGHTERS: A BLACK FAMILY'S ASTONISHING SUCCESS STORY
By Yvonne Thornton and Jo Coudert. Publisher: Plume (Penguin Putnam), 1996. PB$12.95. MVP: The value of hard work, Dreams

Yvonne is one of five daughters who were raised during difficult times in the 1940s. Their father was a ditch digger, among other jobs he held to make ends meet. Despite hard times, he taught his girls the importance of hard work, using their talents and dreaming larger than their present circumstances. It worked. His girls used their musical talent to put themselves through school and grew up to become doctors, of which the author is one, lawyers, and other skilled professionals. This book is a testimony to the fact that we can rise above any situation to achieve greatness as long as we have direction, faith, love, and support.

Explore These: How did the father in this story teach his children the value of hard work? Did you learn anything new? Did the girls' ingenuity and success inspire you toward a goal of your own? If so, tell how.

DREW AND THE BUB DADDY SHOWDOWN
Written and illustrated by Robb Armstrong. Publisher:
HarperTrophy (HarperCollins), 1996. PB$3.95
US/$5.25CAN. MVP: Knowing your self-worth.
Read Aloud

In this funny contemporary novel by Robb Armstrong, creator
of the nationally syndicated comic strip *Jump Start,* a young boy
learns a valuable lesson about self-esteem through his brother's
accident and feud with a local bully. Drew is an ordinary eight-
year-old boy, until one day a cast is removed from his broken arm
and he suddenly discovers that he can "draw like a real artist."
One day he creates a comic strip about a superagent he names
Mason Stone, and receives such overwhelming praise for it that
he and his friends begin to sell it to the neighborhood kids.
Drew, who has always felt that he lived in the shadow of his daredevil older brother, Kyle, exults in the praise and attention. But a
frightening accident his brother has while doing a reckless stunt
soon puts a damper on his success. Drew is convinced that Skipper, a local bully, caused the accident, and accuses him. In the af-
termath, Drew not only learns the truth about the accident, but
learns that respect doesn't need to come from daredevil stunts or
from special talents.

Explore These: What did Drew learn about Kyle at the end of
the story? Why do you think Kyle was relieved to find out that
Skipper didn't do it? Explain what self-worth is and ask, Where
did Drew find that it really comes from?

---

*"I like to read because it's interesting to see how the characters act out
their emotions. A really good book makes me feel like I'm in the story.
When the characters are funny, it makes me laugh; and when they
are sad, I am too."*

—**Ebony,** age eleven

DREW AND THE HOMEBOY QUESTION
Written and Illustrated by Robb Armstrong. Publisher:
HarperCollins, 1997. PB$3.95 US/$5.25 CAN. MVP:
Strength of character

This is a frank and humorous book about a boy's reluctant feelings as his parents switch him from his black public school to an all-white private school. Robb Armstrong's cartoon-style illustrations enhance the appeal of the book, especially to children this age who love to read comics. The main character, Drew, is a budding comic illustrator himself. He created the character Mason Stone Superagent, and his friends from 'round the way eagerly await each new installment. In time, though, Drew must say goodbye to his faithful boyz when his parents decide to transfer him to a better school. Will he lose his homeboy status when he dons his new navy blue school blazer with the antlers embroidered on the pocket? Drew wonders fearfully. Or, worse, will he start to "talk and act white," like his cohorts predict? Still unsure, Drew extends himself to a disheveled but rich white boy who needs help while on a visit to the new school. His kindness returns to him when he least expects it and he makes a new friend in the process. Even his homies come around eventually and promise to stay in touch. Maybe prep school won't be so bad after all. A good book to give a child who is having angst about changing schools.

Explore These: Why didn't Drew want to go to the new school? Ask a child: Have you ever felt sad when you had to leave old friends or classmates? Describe the circumstances. Did you stay in touch? Make new friends? Have you ever been one of the only blacks in a school or neighborhood? Did you find yourself acting differently? How can you stay strong even when you stand alone?

ESCAPE TO FREEDOM: A PLAY ABOUT YOUNG FREDERICK DOUGLASS
By Ossie Davis. Publisher: Viking (Penguin Putnam),
1990. PB$3.99. MVP: The importance of reading.
Classic

History comes alive for children when it is made interactive. This play captures the life of the great orator, editor, and U.S. ambassador Frederick Douglass, from his childhood as a slave to a young white boy to his eventual escape to freedom disguised as a sailor. In between, Frederick discovered the hard way how crucial it was that he—and every enslaved black person—learn to read. The conspiracy among white slaveowners to forbid slaves from even holding a book or trying to understand printed numbers or words is brought out with haunting clarity. Even the sympathetic white mistress who introduced Frederick to reading was severely reprimanded by her slavemaster husband, who insisted she stop immediately. Of course, all of this fuss about *not* allowing slaves to read only served to convince a determined Frederick that he must learn—or die. The staging for this play is simple and well constructed and it requires only a few simple props. Five children can perform this play with two playing dual roles, or seven children each playing one role. The music for the play consists of hymns sung by cast members; the melodies can be made up or the actual hymns can be researched and practiced.

Explore These: Explain what a play is—that it is meant to be performed, not read; use the book to show the format of a play script. Read through the play informally; assign parts to each child and encourage them to bring feeling to their characters. (If you want to perform the play publicly you must obtain permission in writing from the source listed in the front of the book.) Take children to the dress rehearsal of a community or regional theater production and discuss the interactions they see between the performers, director, and other production staff.

"There's nothing I enjoy more than reading a gripping, intriguing mystery."

—**Nancy Wilson,** Grammy and Emmy award–winning songstress who enjoys Robert San Souci's folktales

---

THE FAITHFUL FRIEND
By Robert D. San Souci. Illustrator: Brian Pinkney.
Publisher: Simon & Schuster, 1995. HC$16.00
US/$21.50 CAN. MVP: Unselfishness, Interracial
friendship. Caldecott Honor

This beautiful rendition of a West Indian tale has all the elements of a great story: loyal friendship, pure romance, perilous adventure, and a happy ending—all in a lush tropical setting (the island of Martinique) depicted by brilliant illustrator Brian Pinkney. Clement and Hippolyte are best friends from childhood, the former black, the latter white. A welcome twist is the fact that Clement's well-to-do black family owns the Big House, and invites Hippolyte's working-class French mother to live there. With slavery ending in the Caribbean much earlier than it did in the U.S., black families were able to rise to prominence and become landowners more readily. The two boys are caught up in intrigue when Clement falls in love and enlists Hippolyte's help to win his bride, Pauline. Her disapproving uncle conjures up trouble for the new couple in the form of beautiful forest zombies that set death traps for Clement and Pauline. San Souci notes that the identification of these spirit-like troublemakers as zombies makes the story distinctly West Indian. Loyal to the end, Hippolyte takes the fall in order to save his friends' lives and they watch, horrified, as he begins to turn to stone (the punishment for disrupting the zombies' plan). A surprising character arrives to save the day and restore Hippolyte back to life. Everyone marries, has children, and lives happily ever after—together. A wholesome tale of cross-racial harmony and friendship.

Explore These: Why didn't Pauline's father approve of Clement? What did Hippolyte do to help his friend? Ask a child: What is a friend, in your own words? How far would you go to help a friend? How far *should* you go? Have children pronounce the French words in the glossary that appears at the front of the book. Encourage an interest in learning French words by borrowing language tapes from the library. Suggest a creative project about the island of Martinique and its people.

Black Illustrators' Notebook: Brian Pinkney has illustrated many books for children, including *Alvin Ailey* (see page 116), written by his wife, Andrea Pinkney, who is a children's book editor. He won a Caldecott Honor for *Faithful Friend* and has received awards and honors for several of his other books for children.

FAST SAM, COOL CLYDE, AND STUFF
By Walter Dean Myers. Publisher: Viking (Penguin Putnam), 1975. HC$10.95/PB$3.99. MVP: True friendship. Classic

This admirable group of ordinary young 1970s teens is experiencing some of the harsher realities of life, like the death of a parent and the dashing of dreams. When they get hit hard, these kids decide they must support each other through thick and thin and even offer help to other teens around them who seem on the brink of disaster. The friends form a club called the Good People, admittedly the corniest name they could think of. It's nice to see them stand up for what they know is right and put themselves out on a limb emotionally to talk openly about their fears and doubts. In between all the sharing, they are normal, basketball-stuffing, boy/girl-watching, school-hating teenagers, but they've got one up on everyone else—they've created a safety net for one another. Good writing by Myers pulls it all together into a very believable and inspiring story.

Explore These: Why did they decide to form the Good People club? Ask a child: Do you and your friends talk about problems at school and try to help each other? Is a Good People club a good idea? What purpose would it serve in your life and the lives of your friends?

FOLLOW THE DRINKING GOURD
Written and illustrated by Jeanette Winter. Publisher: Alfred A. Knopf, 1992. PB$7.99. MVP: Hope

Something about the travesty of man's inhumanity to man must have tugged at the heart of Peg Leg Joe, a white man who went to great lengths to help enslaved blacks escape. Joe took a job as a carpenter on a plantation just so he could be near enough to teach the slaves, in code, the way North. He put the directions in the form of a song whose lyrics told of star formations (the Drinking Gourd is the Big Dipper), marked trees and other signs that would aid the journey. It also told of "safe houses," stops along the Underground Railroad that would have a lamp on in the window so they could be recognized. But as this book emphasizes, even with assistance, the journey, which could last for weeks, was still perilous. The travelers walked through the unfamiliar woods by night and rested by day—but who could sleep with the faint sound of barking, snarling hound dogs in the distance? Often there was no food for days and no stars to guide them between landmarks; they felt lost many a time. Once they entered free states in the North, they were shuttled from house to house, hidden in barns, cellars, and secret rooms where they were fed, and were able to bathe and rest in the homes of benevolent white and black families. But how relaxed could they be? If they ventured outside, they could be spotted, caught, and recaptured at any time, if someone had a mind to report them. Finally, after crossing the lake into Canada, the enslaved families knew they were really free.

Explore These: What was the Drinking Gourd? What were some of the dangers the escaping families faced on their journey? What do you think motivated Peg Leg Joe to help the slaves? Explain that abolitionists were people who believed that slavery was ungodly and were willing to take risks to assist the slaves in finding freedom. Ask a child: Has a person of another race ever helped you with something that was important to you? Have you done similarly? Talk about it. What is freedom? What are some other freedoms our forebears fought for that we enjoy today? Point some out and discuss with your child.

THE FRIENDSHIP
By Mildred D. Taylor. Illustrator: Max Ginsburg.
Publisher: Puffin Books (Penguin Putnam), 1987. PB:
$3.99 US/$4.99 CAN. MVP: Dignity. Coretta Scott King
Award, ALA Notable, Hom Book Award

If you are familiar with Mildred Taylor's excellent books about the Logan family, you'll know that the white-owned Wallace store was not the place to shop if you were black and living in Mississippi in 1933. But when a sick neighbor needs some medicine, the Logan children decide to pick it up for her. A shiny glass cabinet of new items catches the eye of the youngest boy, called Little Man, who is nastily reprimanded by the store owner's son Dewberry, "Get your filthy hands off my case! Look at ya, skin's black as dirt!" Little Man, scared to death, holds his clean little hands up to the owner and says, innocently, "They ain't dirty! They clean! See?" Ignoring him, Dewberry's brother chimes in, laughing, "They so filthy better just chop them hands off!" The scar of that incident remained deep in Little Man's heart. *Was* he dirty? he wonders. As they turn to go home, they meet Mr. Tom Bee, an older black man who doesn't take any guff. When he goes into the store asking for "John" to place his order (instead of "Sir"), tempers are at a boil. The racist storekeepers are poised for a fight, but Tom is an elder with nothing to lose, and decides to defend his dignity, whatever the cost. The children learn a harsh lesson about the price of respect as they watch the tense scene with Mr. Tom Bee and John unfold. See also *The Gold Cadillac* and *Mississippi Bridge.*

Explore These: Why did the store owner tell Little Man his hands were dirty when they weren't? How did that make him feel? Do you think Mr. Tom Bee did the right thing? Ask your child to: Describe a time when someone said something untrue about her that hurt her feelings. How did she handle it? Describe a promise made to someone that was hard to keep. How did it turn out? *Parent/Teacher Note:* It is important to first explain to children what was going on between blacks and whites in the South at the time this book is set. The book does not have a traditional happy ending, but it provides an excellent opportunity to discuss a number of values: racial equality, respect for elders, self-image, keeping one's word and dignity.

GIFTED HANDS: THE BEN CARSON STORY
By Ben Carson, M.D., with Cecil Murphey. Publisher:
Zondervan (Harper Collins), 1990. PB$10.99. MVP: Faith

This inspiring story talks of the things many children face—struggling with poor grades, getting by with little money, battling racism and peer pressure, and longing for the absent father—but Dr. Ben Carson's story is one of triumph through courage, faith in God, and belief in himself. Dr. Carson is famous for his part in performing the first successful separation of Siamese twins joined at the head. His remarkable journey from ghetto-raised F student to brilliant surgeon and director of pediatric neurosurgery at Johns Hopkins University Hospital is one that readers will relate to and be encouraged by. Dr. Carson offers gripping personal stories of how God pulled off miracle after miracle to make him the success and the role model he is today.

Explore These: What kept Ben Carson from giving up? How did his brother Curtis, his mother and others encourage him in his chosen profession? What are some of the principles that guide Dr. Carson's life? How can you use them in your own life?

GREAT AFRICAN AMERICANS IN . . .
Publisher: Crabtree, 1996–1997. PB$8.95 US/$10.95
CAN/£ 4.50 UK. MVP: Achieving dreams

This is an excellent series of books for youth for several reasons: they are colorful, mostly filled with photos of people they know and admire, and are very readable. The book spends two to four pages highlighting the careers of each notable, including growing up, developing skills, and overcoming obstacles. You can tell that the choices of who to include in each volume were made with care—it's nice to see designer Patrick Kelly on the cover of the Business book, Gordon Parks on the Arts book, and former Virginia governor L. Douglas Wilder on the Government book cover, along with better-known luminaries such as Michael Jordan, Oprah Winfrey, Bill Cosby, Florence Griffith-Joyner, Denzel Washington, and Spike Lee. The books emphasize the hard roads many had to walk to achieve their current celebrity or superstar status.

Explore These: Use this book to help a child think about career options intelligently. Emphasize the steps each person took to achieve success; have the child write down his or her dream career and then list a few things he or she must do now to move toward it. The series includes eleven books: *Great African Americans In: Jazz, Government, The Arts, Business, Entertainment, Sports, The Olympics, Music, History, Civil Rights,* and *Film.*

"My favorite she-ro in Great Women of the Struggle *was Rosa Parks. She refused to give up her seat on the bus and started a revolution."*
— **Charles,** age 13

 GREAT WOMEN IN THE STRUGGLE: BOOK OF BLACK HEROES, VOLUME TWO
Edited by Toyomi Igus. Publisher: Just Us Books, 1997. PB$10.95. MVP: Appreciating the contributions of black women. Reading Rainbow

Sheroes of the eighteenth century sit right alongside contemporary sisters of excellence in this tribute to ninety black women who have made history in all walks of life, from freedom fighters to athletes. The book devotes one page to each heroine, and their biographies are accompanied by a photograph and a quote. The information presented is interesting and illuminating. Who knew that Pulitzer prize–winning novelist Alice Walker once worked in New York City's Welfare Office, for instance? Or that famous educator Mary McLeod Bethune sold sweet potato pies to help finance her school for girls? Or that Oprah Winfrey gave a speech in her church at age two? Many more facts about these and other famous African-American women are included in this excellent and easy-to-read historical volume. An extensive chronology at the end of the book highlights significant events in our history from 1500 to 1990. This can be a great quick resource for short reports, school projects, and general knowledge.

Explore These: Encourage your child to choose sheroes in her area of interest and make an inspirational poster that can encourage her toward her goal each time she looks at it.

THE HUNDRED PENNY BOX
By Sharon Bell Mathis. Illustrators: Leo and Diane
Dillon. Publisher: Viking (Penguin Putnam), 1975.
HC$16.99/PB$4.99. MVP: Empathy

Aunt Dew is one hundred years old. Because of her loss of memory and frailty, she has recently moved in with her nephew John and his wife, Ruth. Their son Michael is Aunt Dew's biggest fan. He doesn't even mind that she forgets who he is and calls him "John-boy" after his father. Most of the time Aunt Dew sits in her rocker and sings "Precious Lord Take My Hand," but sometimes she'll ask Michael to play her records on the record player or, better yet, open her Hundred Penny Box, which contains a penny from every year of her life. Michael gladly obliges, counting the pennies out as Aunt Dew says, "Stop right here, boy," and asks, "You know what that penny means? 18 and 74 was the year I was born. 19 and 01 . . . I was twenty-seven years. Birthed my twin boys." And so on. Michael learns of Aunt Dew's valuable years on this earth. Michael has a hard time understanding why his mother treats Aunt Dew like a child—making her take naps, and discarding her possessions that his mother feels Aunt Dew doesn't need. When his mother mentions burning the Hundred Penny Box because it is so old and beat up, Michael explodes. Mother just wants Aunt Dew to "go forward and try to have a new life," but Michael feels that his mother "didn't understand that a new life wasn't very good if you had to have everything old taken away from you." The conflict is certainly complex, and Ms. Mathis's remarkable dialogue enables us to sympathize with each character. The illustrations are shadowy and haunting, not quickly forgotten. This story offers children a probing look into growing old and a protagonist who is to be admired for his loving, empathetic actions toward his great-aunt.

Explore These: What's the significance of Aunt Dew's penny box? Ask a child: Can you remember something important that happened in every year of your life? Is there an elderly person in your family? What fears and concerns might they be feeling as they grow older? How can you encourage and support them in their "golden years?" Take a trip to a nursing home and bring a bouquet of flowers or a bag of lollipops to share with the residents. Ask them to tell you a story.

I HAVE HEARD A LAND
By Joyce Carol Thomas. Illustrator: Floyd Cooper.
Publisher: HarperCollins, 1998. HC$14.95. MVP:
Hope, Vision

The story of African-American pioneer families who helped settle the Wild West is not often heard, but is richly described in this warm and lushly illustrated book by award-winning author Joyce Carol Thomas. The book was inspired by the story of the author's great-grandparents, who were among a tide of African Americans who joined the race for free land in the Oklahoma Territory 1889 and 1893 land runs. Thomas's poetic language describes the promise and dreams her ancestors saw turn into realities as they staked their claims on the prairies, dug starter homes out of sod, and raised log cabins by hand with their neighbors to endure the harsh winters. The book resonates with the strong sense of independence and family unity that our brave forebears surely must have reveled in after their flight from the South. Freedom gave added joy to simple pleasures such as singing praise songs "under an arbor of bushes" and eating flapjacks and honey at a family breakfast on a cold, snowy morning. These scenes are perfectly depicted by Cooper's warm, textured illustrations (Cooper's family also laid a claim in the land runs). An author's note at the end of the book describes some of her family's personal stories.

Explore These: Why did black families go to Oklahoma? With your child, make a list of all the things the pioneers would have to do and learn in order to survive in the new land (i.e., plant food, harvest food, sell it, hunt wild animals, build a log home). Explain how with determination and faith, the settlers learned these new skills. Read a parallel "promised land" story, such as the biblical story of the Israelites at Jericho. One Sunday morning, sit together as a family and sing spirituals; have each person share a brief "sermon," in their own words.

... IF YOU LIVED AT THE TIME OF MARTIN LUTHER KING
By Ellen Levine. Illustrator: Anna Rich. Publisher: Scholastic, 1990. PB$5.99 US/$7.99 CAN. MVP: Black history, Martin Luther King

This brightly illustrated, easy-to-read book puts children right in the action in the midst of segregation and the growing civil rights movement. The role children played in the struggle is highlighted in several instances, making young readers feel included. One illustration shows how children distributed flyers to people urging them to join the Montgomery bus boycott; others show young people picketing in front of Woolworth's, holding hands singing "We Shall Overcome" as part of SNCC (pronounced "snick," for Student Non-Violent Coordinating Committee); and another shows a boy looking in from outside the fence as white people picnic—the sign above him blaring "NO COLORED." An effective way to teach black history to children as a living, breathing, ongoing saga, one in which they play a significant part.

Explore These: When did the civil rights movement begin? Were children involved in the protests? What part did they play? Ask a child: Do you see ways that you benefit today from the work of yesterday's black children? What can you do now to benefit your own children someday?

Black Illustrators' Notebook: Javaka Steptoe won his first Coretta Scott King award for illustration with *In My Daddy's Arms I Am Tall*. He is the son of the late artist John Steptoe, who also won a King award in 1982 for his illustrations in *Mother Crocodile* (see "Oops" List, page 232).

IN MY DADDY'S ARMS I AM TALL: AFRICAN AMERICANS CELEBRATING FATHERS
By Javaka Steptoe. Publisher: Lee & Low, 1997. PB$15.95. MVP: Honoring Fathers. Read Aloud, Coretta Scott King Award

This is a powerful collection of poems by new and established black writers speaking from their hearts about their fathers. "When you follow in the path of your father you learn to walk like him," an Ashanti proverb tells us at the book's beginning. Javaka Steptoe should know. He is the artist son of the late John Steptoe, a distinguished illustrator. "I was able to think about my father and how he affected me and how I affected him," says Javaka on writing his first book, in his father's honor. The art is superb, three-dimensional mixed media that seems almost touchable. Steptoe uses beads, buttons, pennies, torn paper, leaves, dirt, bits of cloth, and even a painted basketball to create his full-color collages. The poems are evocative, reminding us that we are the "crop," the fruit of our collective fathers' loins. Will we be "big, strong, and proud like him," as one poem asserts? Older children will really enjoy and be enriched by reading these, though it may bring up some deep issues for those without relationships with their fathers.

Explore These: Which one of these poems make you think about your dad? Tell why. What's different about your relationship with your dad as opposed to your mom? If your dad is absent and you could have changed the past, what would you like your relationship to be, if any?

AN ISLAND CHRISTMAS
By Lynn Joseph. Illustrator: Catherine Stock. Publisher: Clarion Books, 1992. PB$5.95. MVP: Helping out at home, Making holidays special. Read Aloud, Audio

Anyone who appreciates West Indian culture will like this book for a child. It is written in mild dialect and is filled with large watercolor illustrations of an island family preparing for Christmas. Just like in America, there are special meals, drinks, cakes, and music to be made in preparation for the big day—mashed potatoes for fried alloe pies, fresh soursop to make ice cream, and rum-soaked currants for black Christmas cake. The red sorrel leaves that decorate the book's opening page are a Caribbean staple; steeped in water, they make a wonderful drink. It is a warm and endearing experience watching the children put homemade decorations on their modest but unique guava branch Christmas tree, "hearing" the parang band play in front of each house, and watching dad sneak off to town on his bike to pick up a last-minute gift—a steel band drum for his daughter, Rosie, who is our narrator. The way the children willingly pitch in to help their parents prepare the house for visiting relatives is an underlying lesson in this pleasant and unique story.

Explore These: What are some of the treats Rosie's family prepared for Christmas? Talk about the fact that black Americans can come from many places—the Southern U.S., the Caribbean, Africa, South America, and other countries. Show children where the West Indies is on the map and read the author note at the end where he explains the traditions of his home island, Trinidad, on which the book is based. Explain that though Rosie's family didn't have a lot of money for expensive gifts, they still had a great Christmas.

 JACKSON JONES AND THE PUDDLE OF THORNS
By Mary Quattlebaum. Illustrator: Melodye Rosales.
Publisher: Bantam Doubleday Dell, 1994. PB$3.99.
MVP: Friendship, Ingenuity

Jackson Jones is a city kid with big ambitions and a huge dose of self-confidence. On his tenth birthday, his hope for a new basketball is shattered when his country-raised mother gives him a gift that she hopes will represent a piece of her childhood: a small city garden plot. Jackson's initial disappointment fades as he and his friend Reuben begin scheming about how they can make that garden plot turn a profit, earning money for the basketball with change to spare. But conflict arises as Jackson's money-making ambitions begin to get in the way of his friendships, and the neighborhood bully begins to harass him in the process. Jackson's descriptions have real spunk—". . . my tenth birthday had flattened like a basketball hit by a Mack truck. PP!-fssssss . . ."—which will make the story interesting and believable to a child this age. He learns the value of swallowing his pride and his profits for the sake of keeping his friendships. Quattlebaum fills the story with vivid and colorful glimpses of city life—his bilingual Colombian neighbors, and the woman whose "lips were the color of zinnias and her eyes blue-painted up to the brow." The story shows the importance of the close relationships formed between neighbors in Jackson's inner-city apartment building.

Explore These: Why was Jackson disappointed at first? What did the garden plot have to do with him getting a new basketball? Ask a child: How can you work to contribute to the purchase of something you want? Figure out how much you need to make and by when in order to buy the item. Help your child make her own "garden of flowers," whether in the yard or on the fire escape or windowsill. Watch with her the progress from seed to blooms and explain how the process works.

Black Illustrators' Notebook: Jerry Pinkney is a three-time Caldecott Honor Medalist and is the only artist ever to have won five Coretta Scott King Awards for illustration, including one for *Minty* (see page 81), and two Coretta Scott King Honor Awards. *John Henry* won a Caldecott Honor Medal for illustration.

 JOHN HENRY
By Julius Lester. Illustrator: Jerry Pinkney. Publisher: Dial Books (Penguin Putnam), 1994. HC$16.99. MVP: Determination

This is the incredible legend of a boy-turned-man named John Henry. Even as a baby, John was big—doing arm-lifts with his own cradle, as Jerry Pinkney humorously depicts. As a youngster, he was taller and stronger than everyone his age and people came from miles around just to see him. He could even outlast the sun and outrun a man on a horse. When the time came for John to leave home to seek his fortune, his father gave him two huge sledgehammers that had been passed down to him. John Henry joined a road-building crew, where there was a big boulder, "hard as anger" sitting in the middle where the road was to be. The men tried dynamite to blast the rock, but nothing moved. John Henry commenced to swinging his hammers so fast and hard, huge clouds of dust and rainbows appeared around his shoulders, "shining and shimmering in the dust and grit like hope that never dies." When John Henry finished a job, he walked off into the sunset like a cowboy after a battle won. The next crew needed a hole blasted in the side of a mountain to make a tunnel—guess who worked faster than even the steam-blasting machine? After John Henry's death, the townspeople learned a lesson about a life well lived. And folks talk about, and sing about, him still, they say.

Explore These: Who was John Henry and what did he do best? Help your child to think about something they do very well, better than most. Help them explore the things they can do or be using that talent when they grow up.

 JOURNEY TO JO'BURG: A SOUTH AFRICAN STORY By Beverley Naidoo. Illustrator: Eric Velasquez. Publisher: HarperTrophy, 1988. PB$4.95 US/$6.75 CAN. MVP: Determination, Love for siblings

Through the story of thirteen-year-old Naledi and her younger brother Tiro, which was awarded the Children's Book Award, we learn a lot about what life was like in South Africa during apartheid. More than that, we learn that life in the small village where the children live is very different from the bustling and dangerous city of Johannesburg where everyone works. Naledi and Tiro's mom works as a live-in maid for a wealthy white family in Jo'burg, many miles away. Their youngest sister, Dineo, has been sick and none of Granny's remedies have helped. There was no money for a doctor and no guarantee that a white doctor would treat Dineo. They must go tell their Mma (Mother, in the Tswana language). The two take the risky journey on foot, and along the way encounter both kind helpers and perilous situations with the South African police. It is noteworthy how Naledi takes care of her younger brother throughout the journey, and how much they sacrifice to help their sister get well. Also, if it were not for the kindness of several friends and strangers, the children would never have made it to their destination. Eventually, the two do find their Mma, and they are changed by what they see in Jo'burg. Naledi now understands that freedom in South Africa will be costly, but she vows to be a part of it.

Explore These: Why did Naledi and Tiro make the long trip? Ask a child how they would plan if they had to make such a long and dangerous journey. What was the police scene at the train station all about? Use the glossary in the back of the book to help a child learn the African words. Show children where South Africa is on a globe or map. Talk about the importance of the South African liberation that took place under President Nelson Mandela.

Black Writers' Notebook: Mildred Pitts Walter is the author of more than a dozen books for children and young adults, including *Justin and the Best Biscuits in the World,* winner of the 1987 Coretta Scott King Award. She is also the author of *My Mama Needs Me.*

 JUSTIN AND THE BEST BISCUITS IN THE WORLD
By Mildred Pitts Walter. Publisher: Bullseye Books
(Random House), 1986. HC$16.00/PB$3.99 US/$4.99
CAN. MVP: The importance of being thorough. Coretta
Scott King Award

Justin hates chores—he thinks only women know how to do things like clean, cook, make beds and be on time. But a week at his grandfather's big Missouri ranch changes all that. Grandpa has a plan. He will teach Justin how to do "men's work" like fixing fences and handling horses, plus show him by example how to do his household chores excellently. Justin notices how Grandpa's bed is always crisp, his room clean, and his pants always ironed. On top of that, Grandpa makes a delicious meal from scratch when they're out camping. Justin sees first-hand that being a man means more than he thought. He also learns about his great-great-grandfather's life as a black cowboy and gets to attend a real rodeo. Justin goes home with a great recipe for biscuits under his belt, and some valuable lessons that will serve him for a lifetime.

Explore These: Why do you think Justin was having such a hard time with his chores? What finally helped him? Ask a child: What did you learn about black cowboys? About running an animal farm? What are some benefits of taking the time to do chores thoroughly instead of halfway? Show your child by example the proper way to clean his room and do other chores. Project: Plan to visit a rodeo or farm. Take out a book on black cowboys. See *Black Cowboys, Wild Horses* by Julius Lester, page 118.

 KIDS' BOOK OF WISDOM
Compiled by Cheryl and Wade Hudson. Illustrator: Anna Rich. Publisher: Just Us Books, Inc., 1996. PB$5.95. MVP: Living values

A compilation of quotes, proverbs, and sayings recognizes the virtues passed on from the great history of African-American tradition. The book organizes the quotes according to a specific virtue such as ambition, loyalty, patience, trust, and so on, first defining the virtue, offering a brief explanation or anecdote, and then listing the quotes. The great diversity encompassed in black culture and tradition is emphasized here. The quotes are compiled from famous black contemporary and historical figures, adages from various African countries, blues lyrics, and more. Some are humorous (on friends and family: "Everybody that grins in your face ain't no friend to you"), some are inspirational (on courage: "The strong man is the man who can stand up for his rights and not hit back"—Martin Luther King Jr.)—all are enjoyable. Children will love this small book just to read on their own or as a beginning resource for homework assignments.

Explore These: Which were your favorite sayings and why? Invent your own axiom or saying to represent a common virtue. Pick two or three favorite quotes to put up in your bedroom or on the refrigerator door.

KWANZAA
By A. P. Porter. Illustrator: Janice Lee Porter. Publisher: Carolrhoda Books, 1991. PB$5.95 US/$8.50 CAN.
MVP: Appreciating African family values

Not only does this book explain what Kwanzaa is, it offers a history lesson about our people. Children learn about the slave trade, about Maulana Karenga, and the fact that Marcus Garvey created the red, black, and green flag, the bendera. The words used to describe the seven principles are simple, but clear and thoughtful. "Ujamaa means buying from each other. African-Americans buy most things from people that are not black. Going to stores and clinics owned by black people makes the African-American community stronger." See also *Seven Candles for Kwanzaa* by Andrea Davis Pinkney and *The Story of Kwanzaa* by Stephen Taylor.

Explore These: Ask a child: In their own words, what does Kwanzaa mean to them? What are the seven principles of Kwanzaa? What are some specific ways they can live out some of these principles every day? Activity: Help your child host a Kwanzaa celebration for his friends.

Let's revive our storytelling tradition! Prolific author **Julius Lester** notes, "Storytelling creates and re-creates community, making a bond between the living and the living, the young and the old, the living and the dead, the human and the animal, the human and the vegetable and the mineral." The act of a parent, relative or teacher taking the time to sit down and tell a child a story cannot be replaced by handing him a storybook and hoping he reads it, no matter how well written or beautifully illustrated it may be. A child may forget the details of the story told to him, but he will remember the relationship. To learn more effective storytelling, see books in Great Reading Resources.

 THE LAST TALES OF UNCLE REMUS
As told by Julius Lester. Illustrator: Jerry Pinkney.
Publisher: Dial Books (Penguin Putnam), 1994.
HC$18.99. Theme: African-American folk tales.
Read Aloud

Unfortunately, storytelling may be a dying art in today's modern black family. As Julius Lester points out in the Introduction to this book, the fourth in the award-winning remade series of Uncle Remus Tales, storytelling "is a human event." Lester has again attempted to preserve for our children, and future generations, the wonderful old stories about Brer (short for brother) Rabbit and his friends. His desire was also to redeem the image of Uncle Remus, which is associated with servility and plantation life, and preserve the largest group of African-American folktales in existence. In these stories children meet crafty and delightful characters like Grandaddy Cricket, who is the size of a goat, Minnyminny Morack and Follamalinska, the dogs who save a little boy from becoming a bear's dinner, and poor Doofus McGoofus, who got on the wrong side of the ever clever and triumphant Brer Rabbit. The thirty-nine stories are wonderfully told—in a way that makes you feel you're getting the inside scoop on each character by Uncle Remus—and they are short enough to keep children giggling and wanting more. See also *Tales of Uncle Remus, Further Tales of Uncle Remus,* and *More Tales of Uncle Remus.*
Explore This: Do you notice which character-animals seem to

always come out on top? If your child has a pet: Ask her to imagine what it would say if it could talk, what kind of clothes it would wear and what its personality would be like. She could write a story about it or draw its portrait.

 LIZA LOU AND THE YELLER BELLY SWAMP
By Mercer Mayer. Publisher: Aladdin Paperbacks
(Simon & Schuster), 1997. PB$5.99. MVP:
Resourcefulness, Bravery. Classic, Read Aloud

Who's afraid of the big bad swamp creature? Not "bold as brass" Liza Lou. With her "fancy thinking" she frees the Yeller Belly Swamp from the likes of the Confederate Swamp Haunt, Gobbledygook, Swamp Devil, and the Swamp Witch. The text is often in colloquial dialect ("meaner than a stomped on pole cat"), with many references to Southern "swamp culture," such as poling through the swamp to visit a family member and daily encounters with swamp animals such as bobcats, alligators, or cottonmouth snakes. Liza Lou displays the wit and bravery that kids will love. What child doesn't long to possess the power to overcome their fears and look those "monsters" in their lives square in the face? Mercer Mayer's hilarious illustrations of Afro-headed Liza Lou and the various crazy-looking creatures she encounters are irresistible.

Explore These: What are some of the ways Liza Lou outwitted her foes? Ask a child: How could you outwit any mean "creatures" you encounter? Here is a great opportunity to point out how Liza Lou used brain, not brawn, to overcome adversity. Compare life in the old swamp (boiling clothes to get them clean and so on) to our conveniences of today.

Black Writers' Notebook: Famous children's book author **Countee Cullen** (1903–1946) spent much of his short life reading books at the library in Harlem. After receiving his master's degree from Harvard, Cullen taught English, French and creative

writing to high school students in New York. He loved writing
books that made reading fun and enjoyable for children.

 THE LOST ZOO
Christopher Cat and Countee Cullen. Illustrator: Brian
Pinkney. Publisher: Sliver Burdett Press (Simon and
Schuster), 1991. HC$12.95, Library edition. MVP:
Human frailties. Classic, Read Aloud

This classic version of Noah's Ark was thankfully rescued from
the out-of-print file by Silver Burdett and revived with swirling
scratchboard illustrations by Brian Pinkney. It is a wonderfully
strange and creative story about how the animals were chosen for
the Ark, and what happened to the ones that didn't make it. It is
written from the perspective of Cullen and his over-intelligent
cat, Christopher. The back-and-forth banter between the two at
the beginning and end of the book is very entertaining and
funny. Christopher begins telling Countee the story of the animals in the Lost Zoo that didn't make it onto the Ark—animals
like the Squililigee, the Lapalake and the Ha-ha-ha—and the
two decide to write a book of rhymes about them. Though the
clever rhymes are about animals, they really tell about the human
frailties we all exhibit from time to time—arrogance, lateness,
shyness, and so on—that can keep us from achieving our goals.
According to his story, when Noah got the word from God that
there was to be a flood, he sent invitations to each member of the
animal kingdom asking them to choose the best two of their kind
to send to the Ark. Well, this invitation creates quite a stir because certain animals don't want to be seated next to certain others, and they write Noah back to tell him so. After that gets sorted
out on the ark, we hear the humorously sad tales of the many
strange animals who were invited to the Ark, but because they
were either too busy, too sleepy or too something-else, "missed
the boat" that could have saved their lives.

Explore These: What negative character traits did the various animals exhibit? How would those traits create problems in real life? Create an animal, give it an appropriate silly name, and write a story about how your animal missed the Ark and why.

 MAKE A JOYFUL SOUND, POEMS FOR CHILDREN BY AFRICAN AMERICAN POETS
Edited by Deborah Slier. Illustrators: Cornelius Van Wright and Ying Hwa Hu. Publisher: Scholastic Professional Books, 1996. HC$13.95. MVP: Perseverance, Black beauty, strength

The poems in this book reflect the richness, strength and beauty of African-American people and their heritage. Poets such as Langston Hughes, Eloise Greenfield, Karama Fufuka, and Nikki Giovanni are represented here, along with many others. Some poems praise the beauty of our multihued skin, as in, "Black Is Beautiful" by Useni Eugene Perkins or "What Color Is Black" by Barbara Mahone. Others reflect the virtues that have allowed us to persevere, such as Langston Hughes's "Mother to Son": ". . . Don't you fall now—For I'se still goin', honey, I'se still climbin', and life for me ain't been no crystal stair." The collection reverberates with poems that share a love for nature ("I Love the Sea" by Alfred M. Cruishank), humor ("Willimae's Corn-rows" by Nanette Mellage), and history ("A Protest Poem for Rosa Parks" by Abiodun Yewole). Children will enjoy the book's illustrations, which creatively frame and interpret the poems, making them more tangible to children who are new to poetry.

**MAMA'S BOYZ: AS AMERICAN AS SWEET
POTATO PIE!
By Jerry Craft. Publisher: American, 1997. PB$9.95
US/$14.95 CAN. MVP: Humorous life lessons**

You know Jerry Craft's work is "on point" just by reading the comic strip on the back cover of this book. It depicts a department store scene, with Yusef and his brother Tyrell shopping—or trying to shop—as they are being covertly watched by every salesperson in the store. The copy asks, humorously, "Can you count how many people are watchin' me and my brother Tyrell as we try to shop?" This comic strip collection is built around the lives of the Porters: teenagers Yusef and Tyrell, their mother, Pauline (or Ma), their grandparents and their uncle, Greggo. Their hilarious experiences in everyday life represent those of most families with teenagers: they love sneakers and extra-large clothes, like the opposite sex, hate homework and want to be grownups—now. In one strip, "Mom's Movin' Out!," their single mother decides she needs a vacation. She announces to her boys that she thinks they're old enough and mature enough now for *her* to get her own apartment. The boys discover just how much they still need their Mommy! Other full-length sketches include "Uncle Greg's Blind Date," "Mom's New Pumps," and "My Date with Density," in which Tyrell wins a rap contest and gets to meet Ice Milk, "the dopest rapper in all the world." Shorter strips also appear throughout the book. More serious topics like the real meaning of Black History Month are also well presented. Craft's quick wit, artistic skill and deft use of youth language to bring out life lessons are sure to capture a young person's interest. (See Great Websites for ordering details.)

Explore These: Read the page about Jerry Craft's career as a cartoonist. Encourage children to think about what they would have to do to achieve their own career dreams. Have each child think about ordinary things in life that can be made humorous. Then have them create their own short cartoon, with text, simple drawing(s), and a title, placed in a boxed comic strip format.

A MILLION FISH . . . MORE OR LESS
By Patricia McKissack. Illustrator: Dena Schutzer.
Publisher: Dragonfly Books (Alfred A. Knopf), 1992.
HC$6.99 US/$9.50 CAN. MVP: Using your imagination

In this creative and madcap story, children are given an example of how an unfettered imagination can shape a story, and are introduced to the tradition of tall tales. The story's illustrations are memorable, almost jumping off the page in their brilliant colors and bold brush strokes. Hugh Thomas is fishing one morning on Bayou Clapateaux when Papa-Daddy and Elder Abbajon come rowing by and warn him that the bayou is "a mighty peculiar place." They also tell him a wild story of the time they caught a five-hundred-pound turkey there. Skeptical, Hugh Thomas watches them leave, catches three small fish, then proceeds to catch a million more fish in the next half hour! But in trying to take them home he is confronted by Atoo, the grandfather of all the swamp alligators, a host of pirate raccoons, and a legion of thieving fish crows—who each manage to relieve Hugh Thomas of a large portion of his fish. After a final run-in with the neighbor girl's cat, who tricks him into leaving while she steals his fish, all he has left to bring home are three little fish and the story of where the rest went.

Explore These: What happened to all the fish Hugh Thomas caught? Make the fish collage according to instructions in the front of the book. Read the explanation of tall tales in the back inside cover and help a child make up his own tall version of something that really happened. He can test it out on family or friends when it's finished. (Explain that this should only be done when they are telling a story to entertain.)

MUFARO'S BEAUTIFUL DAUGHTERS
Written and illustrated by John Steptoe. Publisher:
Lothrop, Lee & Shepard, 1987. HC$16.00.
MVP: Inner beauty. Caldecott Honor, Horn Book
Award, Audio

This stunning book illustrates the African tale of a father and his two beautiful daughters, Manyara and Nyasha. One has a haughty, mischievous spirit, the other a sweet, pleasant one. Both want to be chosen as queen of the land, but they each choose a different means of obtaining their prize. Manyara scoffs at opportunities to be kind and helpful to others along the way, and Nyasha extends herself to those in need and heeds the wisdom of her elders. Needless to say, she is crowned queen and the sister merely becomes the castle servant girl. It's nice to see the illustrations of the father as a regal and handsome African king. He loves both of his daughters equally, despite their differing temperaments.

Explore These: Did Manyara and Nyasha's father love them both the same? What do you think about the way Nyasha treated her sister? What specific actions lead to Nyasha becoming queen? Ask a child: Which girl would you rather be like or have as a friend?

NATHANIEL TALKING
By Eloise Greenfield. Illustrator: Jan Spivey Gilchrist.
Publisher: Black Butterfly Children's Books, 1988.
PB$6.95. MVP: Self-image. Coretta Scott King Award

Children will enjoy the rap beat of some of these spirited poems and rhymes about everyday issues. Nathaniel is a young boy who loves being nine, misses his mama (who passed away), is proud of his dad, and dreams about his bright future. But Nathaniel also picks up on very sensitive things in his world, as only children seem to do. Like the fact that his Aunt Lavinia is hiding from the family because she's ashamed of her life; that adults always seem to be competing to be the best, instead of just enjoying themselves; and how his lonely neighbor always looks like she's got the weight of the world on her shoulders. The book's down-to-earth prose offers glimpses from a child's mind's eye . . . maybe *your* child's.

Explore These: Talk about some of the things your child thinks about adults and the adult world.

NIGHT ON NEIGHBORHOOD STREET
By Eloise Greenfield. Illustrator: Jan Spivey Gilchrist.
Publisher: Dial Books (Penguin Putnam), 1991.
HC$13.95. Theme: A child's look at life's hard realities

This batch of poems is no joke. They are gritty, sweet, scary, funny and odd. They are about waiting for what seems like forever for a friend to come home, not wanting to go to bed until you got hugged enough, telling your out-of-work parents a joke to cheer them up and resisting the drug dealer who prowls your neighborhood looking for eager children. Eloise Greenfield does a masterful job of capturing the tiny nuances of a child's thinking and expressing them in words children will understand.

Explore These: Ask a child: What are some things that scare or worry you?

PINK AND SAY
Retold and illustrated by Patricia Polacco. Publisher:
Philomel Books, 1994. HC$15.95 US/$20.95CAN.
MVP: History, Interracial friendship

This is one of the most powerful children's stories I've read. It is a retelling of a true story handed down to Ms. Polacco (who is white) by her great-grandfather Sheldon. Pink (Pinkus), a black soldier, finds Say (Sheldon), a white soldier, wounded in the middle of a field during the Civil War. They both were separated from their respective companies right in the middle of Confederate territory. Pink carries Say on his back all the way home to his mother, who nurses Pink like a son. But there is always the fear that "marauding" Confederate troops will come knocking at the door—which they eventually do. Say, who feels cowardly, looks up to Pink, who has endured much more than he but still wants to return to battle. "Cause it's my fight, Say. Aint it yours, too? If we don't fight," Pink asks, "then who will?" Moe Moe, Pink's mother, is shot by the Confederates after hiding Pink and Say in her root cellar. But before she dies she has taught Say a lesson on bravery that he will never forget. The two compatriots are captured and hauled to a prison camp, where they are separated for the last time. The epitaph sadly notes that while Sheldon made a narrow escape, married and went on to have children and grandchildren, Pinkus was never heard from again. As the story goes, he was hanged that same day, his body discarded in a lime pit. Ms. Polacco wrote this book as a tribute to Pinkus Aylee, "since there are no living descendants to do this for him."

Explore These: First, explain the fact that the North (Union Army), which wanted to abolish slavery, and the South (Confederate Army), which wanted to perpetuate it, were at war. Why did Pink help Say out when he was hurt? Would you have helped Say or just left him alone? Discuss why or why not. **Parent/Teacher Note:** *Make sure the child is emotionally mature enough to handle the disturbing ending.*

RED DOG, BLUE FLY: FOOTBALL POEMS
By Sharon Bell Mathis. Illustrator: Jan Spivey Gilchrist.
Publisher: Viking (Penguin Putnam), 1995. PB$5.99.
Theme: Sports as a metaphor for life

These two female artists collaborated to produce a well-done book of poems designed to appeal mostly to boys. Football is the name of the game in this collection—hard practices, the struggle to learn all the plays, the elusive ball, the broken bones, the thrill of victory and the agony of defeat. The authors included two poems about girls, including one about the one girl on the team who the players say "does everything right/a running back who's outta sight."

Explore These: What are some of the keys to becoming a good football player? How do these skills translate into real life?

Black Writers' Notebook: Born in a Mississippi plantation, writer **Richard Wright** (1908–1960) was the son of a farm worker. He experienced poverty, hunger, and racial prejudice in his early years. Though he longed for books, he was unable to buy them or borrow them from the library because he was black. With his most celebrated novel, *Native Son*, published in 1940, he broke ground for other African-American writers such as Ralph Ellison and James Baldwin.

 RICHARD WRIGHT AND THE LIBRARY CARD
By William Miller. Illustrator: Gregory Christie.
Publisher: Lee & Low, 1997. $15.95. MVP:
Determination, Courage, Love of reading

This is the last in a series of three picture books that share the key turning points in the lives of famous black writers. Richard Wright grew up poor in the segregated South in the 1920s, where books were hard to come by if you were black. However, his mother took the time to read to him from the comics, and Richard read whatever he could from old newspapers and books he found in garbage cans. Richard had a dream—to move to Chicago and start a new life. He got a cleaning/errand boy job in an optician's office to save money for the move. Little did he know that God would use that meager job to allow Richard to achieve his dream. One of his bosses often sent him on errands to the library. Overwhelmed by the vast amount of books available there—but *un*available *to him*—Richard took a big step. Sensing that this man might be sympathetic, Richard asked his boss whether he could take out a few books for himself on his next errand. His boss was cautious, but agreed. The ensuing experience—staying up all night reading Tolstoy, Dickens and other great novelists—changed Richard forever. He would later become an internationally renowned bestselling author, one of the most important of our time. See also *Zora Hurston and the Chinaberry Tree* and *Frederick Douglass: The Last Day of Slavery.*

Explore These: How did Richard first learn to read? Encourage a child to read the comics and the newspaper. Have her cut out her favorite comic or newspaper article and read or summarize it out loud. Talk about what Richard went through just to read a book. Emphasize how fortunate children today are that they can take books out of the library; institute scheduled trips to the library regularly.

I will provide opportunities for learning and will instill a sense of pride in my children by teaching our past and present history.
—From the Black Family Pledge by **Maya Angelou**

ROSA PARKS
By Eloise Greenfield. Illustrator: Gil Ashby. Publisher: HarperTrophy (HarperCollins), 1996. PB$3.95. MVP: Courage of one's convictions

This book will introduce children to the heroic story of Rosa Parks and how her simple and courageous act of refusing to give up her seat on a bus sparked a city-wide, year-long bus boycott, turning Montgomery, Alabama, into "the walking city" and giving national momentum to the civil rights movement. It details Rosa's childhood in pre–civil rights Montgomery and shares defining moments in her life, such as the time when she and her sister were refused service at a soda fountain because of their color. Notable is the how the book carefully describes the process that helped shape Rosa's character—her blossoming involvement with the NAACP and the voters' league, how she preferred to go thirsty rather than drink from a fountain marked "Colored," and how it hurt her to see young black children taught to sit at the back of the bus. After her quiet but heroic decision not to give up her seat on the bus, the story maintains its suspense with the involvement of Martin Luther King, the creation of the Montgomery Improvement Association (which helped provide transportation to those who stopped using the buses), and the final victory given by the United States Supreme Court. Realistic illustrations interspersed throughout the short easy-to-read chapters will also help a young reader move swiftly through the book.

Explore These: Why didn't Rosa Parks give up her seat on the bus? What character traits did she need to do what she did? Did she accomplish her goals alone or with the help of others? Ask a child: What would you like to see changed or improved in your city or neighborhood? This book provides a good example of how the unity, help, and support of the community helped complete the process that her one action started—ultimately changing the laws across the nation.

THE SECRET OF GUMBO GROVE
By Eleanora E. Tate. Publisher: Dell, 1987. PB$3.99.
MVP: Determination

Producing a captivating novel for this age group isn't easy, but this one successfully combines mystery, humor, history, *and* provides moral dilemmas readers can relate to. Young Raisin is a smart, hip girl who likes boys, has a quick wit, struggles with minding her parents, and loves history. When she agrees to help one of the town's elders clean up a forgotten local cemetery, the intrigue begins. It seems that the town has a slave history that no one wants to acknowledge—even her own parents. Moral conflicts experienced by every youngster are well treated. Such as the fact that Raisin's dad tells her to stay away from the seedy but exciting downtown scene, but goes there to shoot pool and buy beer himself. Or the fact that her parents encourage her love of black history—except when it involves members of their own family. Raisin experiences a range of typical emotions for a youngster her age: jealousy toward her sister for entering a local pageant without her, feeling misunderstood by her parents and other adults, wanting to have more freedom and trust extended, etc. Her wit, determination, and good character make her an admirable, likable protagonist.

Explore These: What is Raisin's favorite subject? Why don't her parents want to talk about the past? Project: Help a child create family history; you can attempt to find information on where great- and great-great grandparents may be buried.

 SETH AND SAMONA
By Joanne Hyppolite. Illustrator: Colin Bootman.
Publisher: Yearling (Bantam Doubleday Dell), 1995.
PB$3.99 US/$4.99 CAN. MVP: True boy-girl friendship

This wonderfully written short novel stars an unlikely pair—a girl named Samona ("the wildest girl in the fifth grade") and Seth, a quiet boy from a "proper" Haitian-American family. Samona is from a single-headed household and doesn't always wear the right clothes or shoes, but her precocious nature and crazy-but-harmless schemes keep their friendship lively, though Seth won't admit it. In the end, though, Seth realizes that life without Samona is just plain boring. He comes through for her when she needs a friend most of all—as a frozen-stiff contestant in the Little Miss Dorchester pageant. As a native of Haiti herself, the author uses her personal wisdom to show us what it's like growing up in a Haitian-American family, a glimpse that children this age should find interesting.

Explore These: How did Seth come through for Samona in her hour of need? Ask a child: What did you learn about the real meaning of friendship from Seth and Samona? Do you have a good friend of the opposite sex? What's different about this friendship from your same-sex relationships? This could be a good springboard to talking about the differences between boys and girls. Help your child to find Haiti on the map and read more about the culture. Encourage your daughter to consider entering a local pageant, putting her talents to the test in front of an audience. A boy could enter a talent contest.

SHAKA, KING OF THE ZULUS
By Diane Stanley and Peter Vennema. Illustrator: Diane
Stanley. Publisher: Mulberry Books (William Morrow),
1988. PB$4.95. MVP: Leadership skills, Wise planning

King Shaka Zulu of Africa was a military genius in a class with
Napoleon, Julius Caesar and Alexander the Great, but are our
children studying him in their history classes? Probably not. This
illustrated history chronicles the life of Shaka (pronounced oo-
Shá-geh) Zulu from his childhood as a timid boy to his emergence
as a young, handsome warrior of great finesse, and ultimately to
his rise to become the greatest king southern Africa ever had.
Shaka displayed leadership and management skills in 1824 that
we now clamor to learn through self-help books. He used his
head to plan strategy for his army, something the white traders
couldn't believe possible, designed special assegais, or swords,
that would be more effective in battle, toughened up his men
with long practices and rewarded them handsomely. As a result
of his wise leadership, the Zulu army won battle after battle and
Shaka rose to stardom. Even the "visiting" English were impressed, but not so much as to forget why they came—to trade
and buy or capture land. The tricky Englishmen, feigning friendship, got Shaka to sign a paper that gave them land supposedly
"to settle on." At the same time, Shaka's army was becoming too
large for him to handle himself, and it appears that there was no
one he trusted enough to share leadership burden. As a result,
the men in the army grumbled and plotted against Shaka, and
eventually killed him in a surprise attack. In the end, we see that
even the great Shaka suffered a lot of personal pain.
   Explore These: What tribe did Shaka lead, in what part of
Africa? What were some of Shaka's good leadership qualities?
How can you use some of these qualities in your activities?

THE SINGING MAN
By Angela Shelf Medearis. Illustrator: Terea Shaffer.
Publisher: Holiday House, 1994. HC$16.95/PB$6.95.
MVP: Belief in oneself

Hear the rhythm of the omele drum as Banzar, a West African young man, follows his heart and pursues a music career against the advice of village elders. Banzar's decision isolates him from his village and forces him to leave home. But don't feel too sorry for this young rebel. In fact, readers will cheer him on as he proves to the world and himself that when your heart is in your work, the money usually follows. The story's realistic illustrations put the reader on the road to Otolo with Banzar, where he meets Sholo, a blind singer who travels from village to village singing about African history. Sholo exemplifies the type of mentor parents would want for their children. His character helps prove that success in life comes from teamwork and emulating successful people. Through Sholo's example, Banzar also realizes the importance of working with passion toward a worthwhile goal. In time, Banzar, known throughout the land as the singing man, gets the ultimate job as the king's personal musician. The story climaxes as Banzar, now a wealthy man, meets his impoverished brothers in a marketplace and ends much like the Bible story of Joseph. Loaded with principles for success, this book reveals to youngsters the importance of having goals and dreams and following them.

Explore These: What did Banzar learn from Sholo? Ask your child: What are some professions that might be considered worthless by some people? Are they still worth pursuing? Can we respect others' opinions and still stick to our convictions? How? Talk about some real-life situations with your child. Expose your child to career opportunities that seem to suit his talents early on by connecting him with adult mentors in various fields.

SISTER
By Eloise Greenfield. Publisher: HarperTrophy
(HarperCollins), 1992. HC$15.00/PB$4.50 US/$5.95
CAN. MVP: Self-identity

Thirteen-year-old Doretha began writing her thoughts down in an old notebook when she was nine. That was when her dad gave her the old book, the same one he used when he was coming up (only he ripped his private pages out first). Daddy always had something in his junk box to make Doretha and her older sister, Alberta, smile on those nothing-fun-to-do-days. Then one day he died without warning. Since then Doretha clings to her notebook-journal as both a remembrance of her dad and a place to find herself. Alberta, the beauty of the family, isn't so fortunate. She has been on a rebellious, self-destructive streak ever since their father's death. Her mother is worried sick about her, on top of being grieved over the sudden loss of her husband. Alberta is hanging around with a crowd that thinks they're grown, she comes home at all hours of the night, and has just announced that she's quitting school—at sixteen. And everyone from teachers to neighbors predicts that Doretha will be just like Alberta. In some ways Doretha wants to be like her sister—pretty, popular, irreverent—but there's no way she wants to be the cause of any more hardship for her Mama. Doretha's clear head and sensitivity to her mom's pain are admirable, as is her valiant struggle to find herself in the midst of it.

Explore These: Why does Doretha keep a journal? Explain to your child the value of writing your thoughts down in a special place. Purchase a blank book for her to begin journaling. Ask a child: Why do you think Alberta began to "act out"? Do you have an older sibling, cousin or friend whom you want to be like? What are some of the qualities you admire about them? How do you think those qualities will help you?

SONG OF THE TREES
By Mildred D. Taylor. Illustrator: Jerry Pinkney.
Publisher: Dial Books (Penguin Putnam), 1975.
HC$15.99/PB$3.50. MVP: Love of, respect for nature.
Classic

Cassie and her family live in Mississippi among a huge forest of luscious old trees that become their friends, "singing" their song as the leaves rustle in the wind. She and her brothers love to play hide and seek among the towering pines (a good "hiding tree"), walnuts, beeches and hickories. To her, the trees had a protective quality, but Cassie could tell from the "eerie silence descending over the forest" that something awful was about to happen. Money is even scarcer now during the Depression. People were stealing the little Papa sends home to the family, and food was on the serious ration. How was Mama going to get her medicine if there was no money? Along came opportunistic Mr. Andersen, who plots to cut the trees down for profit and will stop anyone who gets in his way—by any means necessary. Can they sacrifice their beloved forest for a few much-needed dollars? This is a nice-sized reader with a good balance of illustrations and text for a child this age to really enjoy. It reminds children of the value of nature.
Explore These: Why were the trees so important to Cassie and her family? Why did the men want to cut the trees down? Ask a child: Have you ever felt protective over something you've had for a long time? What did it mean to you? Choose a book from the library and learn more about types of trees and how and where they grow. Check out the trees in your neighborhood and identify them, examining the different shapes of the leaves.

THE STORIES JULIAN TELLS
By Ann Cameron. Illustrator: Ann Strugnell. Publisher:
Bullseye Books (Random House), 1981. PB$3.25
US/$4.25 CAN. Read Aloud, ALA Notable

Julian is a great little guy, but his mouth and his antics are always getting him into trouble. Like the time he almost killed the fig tree in the backyard, eating its leaves hoping that they would make him grow taller. Or the time when he told his little brother Huey that ca-ta-logs have magic cats in them that jump off the pages and do your gardening for you. These are hysterical little stories sure to get a smile out of even the toughest young grade-schooler and are perfect for introducing the concept of chapter books to a young reader. Whole-page illustrations make the reading challenge less daunting. Also see *More Stories Julian Tells*, which has slightly larger print.

Explore These: What is your favorite Julian story? What are some of Julian's good and bad qualities? Ask a child: What funny situations have you been in at home with siblings or friends? Describe.

 SUMMER WHEELS
By Eve Bunting. Illustrator: Thomas B. Allen. Publisher: Voyager Books (Harcourt Brace), 1996. PB$6.00 US/$8.00 CAN. MVP: Trust, Being nonjudgmental

Every day Lawrence and his friend Brady check out a bike for the afternoon from Bicycle Man, an older, Mr. Fix-It–type gent who drinks coffee and loves jelly donuts. He runs his unique bike-borrowing service on an honor system: sign a bike out and return it; if you break a bike, you help fix it. This works great among the neighborhood kids, but when a tattered-looking homeboy steps into the garage looking to check out Lawrence's favorite bike, Lawrence is suspicious and angry. Just as he suspected, the boy, whose name is Leon, uses a fake name to sign out the bike and "forgets" to return it. Lawrence is furious at Bicycle Man for being so naive, and for allowing the questionable boy to borrow bikes in the first place. For Leon, "borrowing" and "giving" are one and the same. Lawrence can't wait to see him punished, especially when he returns another bike damaged. But he doesn't get the satisfaction. Bicycle Man is calm but firm—his position is to treat everyone equally, good kids and "bad." He exemplifies the ways we want our children to be treated by others, and the way we want our children to act. He doesn't judge Leon by his appearance, his carelessness or even his smart mouth. He takes the time to search deeper to find out what Leon's problem is, where his pain is, and finds out that he is fatherless. Through Bicycle Man's tender treatment of Leon, he earns the boy's respect and friendship—and even a jelly donut. In the process, Lawrence and his friends learn a valuable lesson about being nonjudgmental.

Explore These: What were Bicycle Man's rules for lending bikes out? Ask a child: What do you think about the way Bicycle Man treated Leon? How would you have felt about Leon if you were Lawrence? Should people be trusted even when they don't seem trustworthy? Describe a situation in which an adult trusted you to do something without watching you. How did it turn out?

 SUSIE KING TAYLOR: DESTINED TO BE FREE
By Denise Jordan. Illustrator: Higgins Bond. Publisher: Just Us Books, 1994. PB$5.00. MVP: Perseverance

We read a lot about the famous nurse Florence Nightingale, but, as this book's jacket notes, "Not many people have heard about Susie King Taylor." She has not been celebrated or given an honorable burial or even a presidential medal, but her story is no less important or valuable. Born enslaved, Susie had the rare opportunity to live with her grandmother, a free black woman in Savannah, Georgia. There she learned to read and write and almost immediately began to take in private students. When the Civil War broke out, Susie switched hats and became a nurse, caring for wounded black soldiers—many without arms or legs. She married a soldier and fellow teacher and became pregnant, only to lose her husband to a fatal accident. Undaunted, Susie tried to teach again, to no avail—everyone was attending public school by then, for free. No opportunities existed for her in hospital nursing, either. The clear message was, "blacks need not apply." She found some success moving to Boston, becoming a maid and a cook, and finally remarrying in 1879. She began the Woman's Relief Corps there, which served the needs of war veterans and their families for many years.

Explore These: Why was learning to read and write so important to Susie's future? Ask a child: In what careers are good reading and writing skills essential? Introduce a child to teaching or nursing careers, using this book as an example, and describe *realistic, everyday* scenarios experienced by people in those occupations. Discuss the important inner qualities needed to be in "helping" professions. Arrange for an interested child to visit a hospital ward to see what nursing is really about.

TALK ABOUT A FAMILY
By Eloise Greenfield. Publisher: HarperTrophy
(HarperCollins), 1993. PB$4.50 US/$5.95 CAN. MVP:
Accepting change, Understanding parents

Genny's parents have been fighting a lot lately, but that's all going to change when her oldest brother Larry comes home from the military. Larry fixes everything, and Genny is sure he can fix this problem, too. But sadly, this is too big a job for Larry, or anyone. Genny grows angry—it wasn't supposed to happen this way, things weren't supposed to change. Daddy wasn't supposed to move out—ever! What did they do to make him leave? Genny and her sister are overcome with guilt; then anger sets in. This is a great book for a child whose parents recently separated or divorced. Through a very special relationship with wise old Mr. Parker, a widowed neighbor, Genny learns that just because families change they don't have to fall apart, they just reinvent themselves into a new shape. Her parents' breakup brings Genny and her siblings closer, and together they help each other cope.

Explore These: What was Genny expecting of her brother Larry when he returned? What does she learn from Mr. Parker? Ask a child: How would/did you feel if/when a big change happened in your life: your family moved, your best friend died, your parents separated? Is there a special person like Mr. Parker to whom you could go to share your feelings and be comforted? What are some ways to cope with things that we don't like but can't change?

TAP-TAP
By Karen Lynn Williams. Illustrator: Catherine Stock.
Publisher: Clarion Books (Houghton Mifflin), 1994.
HC$14.95. MVP: Mother-daughter bonding

Catherine Stock's cool watercolor illustrations draw the reader right into this story of Sasfi, a young Haitian girl who is accompanying her mother to the market. She has gone there many times before, but never with a basket of wares on her head like her mother. Wanting to prove she is old enough to be a helper but yet struggling to keep up, she asks if they could take a "tap-tap" (or minibus) to the market instead of walking. Her mother explains that they do not have the money for a tap-tap and so they continue on foot. Once at the market Sasfi proves her worth by selling all of the oranges they have brought. Her mother rewards her with a new hat and a bit of change. Anxious to spend her fortune, Sasfi wanders through the market passing up all the colorful sights and smells for—you guessed it—a ride home on the tap-tap. If you've ever ridden in a minibus in the Caribbean, you'll appreciate this humorous "education" in Haitian transportation (chickens, goats, babies, furniture, food, and people all ride together). Young readers will be delighted as Sasifi's new hat flies off her head and will wish that getting home could be as much fun as in the story! Why is it called a tap-tap? Because in order to make the driver stop you must tap on the side of the car.

Explore These: Why was Sasfi so anxious to go with her mother into town? What do you do to help Mom and Dad with their chores or their work? What *could* you offer to do? Compare a tap-tap to our modes of transportation. Look at how the tap-taps are decorated in the book and draw your own version. Explain that people call one another *chérie* (a French endearment) in Haiti and learn a few basic French words (like *"allo"* for hello and *"bonsoir"* for good night); make them a part of your everyday conversation.

YOUR DAD WAS JUST LIKE YOU
Written and illustrated by Delores Johnson. Publisher:
Macmillan, 1993. HC$13.95 US/$17.95 CAN. MVP:
Father-son relationships, Overcoming the generation gap

The complex aspects of a father/son relationship are explored in this heartwarming dialogue between Peter and his grandfather. Peter and his father are "always battlin'." After carelessly knocking over "that ole stupid purple thing" on his father's dresser, Peter shows up at his Grandpa's house in search of comfort. Peter has a difficult time understanding why his father "never smiles—he only yells." Grandpa offers no explanation other than to remind Peter that his father was once a boy who played hard and told knock-knock jokes "just like you," until he decided that it was time to be serious. Peter is amazed to find out that as a child his father, above all else, loved to run. His empathy grows as he learns that his dad, while having "trouble in school," sought to win a big school race. Grandpa explains how Peter's father's hopes were dashed when the race was canceled at the last moment. Even so, he ignored the rain and ran the race, fueled by his frustration and anger, until he collapsed in a sobbing heap at the finish line. Peter's grandfather picked up his son, carried him home and fashioned him a purple homemade trophy—the same "ole stupid purple thing" Peter knocked over. Now he understands why it is so important to his father. Peter returns home and fixes the trophy, and this begins the "fixing" of his relationship with his father, too. A child will be engaged by the emotional conflict and resolution between the three generations of men. Johnson's wonderful dialogue is coupled with illustrations that capture the heartache and tender spirit of both Peter and his father.

Explore These: Why were Peter and his father "always battlin'?" Ask a child: Do you ever think that your parents used to be young like you? What do you think they were like when they were little? Take this opportunity to divulge a bit of yourself and your past hopes, dreams and disappointments to your child.

5

Great Books for Preteens and Young Adults

Older children and young teenagers who read independently and for pleasure

Books older readers like have:

- Strong emotion
- Themes that are often about relationships with parents; attraction to the opposite sex; the teenage identity crisis; peer pressures; sports figures
- Straightforward, "cool" language; don't talk "down" to them
- An ironic, sarcastic or even pessimistic voice.

Preteens and young adults can be hard-to-please customers when it comes to books. "Things like MTV and the Internet really take young adults away from reading," says Deborah Brodie, executive editor of Viking children's books, not to mention homework, sports, friends, phone calls, and shopping. It seems that even book publishers are still searching for the magic combination of content and style to inject into books that will capture the interest of today's young adults. A book for the over-twelve set can't have plots that are too predictable or corny. I have included a number of the tougher, grittier "reality books" in hopes that they will hold more appeal. The trick is getting them to actually read the book once you buy it.

Here are some suggestions:

- Buy books on subjects your child enjoys and you can tolerate (yes, even if it's space travel, dinosaurs, or the Spice Girls).
- Leave the book lying around the house in hopes that your teenager will pick it up (many parents say this method works).
- Read some of the book yourself and mention or read an interesting or humorous portion of the book aloud to your teen.
- Let the child pick a book every few months that you both will read (with separate copies) and then talk about.
- Remember to ask a youngster about what he's reading and what he finds most interesting about the book, even if you haven't looked at it yourself.
- Join a book club where they choose the books and receive one a month. "My mother played a useful trick on me to get me to read when I was older," says K. T. Horning, Special Collections coordinator at the renowned Cooperative Children's Book Center of the University of Wisconsin in Madison. "She'd tell me about how good a certain book was and then end by saying, 'Oh, in a year or two you'll really enjoy it.' Of course, I went swiftly to the library to find the book that was so delicious my mother thought I had to wait a year to read it!" Note: Some reviews in this section are abridged due to the length of the books. MVPs may also appear as Themes. "Explore These" appears only occasionally in this section, when a book has clear themes and specific value points. At this age, reading for pleasure will be the main motivation.

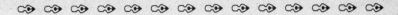

Black Writers' Notebook: Patricia C. and Frederick McKissack, Jr. are the distinguished authors of more than 20 books for children, many of which have been awarded Coretta Scott King, Newbery, and Caldecott Honors. Patricia McKissack comes from a long line of skilled storytellers who encouraged her love affair with words.

AFRICAN-AMERICAN POETRY, AN ANTHOLOGY, 1773–1927
Edited by Joan R. Sherman. Publisher: Dover Publications, 1997. PB$2.95. MVP: Black history, Poetry

This is a small, attractive, and inexpensive collection of 74 poems by black artists. It shows the progression of black poetry in subject and form and includes the work of Phillis Wheatley Peters, Langston Hughes, and many others. For modern poets see *I Am the Darker Brother*, edited by Arnold Adolf, also pocket-sized. *The Black Poets*, edited by Dudley Randall, is a larger, more extensive paperback anthology of black poets and poetry, both historical and contemporary. *Anthology of African-American Poetry* is a collection of poems available on audiocassette.

THE AFRICAN AMERICAN FAMILY ALBUM
By Dorothy and Thomas Hoobler. Introduction by Phylicia Rashad. Publisher: Oxford University Press, 1995. HC$19.95/PB$12.99. Theme: Strong families

The concept of a family album is appealing as a creative vehicle through which to teach children our history. This kente cloth-patterned book is chock-full of outstanding family photographs from north, south, east and west that illustrate the progression of our people from our African homeland to present-day America. It includes a chapter on great contemporary figures in sports, entertainment, literature and media. This album offers a reader-friendly design, balancing text and image with obvious skill. A must for every home library!

AJEEMAH AND HIS SON
By James Berry. Publisher: HarperTrophy, 1991.
PB$4.50 US/$5.95 CAN. MVP: Father-son love,
Overcoming hardship. Horn Book Award

It's disturbing and enlightening to read a story about how our forebears were captured in Africa. This story also gives us a glimpse of normal African life during the slave trade. Ajeemah and his son Atu are strong African warriors. Ajeemah is a skilled leather craftsman and has made a good living for his family. He is looking forward to his son's upcoming wedding to the most beautiful girl in the village, Sisi, where he will present the two pieces of solid gold he has been saving for Atu's dowry. But it is the early 1800s and the slave trade is alive and well in Africa. Just as their festive plans get under way, the two are snatched by white slavers, chained and forced onto a stinking boat bound to who knows where. Ajeemah is stunned. He has never seen white skin before, and further has no idea why he is being treated so roughly. Slowly, after many petitions to his keepers to send word to his family, Ajeemah realizes that there will be no going back. The father and son are brought to the island of Jamaica as slaves. The white slaveowners do everything to break Ajeemah's spirit, and separated from Atu and his family back home, he is sick and lonely. He dreams daily about finding Atu and returning home. Unfortunately, his careful plan of escape is uncovered and his last hope of returning to Africa is dashed. Sadly, on a plantation nearby, Atu commits suicide. Ajeemah must now either learn to live in slavery or die. It is not until he meets and marries Bella, thirteen years after his capture, that he dares to rebuild his life. An intriguing twist to the story is that years later, the couple's daughter, also named Sisi, is given the two pieces of gold that survived the long journey in the sole of Ajeemah's shoe. It is the proudest day of his life when Ajeemah presents his prized possession at his daughter's wedding, along with the story of his painful journey. Sadly, his Jamaican-born daughter, raised in freedom, does not want to embrace her African roots.

Explore These: Explain the importance of the father–son relationship in African culture to help youngsters understand the pain Ajeemah must have felt at losing contact with his sons. Ask, how do you feel about our African roots? In what ways do you relate to them? Discuss. What are some ways we can appreciate the richness and pride of our heritage?

 ANOTHER WAY TO DANCE
By Martha Southgate. Publisher: Laurel Leaf (Bantam Doubleday Dell), 1996. PB$4.50 US/$5.99 CAN. MVP: Finding yourself. Coretta Scott King Genesis Award, ALA Best Young Adult

This story is written from the point of view of a black teenage girl whose dream is to be a prima ballerina. While other girls have crushes on the latest TV hunk, Vicki only has eyes for her hero, Mikhail Baryshnikov. Vicki earns a coveted summer spot at the School of American Ballet in New York City—that means spending the summer living with her actress aunt in the greatest city in the world! Vicki is excited and nervous. It is one thing being the best dancer in her high school, it's quite another story being the only one with brown skin in a top-notch ballet class full of blondes. Vicki begins to notice that her hair isn't silky smooth, her legs aren't as long and slender, and her facial features aren't small and pointy. How will she get through this! On top of that, all of the other girls in the class seem like they've known each other forever. Relaxing her hair takes care of one "problem," and a menu of lettuce and diet Cokes will keep her weight down. Fortunately, the one other black girl in the class befriends Vicki. Stacey is a free spirit who sports a short, natural hairdo and doesn't think too much of the snobby, often racist world of ballet. Her dream is to join Dance Theatre of Harlem. Vicki has never had a close black friend before and enjoys the comfort it brings for the first time. Stacey says the things Vicki has often thought, but never shared. Her budding relationship with Michael—raised in the 'hood, goes to church every Sunday and believes in keepin' it real—gives Vicki new perspectives. Both of her new friends and her aunt all seem to have a freedom with themselves that Vicki longs for. With their help, she discovers that there may indeed be another way to dance.

 BLACK DIAMOND, THE STORY OF THE NEGRO BASEBALL LEAGUE
By Patricia and Frederick McKissack, Jr. Publisher: Scholastic, 1998. PB$5.99. Theme: Great achievers in sports. Coretta Scott King Honor

Any teen who loves baseball will appreciate knowing about the many black men who devoted their lives to the love of the game and the advancement of blacks in the sport. There are captivating photos of Satchel Paige, Jackie Robinson and Willie Mays in action, as well as players with great nicknames like "Cool Papa" Bell and "Stretching Buck" Leonard. The McKissacks thoughtfully include information and photos of blacks who were making inroads in other sports such as boxing and track while baseball was flourishing. Black and white photos of players adorn the appealingly designed cover.

 BLACK ICE
By Lorene Cary. Publisher: Vintage Books (Random House), 1992. PB$10.00 US/$12.50 CAN. MVP: Maintaining your self-identity

How do you make a smooth transition from your middle-class black hometown to the elite white world of prep school? Lorene Cary tells all in this extraordinary memoir—and there's a lot to learn. She spent a lot of time on the "blue couch," the place where most of the black and Hispanic students hung out. And there was always the crew of black kids who "never spoke to us at all because they clearly wanted to assimilate." Her white room-mate wants to know if she feels as "weird" here as she does. Is that possible, Lorene wonders. She had hoped for an escape from her rigid home life when she came to St. Paul's. Instead, she was confronted by more regimentation. Chapel at this time, meetings at that time, homework all the time—it's worse than home! She thought of her little sister, Carole, who felt betrayed and abandoned when Lorene decided to go away to school. Was she scarring her baby sister forever? Her parents had scratched and clawed for years to give their daughters opportunities for advancement. She had to make it work. There was no going back. This book is a great testimony to overcoming your fears, trying new things, and making the decision to be who you are, no matter what.

 BLACK HISTORY FOR BEGINNERS
By Denise Dennis. Illustrator: Susan Willmarth.
Publisher: Writers and Readers Publishing, 1984.
PB$9.00 US and CAN. MVP: Black history primer

This is black history in a form most kids in this age range can really grasp. It is very readable and covers our capture and enslavement in Africa up through the 1970s. What's wonderful is the presentation of the information: well-written tidbits of history are interspersed, almost incidentally, between illustrations, photos and cartoon-style drawings that appear on every page. It's great to see a simple presentation of historical nuances, like Booker T. Washington and W. E. B. DuBois depicted "talking" to each other, disagreeing on the methods blacks should use in order to get ahead. See also *Malcolm X for Beginners*, which uses the same format to discuss Malcolm's life and the civil rights movement.

A BLESSING IN DISGUISE
By Eleanora E. Tate. Publisher: Bantam Doubleday
Dell, 1995. PB$3.99 US/$4.99 CAN. MVP: Dealing with
longing for father, Peer pressure

Zambia Brown is twelve years old, almost a teenager, and she's bored to death. The small South Carolina town she lives in with her aunt, uncle and cousin is dullsville. The only bright spot is the reappearance of her fast-talking father, Vernon "Snake" LaRange. He's back in town flashing wads of hundred-dollar bills, fine jewelry and fast cars and running a nightclub that everybody under twenty-one can't wait to check out. Her aunt and uncle have warned her about Snake, but she can't bear to hear them bad-mouth her dad—even though he's never been a real "dad" to her at all. Zambia idolizes him, and it hurts her to see him paying all of his attention to his other two teenage daughters, who work for him at the club. She would give anything to trade her boring existence for life in the fast lane with Snake, Serrita and Merrita. Not to mention that fine boy, Potsey, who Zambia's had a secret crush on forever. Eventually, she gets to experience a bit of the high life she's fantasized about—and finds much more than she bargained for. Could her idolized father and her cool half-sisters really be involved in illegal scams and drug-running? Will she repeat the mistake her dying alcoholic mother made? Zambia's heart longs for their love and acceptance, but at what cost?

Explore These: Why did Zambia idolize her father so much? When your friends want you to do something you think is wrong, what do you do? What can you do when you're feeling bored? How can you tell whether a boy or girl you like is a good person to get involved with?

THE BLOCK
Poems by Langston Hughes. Collage by Romare Bearden.
Publisher: Metropolitan Museum of Art and Viking
Books, 1995. HC$15.99. Theme: A tribute to Harlem

Through this book, a young adult will be exposed to the work of one of our greatest poets and one of our most inventive artists.

A few of the poems are about budding love and heartbreak, two subjects teens probably know a little about. Others are about dancing, praising, dreaming, speaking out, and getting mad that the white commercial world has "taken my blues and gone ... mixed 'em an fixed 'em so they don't sound like me." Pretty deep stuff, but Langston was always about "keepin' it real."

THE BLUEST EYE
By Toni Morrison. Publisher: Plume (Penguin Putnam), 1970. PB$9.95. MVP: The importance of a strong self-identity. Classic

This is Nobel prize winner Toni Morrison's gripping and often horrifying story of Pecola Breedlove, a dark girl struggling to find her place in blond, blue-eyed America, or even in light-skinned black America. It's a hard life when your father drinks and abuses you, your relationship with your mother is so distant you call her "Mrs. Breedlove," and prostitutes are your only role models. The Breedloves are the talk of the town, and Pecola bears the brunt of it at school, where she is teased endlessly. She sits in her room at the mirror for long hours "trying to discover the secret of the ugliness" and praying, "Please, God, make me disappear." Pecola prays most for God to give her blue eyes like the happy children in her story books or the smiling blond girl on the Mary Jane candy wrappers. As she gets older, this desire consumes her, and she slips further and further away from reality. There is a great lesson in how her "friends" and neighbors react to Pecola's tragic situation. Everyone gossips and wonders and speculates, but few help. "Grown people look away; children ... laughed outright. ... We tried to see her without looking at her ... not because she was absurd, or repulsive ... but because we had failed her. ... The damage done was total." For mature teens only.

THE BOOK OF AMERICAN NEGRO POETRY
Edited with prefaces and critical notes by James Weldon
Johnson. Publisher: Harvest (Harcourt Brace
Jovanovich), 1983. PB$12.00.

This is the classic anthology that first celebrated the creative
genius of black poets Paul Laurence Dunbar, Claude McKay,
Countee Cullen, Langston Hughes, Ana Bontemps, and others
whose names we may be less familiar with, like Gwendolyn Ben-
nett, Joseph Seamen Cotter Jr., and Georgia Douglas Johnson.
The introductions to the work of each poet tell a little bit about
their lives and influences. The prefaces offer valuable context
and information on the development of black poetry. Great for
school reports or just browsing. See also *The Poetry of Black America*, edited by Arnold Adoff, introduction by Gwendolyn Brooks. It
chronicles past and present-day poets such as Amiri Baraka, Nikki
Giovanni, Alice Walker and Julius Lester.

 THE COLOR OF WATER
By James McBride. Publisher: Riverhead Books, 1997.
PB$12.00. MVP: Understanding one's racial identity.
Audio

How often do you read a story about a Polish Jew who forsakes
her family to marry a black man from Harlem? In this poignant,
humorous, and touching story, teens will relate to the identity
struggles that young James McBride undergoes as the product of
biracial parents. The task is compounded by the poverty of the
large family (twelve children) and their white mom's constant
battle for survival and sanity. Though they find themselves in
many unusual situations as a result of their Jewish mother's
worldview, all of the children grow up to be quite successful. The
book is a tribute from James McBride to his mother.

THE CONTENDER
By Robert Lipsyte. Publisher: HarperKeypoint
(HarperCollins), 1987. PB$3.95US/$5.25CAN. MVP:
Perseverance, Discipline, True friendship. Classic

Alfred Brooks is a good kid living in an impoverished neighborhood among friends that walk in the fast lane. He is often the butt of jokes because of his job, sweeping up at a white grocery store, instead of running cons and planning burglaries like the cool guys do. Secretly, they all admire and despise Alfred at the same time. He represents everything they can be, but are too afraid and angry to try. They have good reason—the streets of Harlem are not exactly brimming with exciting job opportunities, especially for young, inexperienced teenage boys. Except for Donatelli's gym. At this famous boxing club Alfred finds his opportunity to be somebody, "somebody special . . . a champion." But it will require a level of physical and mental discipline that he has never known, and even then, Donatelli warns, he may never become a great fighter. As Alfred is exposed to the rough world of boxing, he learns more about life than he ever could in the streets. Whether he can transfer his new mind-set to his friends, who are teeter-tottering on the edge of self-destruction, will be his biggest fight yet.

"I liked reading the author's notes in The Dark-Thirty *where she tells how her grandmother would come home from working in the fields all day and then sit up and tell stories on the porch."*
—**Charles,** age 13

THE DARK-THIRTY: SOUTHERN TALES OF THE
SUPERNATURAL
By Patricia C. McKissack. Illustrator: Brian Pinkney.
Publisher: Alfred A. Knopf. HC$16.00 US/$20.00
CAN. MVP: Coretta Scott King Award, Newbery Honor

During the thirty minutes between sundown and darkness is when Southern children would gather 'round the storyteller on the front porch and prepare to get the willies. I suspect that even Patricia McKissack, whose grandmother told her such stories in just that setting, tossed and turned in her bed the night she finished writing these ten spine-chilling and deliciously suspenseful tales. Each of the stories are inspired by African-American history and range from the time of slavery to the civil rights era. There's "The Woman in the Snow" and her desperately sick baby, who keep reappearing year after year trying to catch a bus to the hospital. The original white bus driver wouldn't allow her to ride, so she haunts each subsequent driver, waiting for the one who will show her kindness. In "The 11:59" we hang out with Pullman porters, known for their ability to spin a tale between shifts, and get reminded that no one can escape the last ride on the 11:59. The storyteller's watch stops at exactly that hour, and death comes on time. Youngsters this age are fascinated with the scary and the mysterious. In this book, they get all of that and learn a lot of black history along the way. Even the cover of this book, done in wonderful detail using Brian Pinkney's unique scratchboard technique, makes you want to run home to hug your mama. The teens in our focus group liked "The Legend of Pin Oak" best. Try it out on yours.

Explore These: Introduce the book by explaining how important storytelling was in our history here (there was no television or radio; many couldn't read; it served to ward off "night loneliness"). Take turns reading the stories with your youngster out loud. Show him how to read with expression, using gestures and facial expressions. Encourage her to write her own dark tale, including surprises, twists and turns. *Parent Note:* Be sure your youngster is mature enough to handle serious suspense without having nightmares!

"I liked the story "The Legend of Pin Oak" in The Dark-Thirty *the best. It's amazing that they actually escaped from their master by jumping off a cliff and turning into birds!"*

—**David,** age 13

DRYLONGSO
By Virginia Hamilton. Illustrator: Jerry Pinkney.
Publisher: Harcourt Brace Jovanovich, 1997.
HC$18.95/PB$8.00. MVP: Historical folklore

The year is 1975. Young Lindy lives with her mother and her father on a drought-stricken farm in Mississippi. Things go from
bad to worse as a dust storm hits, but with the storm comes a boy
named Drylongso. Separated from his family during the height
of the storm, he literally blows into Lindy's home. Ms. Hamilton
explains this character as "part mythical folk hero." When asked
about the strangeness of his name, he explains how, during
droughts, people used to say how it was "dry so long." When he
was born in the middle of that drought, his Ma named him and
pronounced, " 'He comes into the world, and a time of no clouds
will come after him. Where he goes,' she said, 'life will grow better.' " As the story unfolds one sees that Drylongso has a mystical
quality and a keen connection to the earth. "You plant corn on
the full moon," he says. "Plant potatoes in this last of April on the
nights of dark when the moon is going down." How does he
know these things? Drylongso's kind and helpful spirit leads
Lindy's father to a spring in the middle of a dried-up creek, and
the entire family works the soil planting Drylongso's special
seeds. Days later, water comes. After fulfilling what seems to be a
divine appointment, Drylongso leaves as abruptly as he came.
The humanity with which the characters treat each other is a
good lesson to expand on. Ms. Hamilton's colorful descriptions
and masterful illustrations from Jerry Pinkney make even a dust
storm fascinating.

Explore These: Read and talk about the Author's Notes at the
end of the story on the incredible dust storms of the 1930s and
1970s. Talk about other weather patterns that affect only certain
parts of the country at certain times (hurricanes, earthquakes,
floods, El Niño).

THE EAR, THE EYE AND THE ARM
By Nancy Farmer. Publisher: Puffin Books (Penguin Putnam), 1994. PB$4.99 US/$5.99 CAN. Theme: Futuristic adventure in Africa

This adventure story extraordinaire is set in the streets of Harare, Zimbabwe, in the year 2194. The three children of General Matsika, the country's powerful security chief, have been kidnapped by ex-gang members and taken from their comfortable home into the bowels of the city. This is an exciting future world where cars and taxis "fly" in midair and land on antigrav pads, video phone calls are the norm, automatic Dobermans bark and robots answer the doorbell and deliver the newspaper. The three-man detective agency, The Ear, The Eye and The Arm, are hired by the Matsikas to find their children. These men are mutants— all three were born with defects that give them unique abilities: Ear can hear a fly buzzing a block away, Eye can see for miles, and Arm has limbs so long he resembles a creature from *Jurassic Park*. Interestingly, their unusual abilities also make them ultra-sensitive to human suffering. In addition to a great adventure and many comic moments, there are good lessons about love for family, bravery, and compassion cleverly weaved into the thrilling story.

Explore These: Ask a child: What are some of the futuristic things the Matsika children use every day? What is a Mellower? Do you think people like The Ear, The Eye and The Arm could really exist someday? What did you think about life in Resthaven? Would you live there? Why or why not?

FALLEN ANGELS
By Walter Dean Myers. Publisher: Scholastic, 1988. HC$12.95. MVP: Understanding war, Inner conflicts

This is an engaging story about a black soldier's tour of duty during the Vietnam War. Richie Perry needed a way out. He can't afford food and clothing, much less college fees. Richie decides to enlist in the Army as a way to "get himself together." But when he is inadvertently sent to Vietnam instead of quiet desk duty in Germany, Richie experiences fear, hardship, friendship and gruesome death that will change his life forever. He also grapples with racism even as he serves his country. Why are the black men always sent on the most dangerous missions? His inner conflict is that while he's horrified to see his comrades maimed and killed around him, yet he's glad it's not him. This book offers teens a hidden history lesson, offering great details about the Vietnam War within a compelling storyline.

FORGED BY FIRE
By Sharon M. Draper. Publisher: Atheneum, 1997.
HC$16.00/US $21.50 CAN. MVP: Triumphing
over abuse. Coretta Scott King Award

The description of Gerald's life that opens this King award-winning novel is too tragic to imagine. At three years old the child has absolutely no security. His drug-addicted mom might be sweet and loving one day, cussing and swinging the next. He has already learned to judge her moods and knows when to cry and when to stay quiet. Sometimes she left him with that cold, lumpy load in his pants all day, to teach him a lesson, she said. On other days, she forgot to feed him. Gerald learned to hide behind the couch when he was scared, like he was now, seeing his mother passed out on the floor, where she laid all day. The bright flicker of his mom's cigarette lighter always fascinated him, though. Left alone all day with just his GI Joe and the "fire dancer" to play with, Gerald proceeded to flick it on and off, on and off, dazzled by the light. What happens next is predictable, but still affecting. It is this tragedy that gives Gerald a new chance at a normal life with people who love him. That is, until his unstable mother returns, looking shiny and new, wanting him back. Can a small boy take any more disappointment and disaster? This is a hard-hitting story of poverty, child abuse, love, twisted desires, and, ultimately, hope.

FROM SLAVE SHIP TO FREEDOM ROAD
By Julius Lester. Illustrator: Rod Brown. Publisher: Dial Books (Penguin Putnam), 1998. HC$17.99 US/ $25.99 CAN.

Illustrator Rod Brown spent seven years creating the paintings that now appear in this beautiful book about the journey from slavery to freedom. His brilliant, full-page paintings illustrate the glimpses of slave life with incredible detail: the proud, strong, angry Africans, chained together and being led by one puny white man with a gun; the white preacher giving a sermon to the slaves with a Bible in one hand and a whip in the other; an enslaved woman turning back for a last look at a brother hanging lynched, before she resumes her labor; a white missus crying when her slaves are freed; and a baby's rag-bound feet as his family arrives in the North to freedom amid piles of snow. Julius Lester thoughtfully offers three sobering meditations for blacks and whites in the text, in the form of "Imagination Exercises," questions to ask yourself about both the inhumanity of slavery and the joy of freedom.

Explore These: What were some of the horrors the Africans endured on the slave ships? During slavery? In the early days of freedom? Today? Name a few ways you personally are benefiting from the sacrifices of our ancestors. Name a few ways you personally are suffering because of racism that still exists. Do the three Imagination Exercises and discuss. ***Parent Note:*** All of these questions are probing and highly sensitive. Handle with care!

FRONT PORCH STORIES, AT THE ONE-ROOM SCHOOL
By Eleanor Tate. Illustrator: Eric Velasquez. Publisher: Yearling (Bantam Doubleday Dell), 1992. PB$3.99.
Theme: Appreciating our tradition of storytelling

This is a great book for city kids who may not have experienced the late-evening storytelling on the porch, as many country-reared children do. This book is a mixture of stories built on fact, folklore, and African-American history. One summer night twelve-year-old Margie and her younger cousin Ethel find themselves restless and hot. To help escape the biting mosquitoes and pass the time, Margie's father invites the girls to sit with him on the steps of the local one-room schoolhouse, where he makes a rag fire in a metal tub (to keep away the bugs) and spins stories of truth and near-truth for the girls from their family past. Some are campfire scary (the time Grandma saw a light hovering over the couch where her late husband used to doze), and some are humorous (the time Daddy hid a dog at school). In another story, Margie's father describes the memorable and impromptu time he met Eleanor Roosevelt. All ten stories are told from the first-person perspective of Margie, through whom the author weaves the historical background of her own upbringing in Canton, Missouri. At the end of the night, Ethel, who is often teased by Margie, has a story to tell of her own that reminds Margie to appreciate the family she's got.

Explore These: Why does Margie's dad start telling them these stories? Set aside a night to have your own story time outside, if possible. Share one or more stories from your own family past with your child. Ask the child to tell a story from her earliest childhood memories—a special event, how she was once given an exciting present, a favorite birthday party.

GO TELL IT ON THE MOUNTAIN
By James Baldwin. Publisher: Laurel (Bantam Doubleday Dell), 1985. PB$5.99 US/$7.99 CAN

Every teen should read the work of classic black authors such as James Baldwin. In this, his first novel, Baldwin writes the story of a boy growing up in Harlem, the son of a minister. The boy, John, struggles with his own desire to be a writer despite his father's hope that he will follow in his ministerial footsteps. The pressure to obey and do right is intense. John struggles with the strong religious faith his family clings to, his brother's waywardness, his father's coldness and abuse, racism, and determining his own destiny. A must-read.

> *"My father read to us each evening from the comic strips that appeared in our local newspaper. And I remember my seventh-grade English teacher read to us from Shakespeare, standing on her desk and orating, "Friends, Romans, countrymen . . ." She dispelled all ideas that Shakespeare was either hard or incomprehensible. That was the beginning of a lifelong habit."*
>
> **—Henrietta M. Smith,** librarian, historian, editor

 GOD'S TROMBONES, SEVEN NEGRO SERMONS IN VERSE
By James Weldon Johnson. Publisher: Penguin, 1990.
PB$8.95 MVP: Spiritual inspiration. Classic

This book of sermons is small and quite manageable for a teen. It begins with a helpful introduction explaining the tremendous importance of the black preacher as a vehicle for hope and inspiration during slavery—and today. The sermons entitled "The Prodigal Son" and "Let My People Go" are particularly inspiring, and the former is easily applicable to the life of a young man or woman today. Also available on video.

Black Illustrators' Notebook: Christopher Myers is a graduate of Brown University and completed the prestigious Whitney Museum of American Art Independent Studio Program in 1996. *Harlem* was named one of the American Library Association's Top 10 books for young adults. Christopher is the son of distinguished and prolific author Walter Dean Myers.

HARLEM, A POEM
By Walter Dean Myers. Illustrator: Christopher Myers.
Publisher: Scholastic Press, 1997. HC$16.95. MVP:
Poetry, History, Art. ALA Top 10 Books for Young
Adults

This big, bright book, a first collaboration for this father and son team, is filled with poems and collages that depict the sights and sounds of life in Harlem. Folks came from everywhere to seek their fortunes—and to exhale—in a place where they heard black people ruled. Harlem was heaven for whose who yearned for "a place where a man didn't/Have to know his place/Simply because he was/Black." There were all colors and hues on the faces in Harlem, faces that were itching to gather around the radio to find out how, "Jack Johnson/Joe Louis/Sugar Ray is doing with our Hopes." There was music and cooking and rent parties, hair combing and funerals in Harlem, all beautifully expressed in Christopher Myers's careful cut-and-paste style artwork. Teens should really appreciate the art and enjoy the imagery in the poems.

**HARRIET TUBMAN, CONDUCTOR ON THE
UNDERGROUND RAILROAD**
By Ann Petry. Publisher: HarperTrophy (HarperCollins),
1996. PB$4.99 US/$6.75 CAN. MVP: Courage

Ann Petry has done a remarkable job of taking the reader into the realities of slave life. Young readers will marvel at how on one hand Harriet, or Minta, as she was called, was so ordinary, but on the other how her uniqueness prepared her for an important place in history. Like any teen, it seems Harriet detested household work, and she loved the outdoors, preferring the manual labor reserved for the men slaves. While allowed to toil in the fields, Harriet had the opportunity to work side by side with her father, who with premonition taught her to survive in the woods alone, lest she decide to try and escape. This keen ability would sustain her and hundreds of others in the years to come! Her own journey toward freedom began the day she stood between a fleeing slave who was about to be caught and his captor. She survived the subsequent beating, but became permanently handicapped. The depth of the characters and the description of everyday aspects of slave life that are interwoven with the plot make this book compelling. Each chapter highlights in italics the significant events going on in the abolitionist movement during this time period. Ms. Tubman's unquestionable courage and commitment to others is nothing short of phenomenal.

HISTORIC SPEECHES OF AFRICAN-AMERICANS
Introduced and selected by Warren J. Halliburton.
Publisher: Franklin Watts, 1993. HC$23.60/PB$7.95.
MVP: Inspiration

Many of our children don't know that our great oral tradition didn't begin with Martin Luther King Jr.'s "I Have a Dream" speech. This collection includes speeches from religious and political leaders such as Sojourner Truth's "Aint I a Woman?", "The Black Manifesto" by James Foreman of the famous Student Nonviolent Coordinating Committee (SNCC), Malcolm X's "Address to Mississippi Youth," Angela Davis's "Lifting As We Climb," and many other rousing and spine-tingling speeches sure to inspire. The book also offers historical background information on each figure. Hopefully, teens will be encouraged to use these treasures in their academic and extracurricular activities. The speeches offer great material to inspire a song or a rap.

ↄ৶ ↄ৶ ↄ৶ ↄ৶ ↄ৶ ↄ৶ ↄ৶ ↄ৶ ↄ৶ ↄ৶ ↄ৶ ↄ৶ ↄ৶ ↄ৶

Black Writers' Notebook: James Weldon Johnson (1871–1938) was a well-known political figure, author, lecturer, diplomat, and university teacher. He was one of the first African Americans to rise to eminence in so many fields. He is the author of "Lift Every Voice and Sing," the black national anthem, and *The Autobiography of an Ex-Colored Man.*

ↄ৶ ↄ৶ ↄ৶ ↄ৶ ↄ৶ ↄ৶ ↄ৶ ↄ৶ ↄ৶ ↄ৶ ↄ৶ ↄ৶ ↄ৶ ↄ৶

I HADN'T MEANT TO TELL YOU THIS
By Jacqueline Woodson. Publisher: Laurel Leaf, 1994.
PB$3.99 US/$4.99 CAN. MVP: Black-white friendship,
Coping with loss and abuse. Coretta Scott King Honor,
ALA Notable, Horn Book Award

Every child knows a girl like Lena—someone who doesn't fit in at school, isn't cool, doesn't wear the right clothes or say the right things. In this beautifully written story of friendship and shared secrets, we meet Marie, a black, upper-middle class girl whose mother left her and her dad because "there wasn't enough air." Lena, the misfit new girl in school, is poor, self-declared "white trash." Her mother passed away and left her and her sister to live with a physically abusive father. Despite herself, and the protests of her other well-to-do school pals, Marie strikes up a friendship with Lena, and soon they are practically inseparable. Marie also has hurt feelings about her dad—he has been distant and sad since her mother's departure. It is nice to see Marie, living in a swank home with a tenured professor father and a trust fund, introducing Lena to the finer things in life. Marie wonders if her dad will be accepting of her new "low-class" white friends, instead of the other way around. But though Marie has other physical comforts, she still wonders what it's like to be hugged by a father. Through sharing their deepest feelings of anger, sadness, violation, fear, and loneliness, the girls offer each other encouragement and healing as best they can.

Explore These: Do you have any white friends whom your black friends resent or dislike? How do you handle it?

"I love to read because stories allow me to imagine, to create and to learn. I dreamt about going on exciting expeditions and created my own adventures. I also learned how to be brave and goal-oriented. All this by just picking up a book and reading!" Favorite Book: I Know Why the Caged Bird Sings *by Maya Angelou.*
—**Tia Mowry,** actress, co-star of *Sister, Sister*

I KNOW WHY THE CAGED BIRD SINGS
By Maya Angelou. Publisher: Bantam, 1983. $5.50.
MVP: Triumphing over hardship and abuse

This is the brilliant story of the childhood and coming of age of award-winning author Maya Angelou. It is the 1930s, and a young Marguerite and her brother Bailey are having their world turned upside down. They are being sent to visit their mother, who left their small town of Stamps, Arkansas, to seek her fortune in bustling St. Louis, minus her two children. They are scared to leave the security of their loving grandmother and uncle, but also hope to establish the relationship they never had with their glamorous and sophisticated mother. But mom has no real time for children in her fast-paced life. Then a devastating thing happens to Maya at the hands of her mother's "boyfriend." As a result, she stops talking for five years. But she still continues to listen to life, probably better than most talking people did. She also always listened to what her enterprising grandmother told her: "Words mean more than what is set down on paper. It takes the human voice to infuse them with the shades of deeper meaning." This helped Maya not only triumph over her tragedy, but made her the gifted writer she is today.

"Stories, in my opinion, make you feel as if you're a fly on a wall, listening in on wonderful adventures you'd never be a part of. I also love reading because it exercises my brain and enhances my vocabulary." Favorite Book: I Know Why the Caged Bird Sings *by Maya Angelou.*

—**Tamera Mowry,** actress, co-star of *Sister, Sister*

I SEE THE RHYTHM
By Toyomi Igus. Illustrator: Michele Wood. Publisher: Children's Book Press, 1998. HC$15.95.

This is a very creative book of poems that tell our musical history. There are brilliant paintings of Harlem at its best, kentéclothed African drummers and the musicians who have enriched us and spoken for us in song. It is both a series of poems and a bona fide history book. Each spread tells us about another era of music: blues, ragtime, jazz, swing, bebop, gospel, R&B, black rock, funk and hip-hop. Timelines run across each page reminding us of significant achievements in the music world, as well as historic facts, like the desegregation of the armed forces by President Truman in 1948, and Dizzy Gillespie being sent on a world tour by the U.S. State Department in 1956. Little boxes explain valuable things, like the difference between swing and bebop (one is for listening rather than dancing). There is also a tribute to female jazz artists. A nice setting in which to learn our musical history.

I THOUGHT MY SOUL WOULD RISE AND FLY, THE DIARY OF PATSY, A FREED GIRL
By Joyce Hansen. Publisher: Scholastic, 1997. HC$9.95 US/$13.99 CAN. MVP: Patience

It's always compelling to read a story in the first person, especially when reading it transports you back in time. Through this treasure of a book we learn the inner thoughts of Patsy, a former slave girl, at a crucial time in her life and in our history. Her diary begins the year the slaves were freed. You wouldn't necessarily know it from the way things look around Davis Hall, the Big House were Patsy works as a nanny. Many of the house help and field hands don't know exactly what to do now that they're "freed," some don't believe it's true, and others wonder if it applies to all or just some. Besides, being black and free on paper doesn't mean you can walk into a grocery store or even get a ride into town to see about a job. Patsy has a plan, however. She is teaching herself to read by playing the dunce while her charges are being taught. Little do they know, she's taking in all their lessons and reading their books while she dusts the bookshelves. One by one, the cooks, butlers and other former slaves disappear from the plantation, some without as much as a goodbye. Patsy has to keep from laughing as she watches "Mistress" (who she now only calls Ma'am) try to cook with no idea of how a kitchen works. Same goes for Master, now called Sir, who is unable to even keep himself groomed after his faithful manservant takes off. Patsy's learning compels her to teach others, which she does with great success. It's wonderful to see her blossom as a teacher, gaining self-confidence and triumphing over her stammering. She has never had a choice about anything in her life before, not even how to worship God. In the end, Patsy leaves, marries and serves her new community until a ripe old age.

Explore These: Why did Patsy keep a diary? Why didn't she and all the former slaves leave as soon as they were freed? Start a journal of your own and write about your days, hopes, disappointments and goals. Decorate it specially, so it's distinctly yours. See also *A Picture of Freedom, The Diary of Clotee, a Slave Girl*, by Patricia C. McKissack.

THE INNER CITY MOTHER GOOSE
By Eve Merriam. Illustrator: David Diaz. Publisher: Simon and Schuster Books for Young Readers, 1996. HC$16.00 US/$21.50 CAN. MVP: Urban poetry

Many of us grew up reciting Mother Goose rhymes like "Little Jack Horner sat in a corner," but did we ever realize that we were making social and political commentary? Just as those rhymes gave voice to the peasants or poor people of the day, mostly making fun of the "establishment," Eve Merriam sought to let teens in the inner-city know that their concerns were worth rhyming about, too. These biting, sharp, and humorous rhymes cover topics "we dare not close our eyes to," like inadequate housing, unemployment, violence, police corruption, prostitution—and the fact that a black person still can't get a taxi to take him to Harlem. "Mary, Mary, quite contrary" becomes "Mary, Mary Urban Mary, how does your sidewalk grow?" in this clever book. And how's "Now I lay me down to sleep/I pray the double lock will keep" for a nursery rhyme? Some of the rhymes, which are intended for teens and adults, were controversial, even banned, for seemingly condoning violence, but I think you will find much more good here than offensive. First written in 1969, this colorfully illustrated revised version has been the basis for a Broadway musical called *Inner City*.

"My parents loved to read and recite poetry and there were always lots of schoolbooks around the house. My father would read out loud to us from the newspaper. Myself and my three brothers were always expected to be "on program"—which meant able to recite from the Bible or memorize short speeches. I guess you could say we were raised in a language-rich environment."
            —**Cheryl Willis Hudson,** Just Us Books,
                    vice president and publisher

 IN PRAISE OF OUR FATHERS AND OUR MOTHERS: A BLACK FAMILY TREASURY BY OUTSTANDING AUTHORS AND ARTISTS Compiled by Wade Hudson and Cheryl Willis Hudson. Publisher: Just Us Books, 1997. PB$17.95. MVP: The importance of family

This unique book is best described as a "black family album," complete with photographs, illustrations, cartoons, essays, interviews and poems in which sons and daughters pay tribute to their mothers and fathers. These are the children of famous authors and artists, or in some cases the famous artist or author themselves, celebrating their parents—49 in all. Most of the stories are intensely personal and riveting, truly a testament to the persevering nature of our people. Its large format and use of color art help to move the reading along.

Explore These: Which story did you like best? Why? Who's the most "famous" one in your family? What special thing did they do? Project: Have your child write about a relative he admires and why, using any writing style he chooses. He can accompany the tribute with a photo or drawing and give it as a gift.

IN SEARCH OF SATISFACTION
By J. California Cooper. Publisher: Doubleday, 1994.
HC$21.95 US/$29.95 CAN. MVP: The rewards of
patience

Ms. Cooper has long had a knack for delivering moral truths, plain and simple, while illustrating them parable-like in the lives of her many interesting characters. This story is set just after slavery was abolished, and readers enter the lives of both white and black families who have become intertwined due to a slave-mistress relationship that results in a baby. Yin is the mulatto daughter of Josephus, now a freed slave, and Ruth Mae is his daughter with a black woman. The two girls grow up side by side, not knowing they are halfsisters. Yin is loved and doted on by her father, but is unloved by her white mother. Ruth has a much harder life, but grows up a fine girl. When Yin leaves home in a cloud of suspicion to seek her fortune, she runs into a cast of characters, some of whom lead her astray and others who offer her kindness. Unknowingly, she befriends her own halfsister's daughter, and the intrigue continues. In a tale of mystery, hope, misguided love, deception, and fierce loyalty, Ms. Cooper shows us how easy it is to confuse right and wrong in our quest for self-satisfaction.

JUNEBUG
By Alice Mead. Publisher: Bantam Doubleday Dell,
1995. PB$3.95 US/$4.99 CAN. MVP: Courage, Hope

This book's cover art and title wouldn't necessarily lead you to think it is a realistic depiction of a child's life in a neglected ghetto housing project, but it is. In Junebug's story, Mead offers a moving and accurate depiction of the struggles, dreams and choices that this boy must make. Nine-year-old Junebug lives in a bleak, gang-ridden housing project in New Haven, Connecticut, with his mother, young sister, and aunt. Mead enters the mind of a nine-year-old well: one day he dislikes and is ashamed of his indifferent and selfish aunt, the next day a few friendly words from her fuel a hope that perhaps she really cares about him. Junebug walks a difficult road, trying to avoid the pitfalls that his mother warns him against, while all the things that would offer any child security are constantly threatened. Junebug's aunt begins dating a drug dealer and his friends begin carrying guns and hanging around older men who ask them to run "errands" for money. The library he goes to after school closes because of a violent incident. Darnell, the one older boy he respects, runs away to escape project life. When his mother falls down the stairs while arguing with a drug dealer and goes to the hospital, his world spins out of control. His hope lies in putting messages in bottles, waiting for the day he can launch them at sea so someone will rescue him. But in his moment of real crisis, Junebug must find the courage to face his fears and allow himself to dream big.

Explore These: What was Junebug's biggest dream? What dreams have you had that seem impossible to fulfill? List three ways you can work to make those dreams become a reality. Keep a journal to note what you have done each week to help accomplish your dream(s), an excellent habit for success.

 THE KIDNAPPED PRINCE, THE LIFE OF OLAUDAH EQUIANO
By Olaudah Equiano, adapted by Ann Cameron.
Publisher: Alfred A. Knopf, 1995. HC$16.00. MVP: Courage

This historical account of a young African boy kidnapped, enslaved and brought across oceans is compelling, and even more so because of the introduction by Harvard professor Henry Louis Gates Jr. This is a slave narrative told from the boy's perspective. With so little African history offered to children in public schools today, it is a must read for every child, black or white. Readers will marvel at the drive, determination and faith with which this young African's indescribable hardships are endured. Ann Cameron does a fine job of making the story readable and captivating for the young adult. Olaudah Equiano, a prince from the African kingdom of Benin, was abducted from his village in 1755 at age eleven. Six months later, after having been passed from master to master, he was put on a slave cargo ship headed for the West Indies and sold there at auction. The book has many short chapters detailing the young prince's travels from the Americas to Europe and through the Caribbean. His adventures include fighting in the French and Indian War on a battleship, and becoming a savvy merchant while slaving on a merchant ship. The importance young Olaudah Equiano puts on his education as his ticket to freedom is a great lesson for young readers, and his courage, self-dignity and faith sustain him through horror after horror. His contributions to the abolitionist movement are many, but none so telling as this piece of literature, which exposed the atrocities of slavery firsthand—the premier piece of writing of its kind. It has not gone out of print in two hundred years. This work has influenced the writings of great African-American authors such as Frederick Douglass, Booker T. Washington, and Maya Angelou. NOTE: If you have access to the Internet, the author has some great thoughts recorded on the Amazon.com website about her work on this book. Check it out under the book's title.

 LIKE SISTERS ON THE HOMEFRONT
By Rita Williams-Garcia. Publisher: Puffin Books
(Penguin Putnam), 1995. PB$4.99 US/$6.99 CAN.
MVP: Triumphing over bad choices

Teens and preteens are sure to enjoy this gritty story about a smart-mouthed, "fast" fourteen-year-old girl trying to cope with the bed she's made (pun intended). Young Gayle is the mother of a toddler and finds herself pregnant again. This time her mother has had it and takes her for an abortion. But that only takes care of the physical "problem." Gayle's mind and heart are what need to be changed. She has pushed down so many of her real feelings that all that remains is the sarcastic tough-girl exterior that she believes will shield her from pain. Exasperated, her mom sends her "down Souf" to live in the slow lane with her relatives, who are all born-again Christians. Though Gayle despises the strict, slow country life and vows to get on a bus back home every day, she is also getting to know what it's like to live in a functional family for the first time. Despite herself, she and her baby, Jose, are being loved in a way she has never experienced before, even though she thinks her aunt and cousin are totally corny with their constant "Praise the Lord's." Gayle develops a close relationship with Great, her great-grandmother, and has a special moment with her just before she dies. In the midst of her rebellion Gayle discovers that there really is another way to live, and bigger dreams to dream. The brilliant cover of this book depicts a young girl we all know, holding her baby on her hip and with a defiant but secretly sad look on her face. Gayle's dialogue is written in such true-to-life teenage street language, minus the four-letter words, that it's sure to strike a chord with this age group.

Explore These: Why do you think Gayle had such an attitude? Describe how Gayle's life contrasted with that of her cousin Cookie's. How did Gayle help Cookie in the end? Imagine that you had a baby to take care of at age fourteen. How would it change your life?

 LITTLE X, GROWING UP IN THE NATION OF ISLAM
By Sonsyrea Tate. Publisher: HarperSanFrancisco, 1997. HC$22.00 US/$29.95 CAN; PB$12.00. MVP: The importance of discipline, Practicing what you preach

"Y'all Moozlems sure 'bout y'all's work," is something Sonsyrea Tate heard and felt often growing up in her Washington, D.C., neighborhood. Sonsyrea's grandparents had joined the controversial Nation of Islam, along with tens of thousands of other families, in search of a better way in the 1950s. They found discipline, acknowledgment, and respect there, and were assured that their children would be taught to love themselves, not to assimilate. Sonsyrea attended grade school at the Elijah Muhammad University of Islam. There, surrounded by proud black role models, she learned the importance of self-respect, self-reliance, cleanliness, community, and love of blackness. The group ran bakeries, restaurants, and other businesses, supported by followers who sold the *Muhammad Speaks* newspaper on street corners.

Men and boys were taught to protect their women at all costs, so Sonsyrea always felt safe in her inner-city neighborhood. Neither the Nation's growing reputation for subversive violence nor Elijah Muhammad's reported indiscretions were spoken about too much in Muslim homes, lest it feed a rumor mill and dissuade followers from the cause. But Sonsyrea knew there was a growing dissatisfaction with the Nation among her family members. Some felt the discipline and rules were intrusive and denigrated women; others saw too many "brothers and sisters" talking the talk but not walking the walk. In this daring book, Sonsyrea, who has since left the Nation, offers a balanced view of her and her family's life with the group in captivating detail.

Explore These: What did you learn about the Muslim religion? What did you like/not like about the way Sonsyrea and her family lived?

**LONG JOURNEY HOME,
STORIES FROM BLACK HISTORY
By Julius Lester. Publisher: Puffin Books (Penguin Putnam), 1998. PB$4.99 US/$5.99 CAN**

One point that has not been made loudly enough is the fact that "freedom" for the slaves was a frightening experience. Where should they go? Who will hire them? How can they ever mend the broken relationships with wives and children sold away? How will they live? These are six compelling short stories of unheralded men and women searching for, or trying to cope with, "freedom." They are each based on historical fact. Rambler is a runaway slave-nomad guitar player who can't stop running, even when he finds love. Louis has followed the famous Drinking Gourd that leads North, crossed the Big River and is devastated to realize that he could still be caught and recaptured. If not for a secret attic room and a woman's dress and bonnet, he just might have been. After freedom, Jake walks five hundred miles over three months searching for the beloved wife and mother of his children who was sold away from him years before, only to find her married to someone else whom she doesn't love, but is committed to. "I wish I'd known, Jake," she says, sobbing in his arms, "I wish I'd known." This riveting collection was nominated for the National Book Award.

Explore These: What were some of the tremendous challenges the newly freed slaves faced? Discuss this at length and relate it to our condition as a people today.

MAMA'S GIRL
By Veronica Chambers. Publisher: Riverhead Books (Penguin Putnam), 1996. PB$12.00 US/$17.00 CAN. MVP: Determination to succeed

Veronica Chambers chronicles her childhood, turbulent growing up and college years in this much-acclaimed testament to determination and resilience. Her struggles included an abusive father and stepmother, a sometimes indifferent mother, being the only black in a white private school, and being told she was ugly because she is dark. It seems that her unflinching determination to succeed is the thing that caused her the most pain, though ultimately it became her shining star. Chambers is a former editor at the *New York Times*.

MAYA ANGELOU, JOURNEY OF THE HEART
By Jayne Pettit. Publisher: Puffin Books (Penguin Putnam), 1996. PB$3.99 US/$4.99 CAN. MVP: Triumph over adversity

Many teens have heard of or enjoyed Ms. Angelou's classic autobiography, *I Know Why the Caged Bird Sings*. But in this slim, readable story, we get more details of her inspiring life story as world traveler, performer, activist, lecturer, and teacher. The book opens with Ms. Angelou preparing to speak at President Clinton's inauguration. In front of a crowd of dignitaries and citizens, Ms. Angelou delivered an eloquent and stirring message of hope and new beginnings. It was one reward for a long, often painful, yet remarkable journey that began in the poor rural town of Stamps, Arkansas. Her travels in Egypt and Ghana are of particular interest. She is truly a woman of indomitable spirit.

Black Artists' Notebook: Tom Feelings was the first African-American artist to win a Caldecott Honor, with his illustratons for *Moja Means One* in 1991. He honed his talent for drawing at the School of Visual Arts in New York. He has traveled extensively throughout Africa and the Caribbean, and has trained young artists in illustration in Guyana, South America. Mr. Feelings is currently professor of art at the University of South Carolina.

 THE MIDDLE PASSAGE, WHITE SHIPS, BLACK CARGO
By Tom Feelings. Publisher: Dial Books (Penguin Putnam), 1995. HC(Oversize) $45. Theme: The inhumanity of the slave trade

This amazing book about how we were captured, yoked, tortured and brought to the "New World" has no words, yet its illustrations will leave you speechless. Master artist Tom Feelings uses his trademark pen-and-ink drawings in shades of gray to chronicle our ancestors' haunting and horrific journey in the belly of slave ships. The sixty-four paintings in this book represent twenty years of work on the part of Mr. Feelings. He was forced to confront the history of slave trading while living in Ghana, Africa, in the 1960s. Each giant, double-page illustration should be looked at slowly and carefully, with attention to detail. See and feel the men stifling as they lay side by side for weeks on end, and allow yourself to experience the horror of men and women committing suicide by jumping ship—only to be met by sharks. The Introduction to this book is a must read. It could also inspire a wordless book project in which the emotion of a story and the story itself must both be conveyed solely in drawings.

MOTOWN AND DIDI
By Walter Dean Myers. Publisher: Laurel Leaf Books (Bantam Doubleday Dell), 1984. PB$3.99 US/$4.99 CAN. MVP: Being in love, Chasing your dreams

Motown is a smart orphaned teenage boy struggling to stay afloat in Harlem. Didi is a smart teenage girl with dreams and aspirations far beyond her 125th Street apartment. Both of them deal daily with the adversities of living in the underserved, impoverished neighborhood that they call home. Didi is dealing with a depressed mother, an absent father, and a drug-addicted brother while she waits anxiously for that letter in the mail from the college that she hopes to attend on scholarship—it's her only means of escape. Motown has been bounced from foster home to foster home and has dropped out of high school. He is still determined to do well for himself without turning to the life of drugs and crime that beckons to him each day. Motown lives quietly in an abandoned building, where he reads books about Marcus Garvey and other great black leaders given to him by his mentor, a retired professor and bookstore owner. He searches daily for work and always manages to get some menial job to keep himself going. Amazingly, he has saved $400 in a bank book for his future. He and Didi meet under heroic but unfortunate circumstances: Motown intervenes as Didi is being beaten and almost raped by neighborhood druggie "friends" of her brother's. The two fall in love, though Didi fights her feelings all the way through. She feels she must choose between loving Motown and working to achieve the escape-from-the-ghetto life she's always dreamed of. When the two inadvertently become embroiled in a drug-related incident, it brings their young love to a new level.

MY BLACK ME: A BEGINNING BOOK OF BLACK POETRY
Edited by Arnold Adoff. Publisher: Dutton Children's Books (Penguin Putnam), anniversary edition, 1994. HC$14.99. MVP: Understanding our feelings, Appreciating poetry

This is a compilation of short poems in which noted poets such as Sonia Sanchez, Langston Hughes, Lucille Clifton, Nikki Giovanni and Amiri Baraka reflect on what it's like to be black. The poems express love, pride, fear, grief, dreams deferred, thoughts about God and, above all, a celebration of our black lives. They talk about things children this age can relate to, even though some poems were originally published as early as 1926; their words transcend time. One particularly riveting poem, "Black Is Best" by Larry Thompson, describes a boy telling his unbelieving black mother that black is best. She tells him to hush, and eventually hits him because he won't stop saying it. But he still doesn't stop. Barbara Mahone's poem "What Color Is Black?" sums up the importance of reading black poetry to our children: to nurture their self-esteem. "Our love of self/of others/brothers sisters/people of a thousand shades of black/all one. Black is the color of the feeling that we share/the love we must express/the color of our strength/is black."

Explore These: Choose a few poems to read each week. Ask kids to express their thoughts on the poems. Use the short biographies on each poet at the back of the book to tell a little about the person behind the poem. Take them to a poetry reading, then stage an informal one using their own work or their favorite published poems.

"I liked Nightjohn *because it taught me about the way things were during slavery."*

—**Joshua,** age 13

NIGHTJOHN
By Gary Paulsen. Publisher: Laurel Leaf (Bantam Doubleday Dell), 1993. PB$4.50 US/$5.99 CAN. MVP: Determination. ALA Best Book for Young Adults, ALA Notable

This remarkable account is based on the true story of a man who was determined to help other slaves learn to read, even if it cost him his life—and it almost did. Nightjohn was actually a free man—meaning he successfully escaped to freedom in the North. But he returned to the South time and time again, under cover of darkness, to hold "pit school" in the woods with slaves who wanted to learn to read. He understood the value of learning. Young Sarny did, too, and she began taking secret lessons from Nightjohn. She went to sleep dreaming of the letter "A" and thinking about how it sounded, "Ayyy." Reading and even praying were strictly forbidden for slaves—the punishment was dismemberment. Even so, their determination was nothing short of amazing—Sarny's Aunt Delie would put her head in an iron kettle to muffle out the sound as she talked to God. Sarny and Nightjohn wrote letters in the dirt with a stick and Sarny continued to practice letters in her head until she learned to see words. When Sarny's "dirt writings" were discovered, her aunt was whipped for it, but Nightjohn took the blame. For his honesty, one toe was cut off of each foot. Undaunted, Nightjohn escaped again and returned again and again, bringing with him "the way to know." He was a man ahead of his time. "We all have to read and write so we can write about this—what they doing to us," says Nightjohn. "It has to be written."

Explore These: *Why do you think Nightjohn took such risks just to help people read? Why is the ability to read and write so valuable that white slaveowners forbade it so forcefully?

NORTH STAR TO FREEDOM: THE STORY OF THE UNDERGROUND RAILROAD
By Gena K. Gorrell. Publisher: Delacorte Press (Bantam Doubleday Dell), 1996. HC$17.95 US. Theme: How enslaved blacks escaped North

A cold, tired and hungry runaway slave is told to "try" the house with the green roof for food and shelter. What if they were unfriendly people, or worse, traitors? he wonders. How does one adjust to life in wintry Canada, where many slaves fled, when all you knew was warm or rainy weather? For the enslaved, the South was the only American home they'd ever known; yet the North promised a fragile freedom they had never experienced. For a slave, which side is the enemy? Even after entering the "free" states or crossing the Canadian border, many slaves lived with the fear that they might be recaptured by slave hunters or corrupt neighbors who were willing to be bribed for information. Racial prejudice and ignorance existed "up North" and in Canada as well. Black families were sometimes refused the right to settle in certain towns, or were driven off the land they had already worked to clear. In addition, most of the former slaves were uneducated and illiterate, and found that in Canada their children were forced to attend inferior and segregated schools. This "living history" tells the remarkable story of the people and places that made up the Underground Railroad. Each chapter begins with astonishing first-person accounts of what slave life entailed, from being captured in Africa to being "Free at Last!" These introductions are great jumping-off points for children to understand our ancestors' journey to freedom in a more personal way. Period posters, photos, paintings, and illustrations are in black and white, but are compelling and well placed. The book's stunning cover is a reprint of "The Ride for Liberty" by painter Eastman Johnson.

Explore These: Use the map in the front of the book to illustrate the path of the Underground Railroad. The Chronology at the back of the book can be used to help create a timeline, complete with pictures or drawings, from 1400 when the "people trade" started to 1865 when the slaves were freed, possibly as a school project. The book is filled with anecdotes and highlighted sidebar stories of pivotal or interesting figures in the Underground Railroad such as Henry "Box" Brown. Find biographies about these people in the library and read more about their remarkable stories.

 NORTON ANTHOLOGY OF AFRICAN AMERICAN LITERATURE
Edited by Henry Louis Gates Jr. and Nellie Y. McKay.
Publisher: Norton, 1996. HC$59.95

This is the culmination of ten years of work on the part of the authors to compile a canon of great literary works by African Americans. Many high schoolers are required to use the re-knowned *Norton Anthology of English Literarure* in their English classes; now there is one that focuses solely on black literature. The large book incudes everything from speeches to drama to biographies to short stories and much more in between. An accompanying CD includes audio samplings of the great literature offered in the book, plus Negro spirituals. It is a must have for every black household with young teenagers.

 NOW IS YOUR TIME: THE AFRICAN-AMERICAN STRUGGLE FOR FREEDOM
By Walter Dean Myers. Publisher: HarperCollins, 1991.
HC$17.95 US/$24.50 CAN. MVP: Determination

How often will a child read American history as told by an African American? This book, which chronicles the story of our people from Africa in the 1400s to the civil rights movement of the 1960s, highlights the struggles and accomplishments of many whose names are not likely to appear in the "standard" history texts your child reads in school. The courage and talent of our forebears affected the world of politics, art, literature, music, journalism, and education. If the people on these pages could make amazing contributions given the immense obstacles they faced, every black child today should be able to make his or her mark on the world. This book will both inform and inspire and is perfect for finding subjects on which to write class papers or projects. It should be right on every child's bookshelf, next to the *Norton Anthology of African American Literature.*

OH, FREEDOM!
By Casey King and Linda Barrett Osborne. With a foreword by Rosa Parks. Publisher: Knopf, 1997. PB$10.99 US/$14.50 CAN. MVP: Black History

One way to make children interested in learning history is to put them in the story. In this creative book, roving child journalists interview their relatives about what it was like growing up in the 1960s and taking part in the civil rights movement. It is divided into three sections: Life Under Segregation; The Movement to End Legalized Segregation; and The Struggle to End Poverty and Discrimination. The interviews in each section are preceded by a brief historical summary. In many cases, this is the first time the children have heard their relatives' stories of struggle and oppression, and it seems it may also be a long time since the relatives have been asked about it. This makes for very emotion-packed exchanges, such as when young Alana Brevard hears her mother's story of being ostracized in her grade school classroom because no one wanted to sit next to the "nigger." Alana, obviously horrified, says, "Oh my God, Mommy, that's terrible. . . . Oh Mommy, I'm very sorry," at the end of her interview. There are compelling black-and-white photographs of everything from students being harassed at lunch counter sit-ins to hosings and cross-burnings to children from the YWCA being trained to picket movie theaters. One chilling photo shows young white girls picketing school desegregation. A blonde who looks like the wholesome girl next door is holding a sign that reads, WE LIKE YOU, BUT WE DON'T WANT YOU IN OUR SCHOOL. Good photos, concise, well-edited interviews, lots of white space and a hopeful ending make this book a winner.
Explore These: You may want to have your child read the in-

terviewer portions, while you read the interviewees' answers. Encourage a project in which children prepare thoughtful questions for an older relative and become journalists for a day themselves. Interviews could be tape-recorded to create an oral history.

"I liked Ola Shakes It Up *because it was fun to read about all the clever things Ola did to stop her family from moving out of their old neighborhood."*

—**Damaris,** age 13

OLA SHAKES IT UP
By Joanne Hyppolite. Publisher: Delacorte Press (Bantam Doubleday Dell), 1998. HC$14.95 US/$19.95 CAN. MVP: Adjusting to change

Ola's family is moving to a "better" neighborhood, and she doesn't like it one bit. What's wrong with Roxbury, where they live now? And what's so great about a stuffy historical district where they would be the only black family? Ola has to face the prospect of losing her close friends, her favorite housekeeper and her sense of security all at once—hard things to deal with during the preteen years. Her older brother and sister are sold on the move once they see the big new house, but not Ola. She drives her parents crazy with her weekly plans of rebellion, hoping they will give in and move back to their "normal" neighborhood, where every house doesn't look like every other. Any child who is the "only black one" in her class or on her block will associate with the things Ola encounters when she moves to Walcott—funny stares, fearful glances, unfriendliness, even a few jeers. Walcott Corners is also full of rules and regulations, including no playing outside after dark. What a bore! Ola decides that there's only one way to survive—she's got to spice things up. With the unexpected help of an older white neighbor and inspiration from Lillian, the family's newly emigrated Haitian housekeeper, Ola finds strength and encouragement. What she does next is a shining example of how one youngster's creative energy can add "color" to an entire community.

Explore These: Why was Ola so upset about the move? Have you ever felt like you were the "only one" in a group? How did you handle it? Describe a big change in your life and how it made you feel. How can we get inspiration to face our own difficulties by looking at another person's life? What creative abilities do you have? How can you use them right now to improve your community?

 ONCE ON THIS RIVER
By Sharon Dennis Wyeth. Publisher: Alfred A. Knopf, 1998. $16.00 US/$21.00 CAN. MVP: The cost of keeping secrets

This unique story is set in the late 1700s and tells of a "free" mother and daughter from Madagascar who travel on a slave ship bound for New York City. Monday and her mother, Leslie, are desperate to help free a relative who was captured and forced into slavery there, but they are in constant danger of being enslaved themselves in this strange American city. Along their journey, the two are caught in the tangled web of secrets that have to be kept to protect the innocent—including one about Monday that will change her life. The book contains most of the elements young readers enjoy: mystery, romance, and a dramatic, unexpected ending. Thanks to the author's fascination with the history of African Americans in New York state, the book offers good historical facts nicely hidden within the engrossing story. We don't usually associate slavery with the North, and certainly not with New York. This compelling story, based on research of the period by Ms. Dennis Wyeth, opens our eyes to new truths about what our ancestors in the Big Apple experienced.

Explore These: Locate Madagascar on a globe or map. Trace the voyage Monday and Leslie made to New York. What must it have felt like to be on a ship for that long? What do you think about the family's opposition to Viola and Sampson's marriage? Should people of different classes or different races marry? Would you want to know if you were adopted?

THE PARABLE OF THE SOWER
By Octavia Butler. Publisher: Warner Books, 1993.
PB$5.99US/$6.99 CAN. MVP: Imagination

It is a fact that many teens love sci-fi. So why not encourage them to read the artful and acclaimed work of one of the only black science fiction writers around, Octavia Butler? Her novels are about the most deliciously strange people you've ever encountered. *Star Trek* has little chance against this twenty-first-century author who has been hailed as a "powerful voice in African-American literature and modern science fiction." This book centers around a girl named Lauren who is an empath. That means she feels the physical pain of all of the decaying people around her, if she concentrates on them for too long. The story is set in Los Angeles in the next century, where the haves and the have-nots are separated by thick stone enclaves and no one goes out at night unarmed. Homeless people lie in the streets headless, and emaciated children walk the roads aimlessly. But all that changes when violence strikes and the walls separating the classes come down. Lauren and her friends must try to survive and spread their message of faith and hope where there seems to be none left. See also *Pattern-Master* and *Mind of My Mind*.

PHENOMENAL WOMAN, FOUR POEMS
CELEBRATING WOMEN
By Maya Angelou. Publisher: Random House, 1995.
HC$10.00. MVP: Self-confidence. Audio

This little treasure makes a great gift for a high school girl just maturing into adulthood. The famed title poem, "Phenomenal Woman," will teach a teenage girl that she doesn't have to "shout or jump about or talk real loud" because true beauty comes from "the grace of her style," "the sun of her smile" and her "inner mystery." She'll learn that she can handle anything in "Still I Rise," because our ancestors have already borne the brunt of the pain, paid the price, run the race—and won. So pardon her if she "walks like she's got oil wells pumping in her living room."

Solid, practical rules for balanced living come out clearly in "Weekend Glory." And "Our Grandmothers" will teach her to honor and respect her elders always, because they "shall not be moved." It's kind of a marvelous poetic version of a life's-little-lessons-book.

Explore These: What do you feel when you read these poems? Describe. Do you think you have good self-esteem? In what areas could you improve?

REBELS AGAINST SLAVERY, AMERICAN SLAVE REVOLTS
By Patricia and Frederick McKissack. Publisher: Scholastic, 1996. HC$14.95. MVP: Black history, Great men

While the stories of the abolitionists have been told and retold, the leaders of slave revolts are often left out of history. Men like Nat Turner, who led the longest revolt in history; Cinqué, who led the mutiny aboard the ship *Amistad* (recently given some light in the 1997 mega-movie of the same name); and Toussaint L'Ouverture, Haitian emancipator, strategist and colonel. These great men, and others well profiled in this book, were unwilling to accept any compromise of their God-given freedoms and fearlessly waged war against powerful slaveholders. These grand black brothers are heroes of our history and children must know, read about and understand their important contributions to our lives today. See also, *Amistad: A Long Road to Freedom* by Walter Dean Myers.

Explore These: What motivated each of the men in this book who led slave revolts? Pick one and talk about how he went about his plan. How can we best channel our anger and frustrations about racism and injustice and make changes in our world? How can you be an agent of change in your sphere of influence?

THE RIGHTEOUS REVENGE OF ARTEMIS BONNER
By Walter Dean Myers. Publisher: HarperTrophy (HarperCollins), 1992. PB$4.95 US/$6.75 CAN.
Theme: Wild West

Young people with a sharp sense of humor will enjoy this rollicking Western melodrama by Walter Dean Myers. The hero, Artemis Bonner, receives word that his uncle, Ugly Ned, was killed out West by a villain named Catfish Grimes, and has left a fortune hidden in a safe place. Bonner leaves New York to avenge his uncle's death and search for the treasure, traipsing through places like Tombstone, Arizona, and Juarez, Mexico. Myers writes in classic cowboy-movie, melodramatic style, using clichés with deadpan seriousness and also making good use of a tongue-in-cheek humor: "She spit into the corner and wiped her mouth with a delicate move of her wrist that told me she was a true lady." His final showdown with Grimes ends in victory, but with an unusual and hilarious twist at the end.

Explore These: What is a melodrama? Have the child look up the definition and write a one-page melodrama of their own, perhaps a puppet show or a small play that can be performed. (Make sure there is a hero, a villain, and a dramatic moment of crisis.)

ROLL OF THUNDER, HEAR MY CRY
By Mildred Taylor. Publisher: Puffin Books (Penguin Putnam), 1991, PB$4.99 US/$5.99 CAN. Newbery Medal, ALA Notable

This was the first in an award-winning series of books about the Logans, a proud, land-owning black family living in Mississippi in the 1930s. The land the Logans live on was purchased by Mr. Logan's father years ago, and now it provides security and independence for the family. As long as the cotton doesn't fail, the Logans will always be able to pay their yearly taxes—even if that means some sacrifices. Those sacrifices are hard on the Logan children. They don't understand the value of land-owning and staying your ground as much as the adults do. The children walk to their second-rate school each day as busloads of white kids yell jeers out the windows. Cassie Logan, from whose point of view the story is told, doesn't understand racism and doesn't want to. She speaks her mind when she feels wronged—a dangerous thing to do in the South in those days. When a little white girl makes a scene about an accidental bump (what *is* it about bumping?), Cassie stands her ground. She is angry at her grandmother for asking her to apologize. The explanation of racism that her mother finally gives her in the book is a good example for how parents can handle their children's painful "Why?"s Teens will enjoy this compelling and suspenseful young adult novel as the Logan family copes with all types of racism and discrimination in their daily lives. But do they have enough strength to deal with the ruthless night riders?

Explore These: Why was Cassie Logan so upset about racism? Read the explanation of racism Ms. Logan gives Cassie starting on page 126. Ask an adult any questions you have about it. Don't miss *Let the Circle Be Unbroken*, the Coretta Scott King Award– winning sequel.

 RUNNIN' WITH THE BIG DAWGS
By Robb Armstrong. Illustrator: Bruce Smith.
Publisher: HarperActive (HarperCollins), 1998.
PB$3.99 US/$4.99 CAN. MVP: Friendship

With its fun, cartoon-like illustrations, easy-flowing, large-print text and sports theme, this book will appeal to reluctant readers in this age group. It is the better of two books that feature Patrick's Pals, a basketball trio including sports stars Patrick Ewing, Dikembe Mutombo, and Alonzo Mourning. The three main characters are named after the stars, and lessons about friendship and teamwork are taught in the context of a basketball showdown. The boys talk a lot of "trash" off the court, but which is the best team depends on who can slam the rock (which is one of the names for the ball, in case you're not up on the lingo) in the net. Poor Dikembe has just arrived in the United States from Africa and hasn't learned all the cool phrases yet. "I've only been here two days," he tells the boys, "cut me some slacks!" He's mad tall, but his game needs help and it's Patrick's job to be the "mercy coach." A nice element is that we hear Patrick talking to himself, asking his conscience questions and grappling with right and wrong. A fun little book. The textured cover even feels like the surface of a basketball.

Explore These: What did Patrick learn befriending and coaching Dikembe? If you were in the same situation, would you sacrifice your time to help out a friend? Describe a time when you did that. How did it feel?

 SARNY: A LIFE REMEMBERED
By Gary Paulsen. Publisher: Delacorte Press, 1997.
HC$15.95 US/$21.95 CAN. MVP: Overcoming
tremendous odds, Perseverance

It's difficult not to admire the courage, determination, and sweet naïveté of Sarny, a young enslaved mother of two who flees her plantation during the last days of the Civil War. All Sarny and her friend Lucy know is that they are off to New Orleans—wherever that is—in search of Sarny's children, who were auctioned. Her resolve to get to the city where her children are (three hundred and fifty miles away!) amidst open battles and at great risk of being snatched and resold herself is what captures our hearts. Her compassion—stopping to tend to some dying soldiers and "adopt" an abandoned white child—is nothing short of heroic. Sarny's and Lucy's lives are forever changed when they are taken in by Miz Laura, a well-to-do black woman who passes for white. Tasting freedom for the first time with Sarny is a wonderful and quizzical experience—she has never been to town, used a fork, or seen an indoor toilet or a twenty-dollar bill in her life! The book's rich, twisting, turning storyline will satisfy young readers, especially those who enjoyed the first book, *Nightjohn*.

Explore These: What did Sarny have to overcome to adjust to her freedom? Did any of the details surprise you? Discuss.

> *"My mother was a schoolteacher, so I started reading early. She encouraged and motivated me. I mostly read books having to do with self-esteem–building or anything that has to do with moving my life forward."*
>
> **—Jennifer Holiday,** showstopping singer and Broadway performer

THE SHIMMERSHINE QUEENS
By Camille Yarbrough. Publisher: Putnam, 1989.
HC$14.95 US/$19.50 CAN. MVP: Self-esteem,
Self-confidence

This is ten-year-old Angie's routine: she comes home from school and goes into her "dreaming room," also called the bathroom. As she sits on the edge of the tub, Angie imagines a life where she becomes an actress and an Olympic track star, marries a wonderful, loving man, buys a big house for her mother and sisters, and acquires long, flowing, light-colored hair along the way. She also practices the dancing she loves in the bathroom—that is, until she kicks the door so much that her mother orders her out. Angie is longing for a world where she isn't too afraid to answer the teacher's questions, even when she knows the answers. A world where her hair isn't short, she isn't dark-skinned, her father didn't leave them and her mother doesn't make her stay home from school to babysit because she's depressed and can't get out of bed. Angie and her best friend, Michelle, are trying to make it in a school where kids stomp on the teacher's desk when he's not looking, bring knives to school and taunt each other relentlessly. Angie's Aunt Seatta pays a visit and aims to make sure Angie knows herself and her royal heritage before she leaves—and she does. Angie learns that she has the "get-up gift," to see and dream especially when things look ugly; that her task is to "glory in learning," because our ancestors risked their lives to learn; that she is not to allow "Mr. Fear" to get the best of her; and that she has lovely, "African beauty looks" that she can be proud of. This conversation with Aunt Seatta changes Angie's self-concept forever. It is so impressive to see her living out the principles her aunt shares with her, even in rough situations at school. A caring dance instructor gives Angie the opportunity to see that her warm, "shimmershine" feeling and get-up spirit will take her anywhere she wants to go.

Black Writers' Notebook: Noted and prolific author **Walter Dean Myers** has written more than fifty books for young readers, many of which have received top industry awards, including the 1997 Coretta Scott King Award For *Slam!* Mr. Myers is also the 1994 winner of the American Library Association's Margaret A Edwards Award for his lifetime achievement in writing books for young adults. His travels have taken him to the Far East, South America, and even the Arctic.

SLAM!
By Walter Dean Myers. Publisher: Scholastic Press, 1996. HC$15.95 US. MVP: Confidence. Coretta Scott King Award

What a treasure this book will be to teenage boys who play ball. It is the story of Todd, a smart, young, tough-talking athlete who "can take his game to the bank," it's so solid. It's the off-court part that worries him—particularly algebra. Todd struggles to keep his grades up enough to qualify for a college basketball scholarship at his mostly white magnet school. Typical of a teen player, Todd dreams about getting drafted into the NBA, but, atypically, he is also nurturing his talent as an artist and documentarian in an after-school art program. In the midst of all this, he must deal with teachers who make degrading remarks; a sweet, wise beyond her years, college-bound girlfriend who warns, "Don't fall in love with me" (after he's already fallen); and a best friend and ace ballplayer who keeps showing up in nicer cars and clothes and may have secretly entered "the life." All this happens against a backdrop of sirens in the night and brothers in the gutter around One-two-five Street. Todd's mother is a loving force, and his dad is supportive but busy dealing with his own un-realized dreams. Myers has all the basketball play descriptions and terminology—real and slang—down to a science. (Now I know what "the pill," "the pebbles" and "tap and rap" are. I'm sure it would absolutely stun your son or daughter if you started throwing those terms out with authority!

SOJOURNER TRUTH: AIN'T I A WOMAN?
By Patricia C. McKissack and Frederick McKissack.
Publisher: Scholastic, 1992. PB$3.50 US/$3.95 CAN.
MVP: Determination.

This biography of outstanding abolitionist and activist Isabella Sojourner Truth is excellent because it breaks her extraordinary life down into chewable morsels served up in each chapter. We also learn about a number of other key players—black and white—in the abolitionist movement. There are also a number of compelling black-and-white photos of Sojourner, who stood six feet tall. It is heartening to learn of the many white people who took up Sojourner's cause and offered her support, lodging, money and speaking engagements. The book devotes many pages to the growth of the feminist movement, which was bloom-ing at the same time as the abolitionist crusade; sometimes femi-nists sought Sojourner out for her support. Frederick Douglass, Sojourner's contemporary, who advocated a more militant method for liberating the enslaved, also wanted her to rally for the cause. Though Sojourner empathized, she knew that the cause she was devoted to most was freedom and liberty for black people, and achieving it without bloodshed. The fact that she was a presidential guest at the White House for three administrations as a black woman in the slavery era is nothing short of remark-able. Her story is a testament to the power of faith in God and the determination of one's convictions. (Other Scholastic biographies include those on Colin Powell, Bo Jackson, Nelson Mandela, Jesse Jackson and Martin Luther King.)

Explore These: What do you think compelled Sojourner Truth to keep on speaking even after whites mobbed her at one engagement? Is there anything you feel so strongly about that you would risk your life for?

SOUL LOOKS BACK IN WONDER
By Tom Feelings (with poems by thirteen noted black poets). Publisher: Dial Books (Penguin Putnam), 1993. HC$15.99. MVP: Perseverance. Coretta Scott King Award

Tom Feelings chose drawings of people he sketched in Ghana, Africa, Guyana, South America, and the United States for this book, which he dedicated to "our precious young African sisters and brothers, who are our today and our tomorrow." Most of the poems are ten to fifteen lines, and some have a rap-like rhythm (at least to *me*) that many of our young people will identify with. All speak of our beauty, our creativity, and our united strength. More widely known contributors include Maya Angelou, Langston Hughes, Haki Madhubuti, Alexis De Veaux, and Walter Dean Myers. As Mari Evans asks/says in her poem, "Who can be born black and not exult!"

Explore These: Read the poems first yourself to catch the rhythms, then read them to your children with expression, pausing to emphasize powerful verses. Encourage a child to read a favorite one aloud. Ask them to tell you what they liked about a particular poem. Ask them to describe how it made them feel or what pictures they get in their minds when they hear it.

SOUNDER
By William H. Armstrong. Illustrator: James Barkley. Publisher: HarperTrophy (HarperCollins), 1969. PB$4.95 US/$6.75 CAN. MVP: Loyalty. Classic, Newbery Medal

Many may be familiar with this award-winning story of a faithful dog and his sharecropper family. Sounder was what we would call a mutt—part this and part that. But he was the best raccoon-catching dog in his part of Georgia, and he was loyal to the end. Although times were hard for his family, Sounder still got scraps and crumbs to tide him over. When the winter wind howled, the family give him burlap sacks to sleep in to ward off some of the cold. Sounder was loved, especially by his master, who would take him hunting when the season was right, and his master's son, who took care of him when his dad was away searching for food or work, or both. One day, Dad came home with a country ham and pork sausages—an absolute feast by their standards. Everyone ate well, for a while. But it wasn't long before a white sheriff stormed their meager home and arrested the father for theft. Sounder couldn't bear the sight of his master being shackled and dragged off. He ran barking after the wagon and just as he got close, one of the white men shot him on the side of the head. Sounder was bleeding to death in the middle of the road. But he did not die. Crippled, frightened and minus an ear, Sounder lived and, after he had healed a bit in the woods, came back to his family. The most poignant images in this book are of the boy out searching relentlessly for his father, enduring taunts and physical abuse as he examines the shapes of the men on the various chain gangs, hoping to see his dad. And, of course, the image of Sounder hobbling down the same road where he was shot, to meet his master when he finally comes home years later, is riveting.

Explore These: Ask children how they think the boy felt watching this terrible scene of his dad arrested and his dog shot. Why would the boy risk his life to find his father? What would make either the father or Sounder return to the family, given the horrible state they were in? Who are you loyal to and how far would that loyalty extend in a tough situation? Discuss.

> *"I enjoy reading because it's nice to go off to other places. It stimulates your mind, opens you up to new possibilities and improves your people skills, too."*
>
> —"Downtown" **Julie Brown,** formerly of *MTV Jams*

SUGAR IN THE RAW, VOICES OF YOUNG BLACK GIRLS IN AMERICA
By Rebecca Carroll. Publisher: Crown, 1997. PB$12.00 US/$16.95 CAN. MVP: Determination

This is a stirring and informative collection of first-person stories based on interviews with young black American girls aged eleven to twenty, in twelve U.S. cities. Some are sweet, some are street-tough, some grew up with great parents, some with none—but all of them have already experienced the joys and pains of being brown-skinned females in America, and they have a lot to say. Their personal stories about fitting in, friendship, boyfriends, the importance of church, school, their parents, and life in general are great reads, especially for other teens. They have much wisdom to share with their peers.

Explore These: Which girl's story do you relate to most? Tell why. Facilitated by an adult, this could launch an excellent discussion about teen issues.

SWEET SUMMER
By Bebe Moore Campbell. Publisher: One World (Fawcett/Ballantine), 1989. PB$6.50 US/$7.50 CAN. MVP: Love, Coping with father's absence, Loss

Every time Bebe's dad said, "C'mon, kiddo, let's go somewhere," it thrilled her. She spent much of her childhood summers down South with her dad, after her parents' divorce, and relished the time away from mother, aunt, and grandma. It was her time away from the world of sometimes fussy women, ("The

Bosoms") and into the rugged, spontaneous universe of life with her disabled dad. They laughed together, talked about things, and loved one another. But it wasn't all fun and games. There were family secrets that threatened to unravel her image of her father-hero. After her dad lost the use of his legs in a car accident, he had never been quite the same—and neither had her parents' marriage. What really happened? Was it an accident or a joy ride? And why didn't her father ever want to use the shiny new braces in his closet that could help him walk again? Young Bebe strives to make sense of the painful truths, failures, and fragility in her father's life, while still holding on to the powerful image of him that is etched on her heart.

Black Writers' Notebook: Author **Virginia Hamilton** has been writing children's books for more than twenty years. She wanted to become an author when she was ten years old, and told her sister she was going to be famous someday. She has published approximately 35 books to date, including Newbery Honor book *Sweet Whispers, Brother Rush*.

 SWEET WHISPERS, BROTHER RUSH
By Virginia Hamilton. Publisher: Philomel (Penguin Putnam), 1987. HC$18.99/PB$4.50. MVP: Facing up to past mistakes. Coretta Scott King Award, Newbery Honor, Horn Book Award

What if you were a fourteen-year-old girl who has to keep house and care for a retarded older brother for weeks at a time—alone? That's what Tree does when her mother is away working as a live-in maid for white folks (and escaping her own painful life for a while). Tree's brother Dabney is getting sicker and sicker—a strange illness that makes it painful for him to be touched. Tree is having a hard time caring for him and needs her mother to come home. She then meets a fine young stranger named Brother Rush who helps her uncover some dark secrets in her family's past—secrets that hurt. Hamilton combines vivid and complex characterizations with rich language to weave a haunting story of a mother and daughter coming to terms with themselves, their relationship and their future.

Explore These: What does Brother Rush show Tree about her family? What are some of the secrets that Tree's mother was trying to escape? Are there some "secrets" in your family that no one wants to talk about? What would it take to get them out in the open?

TASTE OF SALT
By Frances Temple. Publisher: HarperTrophy (Harper-Collins), 1992. PB$4.95. MVP: Justice, Courage

Drama, suspense, romance and history are all contained in this highly acclaimed and award-winning book, which is set in modern Haiti during the time of the overthrow of the country's military dictatorship. Djo lived in the streets before he was taken under the wing of Father Jean-Bertrand Aristide, future Haitian president, when Aristide was still just a priest who spoke out for the poor of Port-au-Prince. Jeremie was a bright teenage girl who came from an impoverished family, but has received a coveted Catholic education by working for the nuns. After Djo survives a firebombing of the boys' shelter where he lived, Aristide sends Jeremie to record "Djo's story" on a tape recorder while he recovers in a makeshift hospital, and this is the format in which the story progresses. On a broader level, this book is about children who grow up during a time of revolution, trying to understand the complexities and harsh realities of poverty, injustice and political instability, all the while trying to navigate their own adolescence. The book is skillfully written, interspersing Creole and Spanish words in their stories, told in halting English. Readers will be transported with the author's vivid descriptions of life in the shanty-ridden Haitian slums.

Explore These: What courageous acts did Djo do for the sake of what he believed? What courageous acts did Jeremie do? Look up Haiti on the map in the front of the book, or on a larger map or globe. Find out more about Father Jean-Bertrand Aristide and Haitian history.   ·

A THIEF IN THE VILLAGE AND OTHER STORIES
By James Berry. Publisher: Orchard Books (Franklin Watts), 1987. PB$4.99. MVP: Caribbean culture

It was exciting to find a collection of stories for teens that all centered around life in the Caribbean. Rarely do we get a picture of real life there in children's books. These stories capture the cadences of local speech perfectly, which only enhances their interest. It seems that the characters in many of the stories need some "thing" in order to be happy, and most of them get it. One story is about a little boy who just wants a "mouth-organ," or harmonica, so he can be accepted by his cool friends. Another, ironically, is about a little girl who just wants a bicycle so she can ride with the Wheels-and-Brake Boys. One cliffhanger tells of a boy who runs out of a shelter in the middle of a hurricane and almost perishes. What did *he* want? Basically, some shoes, and some attention, from his father. The references to life in Jamaica, where these stories are set and where the author was born, are refreshing; for example, every cool boy pitches for his cricket team (no basketball in sight); when a child is born his nana midwife sprinkles his umbilical cord with castor oil and nutmeg, buries it and might plant a tree over it; Sunday morning one might wake up to a cock crowing, blooming red hibiscus trees and a breakfast of "akee-and-salt-fish in coconut gravy, callaloo, fried plantain, johnnycakes and roast breadfruit." A very enjoyable book with a nice twist.

Explore These: What are some of the customs or foods of Jamaica that are different from where you live? Can you write a short story in dialect? Choose one and try it out. (It's not as easy as it seems.)

"I plan to read more of Zora Neale Hurston. . . . She is an outstanding writer of remarkable depth. I love all the black women writers, but Zora holds a special place among them."
—**Max Roach,** renowned drummer, composer, and musicologist

THEIR EYES WERE WATCHING GOD
By Zora Neale Hurston. Publisher: HarperPerennial
(HarperCollins), 1990. PB$13.00 US/$18.00 CAN.
MVP: Self-confidence

It took almost thirty years for this classic novel to enjoy the success and acclaim it deserved when it was first published in 1937. Today it is a best-seller and hailed as "one of the finest novels of its time." Hurston's key character, Janie, is a stand-up kind of woman, as they say, who knows who she is and doesn't take no stuff from gossipy women or bossy men. Yet she is sweet, smart, and gentle, too—an inspiring combination of a woman. After several interesting and difficult relationships, Janie finds the real love she always knew existed—even if only for a while.

Black Writers' Notebok: Author **Zora Neale Hurston**'s mother always told her to "jump at the sun" (another way of saying, "reach for the stars"). She studied anthropology at Barnard College in New York. Her celebrated novel, *Their Eyes Were Watching God,* resulted from her many travels down South and in the Caribbean. A new book imprint called Jump at the Sun is headed by children's book editor and author Andrea Pinkney at Hyperion Books, a division of the Disney Company.

TO BE A SLAVE, THIRTIETH ANNIVERSARY EDITION
By Julius Lester. Illustrator: Tom Feelings. Dial Books (Penguin Putnam), 1998 PB$16.99. MVP: Adjusting to change. Classic, Newbery Honor

To say that this book is riveting would be an understatement. Reading it, you feel transported back in time to an intimate dinner party in which one hundred ex-slaves are the invited guest speakers. In his acknowledgment page to this classic Julius Lester notes, "The ancestry of any black American can be traced to a bill of sale and no further. In many instances even that cannot be done." Lester should know. He attempted to trace the roots of his own great-grandparents in the early 1960s, to no avail. What he *did* find in his search, interviews done with ex-slaves in the 1930s, inspired him to write this book, for which he won a coveted Newbery Honor in 1967. Lester masterfully interjects short explanations and clarifications in italics before or after the remarkable accounts from men and women who endured slavery, which make up the body of the text. Along with captivating stories that teach us our history in living color, we learn some truths about life on the plantation, like the fact that most plantation owners lived poorly, keeping twenty or fewer slaves apiece (sometimes just one or two), not the one hundred or more we often see depicted. And we learn that slaveowners often feared for their lives each day, knowing what *they* would do to a Massa if they were slaves. We find that three-fourths of the Southern white people held no slaves at all. We also learn that many runaway slaves lived in the woods for years, never reaching "the North," some deciding instead to live with the Indians. It is heartrending and joyous at the same time to read how jubilant our forebears were when they were told they were free (contrary to popular belief, most *did* believe it was true, says Lester). One account notes, "I remembers one woman. She jumped on a barrel and she shouted. She jumped off and she shouted. She jumped on again and shouted some more," remembers Anna Woods. "She kept that up for a long time, just jumping on a barrel and back off again." We would have, too.

Black Writers' Notebook: Angela Johnson has written more than a dozen books for children and young adults, including *When I Am Old With You* (page 107) and *Toning the Sweep* (below), for which she won a Coretta Scott King Award in 1994.

TONING THE SWEEP
By Angela Johnson. Publisher: Orchard Books, 1993.
HC$13.95 US. MVP: Cherishing good memories.
Coretta Scott King Award

This is an affecting and understated novel about three generations of women, each coping with their frailties in different ways. Emmie's grandfather was shot and killed by the Klan, but no one wants to talk about it. It is a family secret until Emmie decides to do a memory video while on a visit to her grandmother's. Emmie has visited Ola, who is dying of cancer, in the California desert every summer since she was two, and she loves it there. Her mom, on the other hand, hates it and can't wait to leave. For her, it's the place Ola escaped to too quickly after her father's death, not allowing her time to grieve properly. She was the one who found her daddy dead. She resents her mother for that. So Emmie and Ola have more of a mother–daughter relationship than Ola and Mama. Now Ola is coming back East to live with Emmie and her mother because of the illness. If the prospect of losing Ola isn't enough, Emmie certainly doesn't expect to stumble on the details of her grandfather's murder or find his letters, which now makes him so real to her she could almost see him. Finally, before she leaves her beloved desert for probably the last time, she finds she needs to ring his spirit to heaven properly, by toning the sweep (a farming tradition involving hammering twists of metal into the ground). In performing this cathartic ritual, Emmie and her mother are brought together.

THE TUSKEGEE AIRMEN, BLACK HEROES OF WORLD WAR II
By Jacqueline Harris. Publisher: Dillon Press (Simon & Schuster), 1996. HC$22.00/PB$7.99. MVP: Courage

This book will inspire any teen who dreams of being a pilot. It chronicles the lives of pioneering black aviators who battled prejudice at home to become fighter pilots during World War II. Pictures of our dashing airmen in preflight meetings and in the cockpit are particularly appealing and heartening. Also included is a photo and brief biography of Bessie Coleman, the first black woman to become a licensed pilot. The section "Opening the Door to the Air Corps" is an important one that helps us understand whose sweat and tears paved the way for this incredible achievement. See also *Red-Tail Angels: The Story of the Tuskeegee Airmen of World War II* by Patricia and Frederick McKissack and, on video, *The Tuskegee Airmen*, featuring Laurence Fishburne and Cuba Gooding Jr.

UNCLE TOM'S CABIN
By Harriet Beecher Stowe. Publisher: Bantam, 1981. PB$4.50US/$5.50 CAN. MVP: Faith

When this book came out in the mid-1800s it was controversial, shocking, and powerful. Few white writers had dared to write about the human tragedy of slave life. Ms. Stowe, the daughter, wife, and sister of ministers, boldly pointed the finger at Christians for allowing slavery. Many passages in the book are considered downright "preachy," and Stowe attested that "God wrote it"; she merely took down what He showed her. The story is about a slave named Tom who, through his moral superiority and incredible humanity, manages to forgive his oppressors and remain faithful to God even though he has lost everything—including his life—at their hands. Though he is despised and ridiculed by many fellow slaves, in the end, many are changed by having known Tom. The story has been likened to that of the life of Jesus, a man from "low" birth who too was oppressed, yet endured and affected people for generations. The beauty of this book is that it is a story of moral passion, unyielding faith, and, ultimately, triumph.

 THE WATSONS GO TO BIRMINGHAM—1963 **By Christopher Paul Curtis. Publisher: Bantam Books, 1997. HC$14.99/PB$4.99. MVP: The importance of family relationships. Coretta Scott King Honor, Newbery Honor**

The pages just fly by in Mr. Curtis's award-winning first novel, which humorously depicts the goings-on of the Watson family. From older brother Byron getting his lips frozen to a rearview mirror in the dead of winter (he was kissing his handsome reflection) to sister Joetta drooling all over the car as she catches some zzz's, his constant humor is delightful. But the story is deeply moving, too. Kenny Watson and his family are traveling from Michigan to Alabama to deliver his older brother Byron into the hands of Grandma Sands. Her reputation for making children mind has led Momma and Daddy to let Byron, who is headed for trouble, spend the summer under her watchful eye. Alabama is hot with the unrest and excitement of the civil rights movement. The family finds themselves in the middle of a crisis as a local church is bombed during a Sunday service. Nine-year-old Kenny comes face to face with death more than once in this tale based loosely upon a real-life bombing in Birmingham, Alabama, that year. As the story progresses, family ties are strengthened and Grandma Sands straightens Byron right out. But the ending is sobering—there are no promises of living happily ever after, just the comfort of family ties and hope for the future.

WHAT HEARTS
By Bruce Brooks. Publisher: HarperCollins, 1992.
HC$14.89/PB$4.95. MVP: Coping with divorce,
Stepparent

In this book we step into the psyche of Asa, an exceptionally bright boy who is in the throes of a divorce. His parents' divorce, that is, but it's his, too, as is obvious from the first chapter on. Divorce affects half of all homes, so, regretfully, many young readers will identify with Asa's resilient, internalizing nature as he seeks to deal—and sometimes not deal—with an unstable mother and a chameleon-like stepfather who tries too hard to love him because he has to. The issues surrounding divorce are not often black and white, but Asa is truly a remarkable study in resilience despite it all. His coping skills and willingness to never give up keep us believing he'll make it through this. And he does. His mother eventually ditches the mean stepdad, and though Asa and his mom are left to fend for themselves, you get the feeling they'll do just fine. A realistic and inspiring story that should encourage any teen experiencing divorce or a parent remarrying.

WON'T KNOW TILL I GET THERE
By Walter Dean Myers. Publisher: Puffin Books
(Penguin Putnam), 1982. PB$4.99 US/$5.99 CAN.
MVP: Being open to new relationships. ALA Notable

When Stephen turns fourteen he decides to begin keeping a diary. He names it "Twimsy, for To Whom It May Concern." Steve may have had a premonition that he would have a lot to write about this coming year. His parents have decided to take in a foster boy named Earl, with whom Stephen will be sharing his room. After some snooping, Stephen finds out that Earl has a criminal record, even though he's only thirteen. This is definitely going to take some adjustment, and Stephen braces himself for the worst. Who would imagine that obedient little Stephen would be the one to instigate a crime to show off in front of Earl—and get caught by the police, causing himself, Earl and their two friends to serve a sentence doing community service in a nursing home all summer! What Stephen learns about himself, his parents, the feisty senior citizens and, surprisingly, from Earl, changes his outlook on life.

Explore These: Why did Stephen spray-paint the subway car? Remind yourself of some unwise things you've done or said recently just to show off to someone. What made you do it? Recall a time when you learned something from an unlikely person, like Earl or even from an elderly person you figured "didn't have it goin' on."

 WORDS BY HEART
By Ouida Sebestyen. Publisher: Bantam Doubleday Dell, 1996. PB$4.99. MVP: Forgiveness, Courage. Classic, Video

Lena, born near the turn of the century and the daughter of a hired laborer, is impetuous, bright, and headstrong. Lena's father teaches her to use her mind to its fullest and excel in all she does. However, after moving to a town out West, Lena struggles to reconcile the peace and patience modeled by her father with her own sense of justice when poor white neighbors threaten her family. When tragedy strikes, Lena is forced to choose between forgiveness and vengeance—forced to actually live out the words she had memorized in her Bible verses. Another prominent tension in the book is the underlying struggle her father and stepmother have in reconciling their decision to go West. Claudie, her stepmother, prefers to stay in their all-black community in the South, where they were accepted and lived without daily racial tensions and threats. But Lena's father chose to come West for the promise of opportunity, advancement, and equality in the white man's world, accepting the risks that were involved in that decision. The book is full of rich period detail, like Lena examining an indoor bathroom for the first time and having to "boil the rag squares that the baby dirtied every day." In the end, Lena must decide whether to keep a horrible secret that could change everything. Much of the detail and material was mined from the author's own family experiences and struggles in a small Texas community in the early 1900s.

Explore These: Why didn't Lena's father want to live in Scatter-creek? What did Winslow's father mean when he said that Lena's family was "like a wedge"? In what ways is being a wedge good or bad? Why?

THE WORLD OF DAUGHTER MCGUIRE
By Sharon Dennis Wyeth. Publisher: Bantam Doubleday Dell, 1994. PB$3.99. MVP: Appreciating a mixed heritage, Self-confidence

In this day and age, when many of our children come from mixed-race backgrounds and separated families, young people will relate to the very modern problems of Daughter McGuire. Daughter is African-Italian-Irish-Jewish-Russian-American, and has a strange name to boot. (Kids at school say, "Daughter? What kind of name is that?" "It's a beautiful name," Daughter tells them proudly.) Her parents separated, and Daughter must adjust to her father being gone and making friends in a new school. When her teacher assigns a project based on family heritage and traditions, she is nervous, especially when a school bully calls her "zebra." Writing the book from Daughter's perspective, Wyeth navigates carefully and believably through these difficult issues, allowing Daughter to experience a wide range of emotions as she grows in her understanding and acceptance of her family and herself. The story shows that some problems are not solved easily, but illustrates the great benefit of self-confidence and apprecia-tion for diversity.

Explore These: What was special about the name Daughter? Do you have a unique name that people find hard to accept? How do you handle that pressure, or how do you treat people with different-sounding names? Expain what a family tree is and help your child start her own.

THE YOUNG LANDLORDS
By Walter Dean Myers. Publisher: Puffin Books
(Penguin Putnam), 1989. PB$3.99. MVP: Being willing
and available

This is the amazing story of four teenagers in Harlem who end up becoming the landlords for a rundown building in their neighborhood. It is a wonderful story of how the group effort of ordinary teenagers with a desire to see their community improved, can affect change. Paul and his friends form the Action Group and are determined to "do" and not just talk about things, like they used to. The first step is to find out who owned the crumbling building across the street and insist that it be rehabilitated. The white owner, impressed with their interest and happy to have the unprofitable building off his back, sells it to Paul for one dollar. Suddenly the Action Group is in the real estate business. This will certainly be a different way to spend a summer vacation! The teens are smart: they hire a part-time accountant (a strange but amicable fellow), and decide to visit each tenant to introduce themselves and find out what they need. Before they can say "eviction notice," the teens have more complaints than they can handle: backed-up toilets, broken banisters and stuck doorknobs, not to mention dealing with the non–rent-payers and outrageous tenants like karate-chopping Askia Ben Kenobi, who wreaks havoc on the top floor. The Action Group does an admirable job as landlords and learns a lot about people and business in the process. A young romance buds between Paul, the main character, and his co-laborer Gloria, and the entire group gets caught up trying to solve a burglary case in which their friend is implicated. In the end, the whole building pulls together and relationships emerge that none of them ever thought possible.

6

Oops List

*Great books that are out of print may be
available through libraries and for special
order through amazon.com and other sources.*

CHILDREN FOUR TO EIGHT

CARIBBEAN ALPHABET
Written and illustrated by Frané Lessac. Publisher:
Tambourine Books (William Morrow), 1989. HC$15.00
US. MVP: Appreciating other black cultures

In this unique counting book, B is for breadfruit, a fruit found
only in the tropics, but B is also for things found everywhere, like
boats, birds and bananas. C is for cricket, a game played in the
Caribbean, but is also for coconut, cat and cow. A helpful glossary with color illustrations of the more obscure words such as

Junkanoo (a Caribbean festival) and hibiscus (a colorful flowering plant) is found at the back of the book to help you explain.

 DADDY IS A MONSTER . . . SOMETIMES
Written and illustrated by John Steptoe. Publisher:
HarperTrophy (HarperCollins), 1980. PB$6.95
US/$9.50 CAN. MVP: Children understanding parents.
Classic, Reading Rainbow

Bweela and Javaka love their daddy, but sometimes they think he looks and sounds like a scary monster, especially when he's telling them to behave in a restaurant, or to go to bed and stop fooling around. The late John Steptoe's unique illustrations humorously depict each stage as Dad changes into werewolf dad—complete with pointy ears, whiskers and a fierce growl— in the eyes of his own children. The important thing is that the children know that Daddy only seems like he's a monster . . . sometimes. Steptoe gets credit for daring to do a story most parents and children can easily identify with, without in any way condoning parental mistreatment of children.
Explore These: Ask children to describe the times when they feel that a parent is turning into a monster. Explain why you may appear monsterlike at times. Allow this to spur a discussion that can foster better relationships among the entire family.

 THE DANCING GRANNY
Retold and illustrated by Ashley Bryan. Publisher:
Atheneum, 1977. HC$5.95. Theme: Cleverness. Classic,
Audio

Young children will love seeing Granny Anika's uncontrollable dancing attacks—especially if you try to act them out a little. She just loves to "shake it to the east and shake it to the west." The believable "uh-huh"s she utters when she's really getting her groove on are hilarious, as are Bryan's simple drawings of her twisting and turning all over the page (looking a bit like the popular dancing baby on the Internet). But Granny was a hard worker who danced while she worked, singing to herself as she tended her garden. But Spider Ananse (who is really a man in this story, not a spider) was not into working at all. He decided to use his wit to outwit Granny and steal her crop. He knew just how to distract her, too. As Granny falls into her dancing spells, Ananse walks off with the goods again and again, until Granny gets wise and cajoles him into a dance fever of his own.

 THE DOVE
By Dianne Stewart. Illustrator: Jude Daly. Publisher: Greenwillow Books (William Morrow) 1993. HC$14.00. MVP: Creativity, Inspiration

This is a lovely story about a grandmother and granddaughter in South Africa after a huge flood that wipes out all of the crops, and even takes lives. By God's grace, Lindi's grandmother's house withstands the flood and, as in the biblical story of Noah's Ark, a dove appears on their front yard. They feed it and take its appearance as a sign of hope amidst disaster. But still, no one in town wants to buy the beaded souvenirs that grandmother Maloko makes for a living, and their food supply is running out. Then Lindi gets an idea. She asks her grandmother to help her make a beaded dove to sell. Grandma is sad that no one at the Community Art shop wants to buy her usual beadwork—but they have never seen anything like the beautiful beaded dove! They buy it immediately and place orders for more. Grandmother Maloko is so glad that now there will be money for food until harvest time. The dove was a sign of hope after all.

Explore These: Why do Lindi and grandmother Maloko make the beaded dove? Ask a child: Have you ever experienced a flood, hurricane, tornado or fire? What was it like? Were you scared? How would you feel if people didn't like something you took time and care to make? Look up the word *inspiration* in the dictionary; explain it to your child. Ask: Has anything in real life ever inspired you to create something (a drawing, story, song, etc.)?

MOTHER CROCODILE
By Birage Diop, translated and adapted by Rosa Guy.
Illustrator: John Steptoe. Publisher: Doubleday Books
for Young Readers (Bantam Doubleday Dell), 1981.
HC$15.00 US/$18.00 CAN. MVP: Listening to our
elders. Read Aloud, Coretta Scott King Award

Dia, also known as Mother Crocodile, is a wealth of wisdom who tells stories about "the way things were" that her children usually don't want to hear. She has lived a long time in these African rivers and has seen and heard everything—she's gossiped with the fish, overheard the washerwomen and even listened in on the conversations of donkeys and camels who came to the river for a drink. She escaped for her life with her own mother long ago when war broke out and bloody corpses filled the river. One day Dia got into a dispute with Golo, the monkey, and he began telling all the other animals that Dia was crazy and her stories were worthless. Even Dia's children began to believe Golo. As they play and ignore their mother's warnings, war soon breaks out. Dia implores her children to escape with her before it's too late. They refuse. Little did they know that men of war like to bring back tokens of their battles for their wives—tokens like crocodile-skin purses and shoes. The little crocs are petrified. Fortunately, the oldest one remembers the escape plan Dia told them about. They save their hides (literally) by using the same muddy trail at the bottom of the river that Dia and her mother used long ago. I'm sure they listened intently to Dia's stories after that!

Explore These: Why did the little crocodiles decide not to listen to their mother's stories? Ask your child: Is there anyone in your family who tells you stories of things that happened long ago? Do you enjoy them or find them boring? Recall one of those stories. (You could also tell your child a story from your childhood.) What is the lesson in it?

OSA'S PRIDE
Written and Illustrated by Ann Grifalconi. Publisher:
Little Brown, 1990. HC$14.95 US/$18.95 CAN. MVP:
The foolishness of pride.

All small children will enjoy this third story of playful Osa, who learns to give up her pride and realizes that she's "no better than anyone else." When her father does not return from the war, Osa makes up stories of his greatness to cover her loss. But as telling her stories become more important than listening to the stories of the other children, she loses her friends. Instead of learning a lesson there, Osa convinces herself that she doesn't need them, since she, too, is better than them anyway. Parents and children will admire the gentle and creative way that Osa's Gran'ma takes her aside and shows her the foolishness of pride. Gran'ma asks Osa to help her make a story cloth, a garment that has pictures woven into it which tell a story. In it Osa learns the story of Vain Girl, who carries her basket of eggs so high on her head that they all fall out as she walks. In this tale, as in the previous Osa stories, Grifalconi's illustrations are warm and appealing, particularly the vivid, simple story-cloth images woven into the text.

Explore These: Why did Osa brag about her father? With your child, make a "story cloth" out of felt. Help them make up a story and cut out the characters from the fabric. Explain how telling a story can sometimes teach a lesson better than a scolding.

OUR PEOPLE
By Angela Shelf Medearis. Illustrator: Michael Bryant.
Publisher: Atheneum, 1994. HC$15.00 US/$20.00
CAN. MVP: Self-confidence, Creativity

This book is doubly valuable because of the beautiful images of strong black men and the father-daughter bond that it centers around. Daddy tells his daughter about various aspects of our heritage, and she imagines what it would have been like if she were there at different points in history. It has a sweet undertone as the child tells how she would have helped build the pyramids with the same skill she uses to build her house of blocks. She would have discovered new worlds with the great explorers, with the same sleuthing (and flashlight) she uses to fearlessly search through clothes closets at home. Colorful, full-page illustrations show the girl and her dad having fun together as she imagines all that she can be and do.

Explore These: What are some of the great things our people did in the past? Talk about some important times in our history and ask a child: What would you have done if you lived at that time? What are some great things you want to do in the future?

RATA-PATA-SCATA-FATA
By Phillis Gershator. Illustrator: Holly Meade.
Publisher: Little, Brown, 1994. MVP: Imagination.

Rata-pata-scata-fata is a West Indian "nonsense phrase," but in this Caribbean tale that delights in a child's dreams and imagination, it becomes a magical scat that a little boy believes will make his chores take care of themselves. Children will enjoy the glimpses of Caribbean culture and the distinctive torn-paper-collage pictures.

SOMETIMES I DON'T LIKE SCHOOL
By Paula Z. Hogan. Illustrator: Pam Ford. Publisher:
Raintree, 1980. MVP: Problem resolution

A helpful book to draw upon when school anxiety troubles your child. Paula Hogan gently approaches the subject through George, an elementary school-age boy who is avoiding his math class because he just can't get it. With hard work and the help of his parents, George becomes one of the best math-game players in the class. Children will identify with George's avoidance tactics as well as the pride he feels in his triumph.

SOUND OF SUNSHINE, SOUND OF RAIN
By Florence Tarry Heide. Illustrator: Kenneth
Longtemps. Publisher: Parent's Magazine Press, 1970.
PB$3.95 US. MVP: Learning to listen, Living with a
handicap. Classic

What would we do if we couldn't see the sun so we know it is
daytime? Or look into our mother's face or even see to match our
clothes every day? This book is about a blind boy who experiences life through hearing, smell and touch. To him, the anxious, impatient voice of his older sister sounds sharp, "like
needles flying in the air." His mom's loving voice, on the other
hand, sounds "warm and soft as a pillow." Abram, the ice cream
man, befriends the boy one day in the park. Abram explains that
color doesn't matter much, they just serve as "outside covers" for
what's really inside. When a prejudiced lady is rude to the boy
and his sister in the grocery store, he recoils. To him, her voice
sounded like she was "squeezing it out of her like the last bit of
toothpaste in a tube." This book does an excellent job of allowing
a sighted child to experience the world of the blind.
   Explore These: How did the boy get around without his sight?
Why do you think his sister was so impatient with him? Help children to imagine what it's like to be blind by wearing blindfolds
for twenty minutes. Have them use their hands to feel their way
around (make sure it's a safe environment) and count steps to
get from one place to another. Ask them to describe how things
feel, smell and sound.

 THREE WISHES
By Lucille Clifton. Illustrator: Michael Hays. Publisher:
Delacorte Press (Bantam Doubleday Dell), 1992.
HC$15.00 US/$19.00 CAN. MVP: Friendship

What would you wish for if you were granted three wishes?
Many children may imagine this scenario filled with new Nikes
for each day of the week and roomfuls of computer games, but
this book movingly teaches the value of friendship over money or

possessions. Zenobia (Nobie) finds a penny on New Year's Day with her birthday year on it, which means any three wishes she makes will come true. As she stands outside in the winter snow with her best friend, Victor, she wishes she wouldn't feel so cold. Almost instantly, the sun comes out. As they go into her house and ponder what her second wish should be, the two get into a fight. "Man, I wish you would get out of here!" she shouts at him. He does—another wish gone *poof.* As she ponders the weight of that third wish, Zenobia realizes how much she values her friendship with Victor. After a talk with her mother, Zenobia makes her final wish count.

Explore These: How did Zenobia use her three wishes? What would your three wishes be? Use this as an opportunity to explain virtues over wealth—the value of having things that money can't buy.

WHAT MARY JO WANTED
By Janice Mary Udry. Illustrator: Eleanor Mill.
Publisher: Albert Whitman, 1968. MVP: Responsibility

What Mary Jo Wanted, one story in the well-known series by this Caldecott Award–winning author, illustrates how a little girl learns the meaning of responsibility after her father gives her the pet she's always dreamed of—a puppy. When everyone in her family is tired of its cries, Mary Jo uses her head to find a solution that is not only responsible and fun, but allows her to be helpful to her family, too.

PRETEENS AND YOUNG ADULTS

BLACK DANCE IN AMERICA
By James Haskins. Publisher: Thomas Y. Crowell, 1990.
HC$14.95 US/$19.95 CAN. Theme: History of blacks
in dance

Teens will find this companion to *Black Theater in America* and *Black Music in America* helpful for school projects and personal study, especially if they are interested in any form of black dance. The book covers everything from jazz dancing to break dancing and tells the stories of extraordinary performers such as Katherine Dunham, Alvin Ailey, Gregory Hines and Michael Jackson.

LANGSTON: A PLAY BY OSSIE DAVIS
Publisher: Delacorte Press (Bantam Doubleday Dell),
1982. HC$9.95. MVP: Pursuing your passion

Ossie Davis has written a play-within-a-play bringing the story of Langston Hughes to life for a young audience. Langston himself pays a visit to a group of children while they are rehearsing one of his plays in their church basement. The play requires 10 people to perform. Langston's life exemplified the vision, hard work, perseverance and pure passion that are required for success.

A LONG HARD JOURNEY, THE STORY OF THE
PULLMAN PORTER
By Patricia and Frederick McKissack. Publisher: Walker,
1989. HC$17.95. Theme: Great men in our history

Most of us think of porters today as men who mop floors and clean toilets, but the legendary Pullman porters pretty much ran the show on the boxcars filled with rich white businessmen, vacationers, newlyweds, actresses and actors, as well as drunks and ho-bos. These skilled men made beds so fast and crisp you could bounce a dime on them—all with an obligatory grin and a bow that led them to become known as "Ambassadors of Hospitality." But, as the McKissacks note in their informative introduction, "seventy years later the gratitude had worn thin." The men worked long, hard hours for meager pay, something the new clan of free-born black Americans wouldn't accept. After their pleas and complaints went unanswered, the men organized the famous Brotherhood of Sleeping Car Porters union in 1925, to obtain better working conditions. This book highlights the key players, led by Asa Philip Randolph, who helped win the near-impossible battle with the powerful Pullman Company, a historic feat whose effect was felt by black workers everywhere. Great black-and-white photographs illustrate the text.

Explore These: Why did the men form the Brotherhood of Sleeping Car Porters? What did it achieve? What is the value of organizing many people together to voice a concern or make a demand, instead of just one person? What could be some challenges in organizing a large group? Is there a campaign or cause you need to rally support for? Devise a plan for how you'll organize.

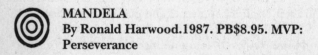

MANDELA
By Ronald Harwood.1987. PB$8.95. MVP:
Perseverance

History can be a hard subject to get teenagers to read, far less enjoy reading. South African writer Ron Harwood skillfully com-bines history and Hollywood in this cleverly formatted book. The compelling story of Nelson Mandela's life in the South African sociopolitical struggle is the main thrust, but the story of how the film *Mandela* was made is also woven into each chapter. There are pictures of Danny Glover (who played Mr. Mandela in the movie) on the set preparing for his various scenes. Pieces of the actual movie script, including staging directions, are included in each chapter.

NINE PLAYS BY BLACK WOMEN
Edited and with an introduction by Margaret B.
Wilkerson. Publisher: Mentor (Penguin Putnam), 1986.
PB$4.95 US/$5.95 CAN. Theme: Plays by black women

This is a just-right-sized collection of nine plays by such noted playwrights as Lorraine Hansberry and Ntozake Shange, who wrote the award-winning works *A Raisin in the Sun* and *For Colored Girls* . . . , respectively. Brief introductions to the stories and their characters' profiles precede each full-length play. The subjects tackled include black/white romance, teenage mothers' dreams, black middle-class pain and discovering black beauty. Most of the plays center on young female characters.

WHEN I DANCE
Poems by James Berry. Publisher: Harcourt Brace
Jovanovich, 1991. HC$15.95. MVP: Black poetry

Inner-city life in England and the Caribbean countryside are the settings for this book of poems, which author James Berry hopes will help bring an even broader sense of unity to the black experience. There are riddle poems and even poems that can be acted out with several parts. Many are humorous, some are somber, but each will inspire a teen to "whip up yourself beyond yourself."

7

Great Reading Resources

Magazines, TV Shows, Websites, Videos, Books and Other Sources That Promote Reading

GREAT MAGAZINES

Magazines that promote reading and feature or regularly include African-American children.

AMERICAN GIRL
Published by The Pleasant Company. Ages: 8–12. Six issues per year. $19.95 per year. 1-800-234-1278.

Refreshingly wholesome, ad-free magazine for girls offers activities, advice, puzzles, sports tips, and stories, plus letters, poems, opinions and ideas from a multi-ethnic mix of girls across the country. A welcome alternative to the gossip about stars and articles on boys and makeup in other girls' magazines.

BOY'S LIFE
The magazine for boys of all ages. Published by Boy Scouts of America. Monthly. $18 per year (add $9 for Canada). Send to: 1325 West Walnut Hill Lane, P.O. Box 152079, Irving, Texas 75015-2079.

Features well-presented information on the things boys like—sports, space, cars, and collecting—and offers how-to's, facts, games, Bible stories, and space adventure comics.

OWL
The discovery magazine for kids. Published by Owl Communications. Age: 8 and up, 9 issues per year. $16.95 per year (add $10 for Canada). 1-800-551-OWLS.

Helps get kids interested in nature, science and the world around them. Features puzzles, mazes, facts about bugs, cars, food and the desert. The Mighty Mites comic strip that runs in the magazine features a black character. *Chickadee* is a sister publication for children aged six to nine; and *Chirp* is designed for children aged two to six.

CONTACT KIDS
Science With Attitude. Published by Children's Television Workshop. Age: 8–14. 10 issues per year. $16.90 per year. P.O. Box 7690, Red Oak, Iowa 51591-0688

Colorful presentation of facts, news, games, puzzles and features about science, nature, math, and technology, including video game and CD-ROM reviews.

 CRICKET
Opens the door to reading. Published by Cricket Magazine Group. Age: 9–14. Monthly. $32.97 per year. 1-800-827-0227.

Offers short stories and activity pages, plus a section for parents. Sister publications include *Spider*, for children ages six to nine; *Ladybug*, for children ages two to six; and *Babybug*, for ages six months to two years.

 HIGHLIGHTS FOR CHILDREN
Published by Highlights for Children. Age: Preschool to preteen. Monthly. About $25 per year. 2300 West Fifth Avenue, P.O. Box 182346, Columbus, OH 43272-2706.

Offers stories, features, puzzles, riddles, articles, poems, projects and reading exercises. Used by many schools as supplementary aid.

 KIDCITY
Published by Children's Television Workshop. Age: 6–9. 10 issues per year. $19.70 per year. P.O. Box 7689, Red Oak, Iowa 51591-0688.

Offers helpful information on the things children enjoy. Lots of creative contests, puzzles and kid polls.

SESAME STREET MAGAZINE
Published by Children's Television Workshop. Age: 3–6.
10 issues per year. $19.90 per year. P.O. Box 7688, Red
Oak, Iowa 51591-0688

Stories and activities that feature the Sesame Street characters
teaching children how to read, count, and draw.

STONE SOUP
Published by Children's Art Foundation. The magazine
for young writers and artists. Age: 8+. 6 issues per year.
$32 per year (for Canada add $6). 1-800-447-4569.

Selects and showcases the writing and artistic talent of youngsters.

GREAT TV SHOWS

*Children's programs that promote reading and regularly
feature or include African-American children*

READING RAINBOW (PBS)

For ages preschool to third grade
Makes reading exciting by exploring the featured book's theme.
Children do their own on-camera book reviews.

LEARN TO READ (PBS)

For ages preschool to adult
Teaches kids and adults the alphabet, vowels, how to sound out
words and read sentences and more, in separate lessons.

MAGIC SCHOOL BUS (PBS)

For ages preschool to third grade
Helps children better understand nature and science by shrinking in size and "becoming" whatever they're studying. Encourages further reading about science.

 WISHBONE (PBS)

For ages preschool to third grade
Puppet acts out stories from classic literature and relates them to real-life situations in a child's life.

 STORYTIME (check local listings)

For ages toddler to preschool
A featured book is read and a puppet asks typical questions a child would ask about the story. A celebrity or guest reads another special book.

 CHARLIE HORSE MUSIC PIZZA (PBS)

For ages preschool to first grade
Great songs, riddles and games that can help kids learn new words.

 WHERE IN TIME IS CARMEN SANDIEGO? (PBS)

For ages first grade to third grade
In a game show format, kids guess answers to history questions.

GREAT VIDEOS

This is a list of thirty-minute videos of actual **Reading Rainbow** *programs hosted by LeVar Burton. Videos listed here include features on African-American children, teens, books, artists and celebrities. To order videos or a catalog, call 1-800-228-4630. All videos cost $45.95. These videos may also be available to borrow through your local library system.*

Follow the Drinking Gourd Runaway slaves journey north along the Underground Railroad by following directions in a song, "The Drinking Gourd." Children are introduced to the history, heroes, stories and music of African-American culture that emerged from slavery. Sweet Honey in the Rock, an a cappella group, performs and shares their historical knowledge. Books on the black experience featured and reviewed in this video include *Follow the Drinking Gourd* by Jeanette Winter; *Shake It to the One That You Love the Best: Play Songs and Lullabies from Black Musical Traditions,* collected and adapted by Cheryl Warren Mattox; *A Picture Book of Harriet Tubman* by David A. Adler; and *Sweet Clara and the Freedom Quilt* by Deborah Hopkinson.

Hip Cat Jazz, America's most original music form, is the topic of this show. Children experience examples of improvisation in music, literature, art and dance, and meet Joshua Redman, a black jazz saxophonist who talks about how music has influenced his life. Books on the black experience featured and reviewed in this video include *Hip Cat* by Jonathan London, read by actress Ann Duquesnay; *Charlie Parker Played Be Bop* by Chris Raschka; and *Willie Jerome* by Alice Faye Duncan.

Mufaro's Beautiful Daughters An African tale of Mufaro's two beautiful daughters, one bad-tempered, one kind and sweet, who go before the king, who is trying to choose a wife. Children celebrate the culture of Africa in New York City's Central Park, learn how African drums are made and played, and watch an African dance troupe, Forces of Nature, perform. Books on the black experience featured and reviewed in this video include *Mufaro's*

Beautiful Daughters by John Steptoe, read by actress Phylicia Rashad; *Jambo Means Hello: Sawahili Alphabet Book* by Muriel Feelings; and the *Jafta* series by Hugh Lewin.

My Little Island A young boy takes his best friend to visit Montserrat in the Caribbean, where he was born. Children experience a plane ride to Montserrat and tour this beautiful island, experiencing its many colorful sights, including shopping in the open market, hearing a steel band, and going on a "mountain chicken" hunt. Books on the black experience featured and reviewed in this video include *My Little Island* by Frané Lessac.

Uncle Jed's Barbershop Sara Jean's Uncle Jed, the only black barber in the county, overcomes racism and other setbacks, including the Great Depression of the 1930s, as he works to save enough money to open his own barbershop. LeVar finds out about making dreams come true with determination and faith as he talks with The Persuasions, an a capella quartet of older black men that has been together for more than thirty years. These friends pursued their dreams in spite of being told that a singing group without musical instruments didn't have a chance for success. Books on the black experience featured and reviewed in this video include *Uncle Jed's Barbershop* by Margaree King Mitchell, *Alvin Ailey* by Andrea Davis Pinkney, and *Zora Hurston and the Chinaberry Tree* by William Miller.

The Wonderful Towers of Watts This book describes how three unusual towers were built in the Watts neighborhood of Los Angeles, California. Children explore the beauty and courage of a black and Latino community challenged daily by violence and learn that an appreciation for the people and structures builds pride in the community. An ex-girl-gang member talks about her life and the positive things she's doing now. Other youngsters from the neighborhood talk candidly about the problems they face and the choices they have to make. Books on the black experience featured and reviewed in this video include *The Car Washing Street* by Denise Lewis Patrick and *Night on Neighborhood Street* by Eloise Greenfield.

Abiyoyo This is a story-song based on a South African lullaby and folk story in which a boy and his father devise a plan to save the townspeople from a giant, Abiyoyo. Children explore some of the ways a story can be told with music, including a look at old music videos from Run DMC and DeBarge. Books on the black experience featured and reviewed in this video include *Abiyoyo*, a story-song by Pete Seeger. The book *Peter and the Wolf*, adapted from the musical tale by Sergei Prokofiev, is reviewed by a black child.

Always My Dad In this book, a black girl treasures the time she spends with her father after her parents divorce. LeVar shares his story of growing up in a single-parent family and children meet the Davis family, which consists of a black father who is successfully raising his four children alone. Books on the black experience featured and reviewed in this video include *Always My Dad* by Sharon Dennis Wyeth and *Boundless Grace* by Mary Hoffman.

Amazing Grace Grace, a young black girl, wants to be Peter Pan in the school play. She runs into obstacles, but refuses to give in. Actress Whoopi Goldberg and an African-American mother both share how they succeeded in nontraditional careers. Books on the black experience featured and reviewed in this video include *Amazing Grace* by Mary Hoffman and *Great Women in the Struggle* by Toyomi Igus, Veronica Freeman Ellis, Diane Patrick, and Valerie Wilson Wesley.

LeVar Burton Presents—A Reading Rainbow Family Special: Act Against Violence In this one-hour special shot in South Central Los Angeles, *Reading Rainbow* host LeVar Burton encourages families to empower children with choices, and challenges them to find more peaceful resolutions to conflict. Children who have been confronted with violence as well as an ex–gang member speak candidly about their hopes, aspirations and fears. The special also profiles teenagers and adults who have experienced violence firsthand and have dedicated themselves to turning young kids in a positive direction. Two organizations that focus on youth development are profiled: Colors United, a support and performance group that promotes self-esteem and reaching out to others, and Teens on Target, an organization of reformed and handicapped gang members. $24.95.

Check out more African-American videos for children, teens and adults at **www.amvideos.com** Samples: *Afro-Classic Fairy Tales*; *Cinderella*, featuring Whitney Houston, Whoopi Goldberg and Moesha; *Dreadlocks and the Three Bears*; plus Bible stories narrated by black celebrities and videos of well-known children's books on the black experience such as *Amazing Grace*; *Roll of Thunder, Hear My Cry*; *John Henry*; *The People Could Fly*; and the Ezra Jack Keats series. Price range: $10.99 and up.

GREAT WEBSITES

Research shows that children who are exposed to computers do better in school and have better attitudes. Approximately sixteen percent of black households have computers in them, according to the National Center for Education Statistics, so let's use them effectively. The Internet can be used to teach our children reading skills and even help our high schoolers find out about college. A few to check out include:

http://www.amazon.com/
Amazon.com online bookstore

http://www.nypl.org/bbranch/kids/onlion.html
This site is sponsored by the New York Public Library, a pioneer in promoting multicultural and African American children's books. For teens there's **http://www.nypl.org/branch/teenteenlilnk.html.**

www.ala.org/yalsa/
This American Library Association website offers lists of great books for all reading levels and subjects. Also available here is "Teen Hoopla," an Internet guide for teenagers.

http://gpn.unl.edu/index.htm
Reading Rainbow's website offers interactive activities related to the television show's topics, as well as audible book reviews given by children on the show.

http://www.cochran.com/theodore/
An interactive storybook about Theodore Tugboat; links to Berit's Best Sites for Children, which offers links to more than 600 sites.

http://www.kidnews.com
Kids from all over the world write stories, poems and letters; help finding a pen pal.

www.reuben.org/craft
Features the hilarious black comic strip, "Mamas Boyz" by Jerry Craft. To order "Mama's Boyz," send $9.95 plus $2.00 to Jerry Craft, 304 Main Avenue, Box 114, Norwalk, CT 06851

www.comiczone.com
Features the syndicated black comic strip "Jumpstart" by Robb Armstrong and comic-related activities and information.

http://www.newghostwriter.com
Features the three characters from the *GhostWriters* television program for children (one of whom is black). Word search puzzles to print out and solve, writing contests, and other activities.

www.surfnetkids.com
A directory of the best websites for children.

http://www.acs.ucalgary.ca/~dkbrown/
The Children's Literature Web Guide

http://www.ascd.org/market/resources/other/ea97.html
Childrens Bookshelf, Reading Is Fundamental (RIF)

GREAT READING RESOURCES

Books and other sources that will help you learn more about children and reading

Coretta Scott King Awards Book, Editor, Henrietta M. Smith

Shadow and Substance: Afro-American Experience in Contemporary Children's Fiction, Rudine Sims Bishop

Information Age by Dorothy Rich

Black Children: Roots, Culture & Learning Styles, Janice E. Hale-Benson

The Real Ebonics Debate: Power, Language & the Education of African-American Children, Theresa Perry and Lisa Delpit

A Parent's Guide to Children's Readers by Nancy Larrick

Reading Begins at Home by Dorothy Botted

For Reading Out Loud!: A Guide to Sharing Books With Children, Margaret Kimmel and Elizabeth Segel

The Misunderstood Child: A Guide for Parents of Children with Learning Disabilities, Larry B. Silver

Different and Wonderful: Raising Black Children in a Race-Conscious Society, Darlene Powell-Hopson and Derek Hopson

You and Your ADD Child: Practical Strategies for Coping with Everyday Problems, Ian Wallace

The Reluctant Reader: How to Get and Keep Kids Reading, Wendy M. Williams, Ph.D.

Books Kids Will Sit Still For: A Read-Aloud Guide by Judy Freeman

The Read Aloud Handbook by Jim Trelease

Comics to Classics: A Parent's Guide to Books for Teens and Preteens, Aretha J. S. Reed

Home: Where Reading and Writing Begin, Mary W. Hill

Pass the Poetry, Please! Lee B. Hopkins

Taking Books to Heart: How to Develop a Love of Reading in Your Child, Paul Copperman

Family Life and School Achievement: Why Poor Black Children Succeed or Fail, Reginald M. Clark

Creative Storytelling, Jack David Zipes

The Art of Story-telling, Marsh Cassidy

MORE READING RESOURCES

Recorded Books, Inc. 1-800-638-1304. 270 Skipjack Road, Prince Frederick, MD 20678. Offers a catalog of unabridged books on audio tape.

Childrens Book-of-the-Month Club. 1-800-233-1066 or (212) 522-4200

Afro-Bets Kids Club, P.O. Box 5300, East Orange, N.J. 07017

CORETTA SCOTT KING AWARD WINNERS

1998   Text: Sharon M. Draper, *Forged by Fire* (Atheneum)

       Illustration: Javaka Steptoe, *In Daddy's Arms I Am Tall: African Americans Celebrating Fathers*

1997   Text: Walter Dean Myers, *Slam!* (Scholastic Press)

       Illustration: Jerry Pinkney, *Minty: A Story of Young Harriet Tubman,* written by Alan Schroeder

1996   Text: Virginia Hamilton, *Her Stories,* illustrated by Leo and Diane Dillon

       Illustration: Tom Feelings, *The Middle Passage: White Ships Black Cargo* (Introduction by John Henrik Clarke)

1995   Text: Patricia and Frederick McKissack, *Christmas in the Big House, Christmas in the Quarters*

      Illustration: James Ransome, *The Creation* (Text: James Weldon Johnson)

1994   Text: Angela Johnson, *Toning the Sweep*

      Illustration: Tom Feelings, *Soul Looks Back in Wonder*

1993   Text: Patrica McKissack, *The Dark-Thirty: Southern Tales of the Supernatural*

      Illustration: Kathleen Atkins Wilson, *The Origin of Life on Earth: An African Creation Myth* (Text: David A. Anderson)

1992   Text: Walter Dean Myers, *Now Is Your Time! The African-American Struggle for Freedom*

      Illustration: Faith Ringgold, *Tar Beach*

1991   Text: Mildred D. Taylor, *The Road to Memphis*

      Illustration: Leo and Diane Dillon, *Aida* (Text: Leontyne Price)

1990   Text: Patricia and Frederick McKissack, *A Long Hard Journey: The Story of the Pullman Porter*

      Illustration: Jan Spivey Gilchrist, *Nathaniel Talking* (Text: Eloise Greenfield)

1989   Text: Walter Dean Myers, *Fallen Angels*

      Illustration: Jerry Pinkney, *Mirandy and Brother Wind* (Text: Patricia McKissack)

1988   Text: Mildred D. Taylor, *The Friendship* .

      Illustration: John Steptoe, *Mufaro's Beautiful Daughters: An African Tale*

1987   Text: Mildred Pitts Walter, *Justin and the Best Biscuits in the World*

      Illustration: Jerry Pinkey, *Half a Moon and One Whole Star* (Text: Crecent Dragonwagon)

1986   Text: Virginia Hamilton, *The People Could Fly: American Black Folktales*

Illustration: Jerry Pinkney, *The Patchwork Quilt* (Text: Valerie Flournoy)

1985   Text: Walter Dean Myers, *Motown and Didi*

Illustration: No award given.

1984   Text: Lucille Clifton, *Everett Anderson's Goodbye*

Illustration: Pat Cummings, *My Mama Needs Me* (Text: Mildred Pitts Walter)

1983   Text: Virginia Hamilton, *Sweet Whispers, Brother Rush*

Illustration: Peter Magubane, *Black Child*

1982   Text: Mildred D. Taylor, *Let the Circle Be Unbroken*

Illustration: John Steptoe, *Mother Crocodile: An Uncle Amadou Tale from Senegal* (Text adapted by Rosa Guy)

1981   Text: Sidney Poitier, *This Life*

Illustration: Ashley Bryan, *Beat the Story-Drum, Pum-Pum*

1980   Text: Walter Dean Myers, *The Young Landlords*

Illustration: Carole Byard, *Cornrows* (Text: Camille Yarbrough)

1979   Text: Ossie Davis, *Escape to Freedom: A Play about Young Frederick Douglass*

Illustration: Tom Feelings, *Something on My Mind* (Text: Nikki Grimes)

1978   Eloise Greenfield, text, and Carole Byard, illustration, *Africa Dream*

1977   James Haskins, *The Story of Stevie Wonder*

1976   Pearl Bailey, *Duey's Tale*

1975   Dorothy Robinson, text, and Herbert Temple, illustration, *The Legend of Africana*

1974 Sharon Bell Mathis, text, and George Ford, illustration, *Ray Charles*

1973 Jackie Robinson, as told to Alfred Duckett, *I Never Had It Made: The Autobiography of Jackie Robinson*

1972 Elton C. Fax, *Seventeen Black Artists*

1971 Charlemae H. Rollins, *Black Troubador: Langston Hughes*

1970 Lillie Patterson, *Martin Luther King, Jr.: Man of Peace*

8

Bookstores in Your Area

These are bookstores, listed by state, that carry African-American books and are members of the American Booksellers Association (ABA). List courtesy of the ABA. Current as of April 1998.

ALABAMA
The Banana Boat
2701 Jefferson Ave. SW
Birmingham, AL 35211-4016

Roots & Wings, A Cultural
Bookplace
1345 Carter Hill Rd.
Montgomery, AL 36106-1421

ARIZONA
Aradia Bookstore
PO Box 266
116 West Cottage
Flagstaff, AZ 86002-0266

Paradise Bookstore
9008 N. 99th Ave. Ste 6
Peoria, AZ 85345

Singing Wind Bookshop
PO Box 2197
Benson, AZ 85602-2197

ARKANSAS
Pickwick Book Store
2610 W 28th Ave.
Pine Bluff, AR 71603-4998

Pyramid Art Books & Custom
Framing
500 East Markham, Ste 110
Little Rock, AR 72201

CALIFORNIA
Adams Books
1353 W. Gage Ave.
Fullerton, CA 92833

African Heritage Books & Gifts
5021 3rd St.
San Francisco, CA 94124
heritagbks@aol.com

Alexander Book Co.
50 2nd St.
San Francisco, CA 94105-3440
http://www.citysearch.com/
sfo/alexanderbook

Capitola Book Cafe
1475 41st Ave.
Capitola, CA 95010-2908
http://www.cruzio.com/~book
cafe/
bookcafe@cruzio.com

Carol's Books & Things
5964 S. Land Park Dr.
Sacramento, CA 95822-3523

Eso Won Books
2235 Lake Ave. #10708
Altadena, CA 91001-2465
http://www.esowon.com
esowon@aol.com

Eso Won Books
3655 S. La Brea Ave
Los Angeles, CA 90016
http://www.esowon.com
esowon@aol.com

Folsom Book Company
418 E. Bidwell St.
Folsom, CA 95630-3117

Groundwork Books
0323 Student Ctr.
La Jolla, CA 92037

Jay 'Day, Inc
PO Box 1000
Altadena, CA 91103

Lewis For Books
7119 Reseda Blvd.
Reseda, CA 91335-4211

The Rainbow Sign
330 East Main St.
Stockton, CA 95202

The Station, Books, Etc.
1434 Santa Monica Blvd.
1 Manager
Santa Monica, CA 90404

Vroman's Book & Stationery
695 E. Colorado Blvd.
PO Box 90217
Pasadena, CA 91101
Vromanbks@aol.com

COLORADO
Cherry Valley Books
726 Cherryvale Rd.
Boulder, CO 80303
http://www.cherryvalleybooks.
com/
custserv@cherryvalleybooks.
com

Hue-Man Experience
Bookstore
911 Park Ave. W.
Denver, CO 80205-2601
http://www.hue-man.com/

Underground Railroad
Bookstore
4878 Chambers Rd.
Denver, CO 80239-5152

CONNECTICUT
American Worlds Books
P.O. Box 6305
Whitneyville Station
Hamden, CT 06518-0305
amworlds@interloc.com

The Baobab Tree
119 Terrace Ave.
West Haven, CT 06516

Black Books Galore Inc
65 High Ridge Rd. # 407
Stamford, CT 06905-3806

Bucket of Books
27 Shore Front Park
Norwalk, CT 06854

UConn Coop
University of Connecticut
PO Box U19
81 Fairfield Rd.
Storrs, CT 06269-2019

FLORIDA
Afro-In Books & Things
5575 NW 7th Ave.
Miami, FL 33127-1401

Montsho Books Etc.
2009 W. Central Blvd.
Orlando, FL 32805-2128

Rubyfruit Books, Inc.
739 N. Monroe St.
Tallahassee, FL 32303

Univ. of South Florida
Bookstore
4202 E. Fowler Ave. BR 097
Tampa, FL 33620

GEORGIA
Brothers '3' Bookstore
1151 Shannon Southpark
Union City, GA 30291

Engineer's Bookstore
748 Marietta St. NW
Atlanta, GA 30318
http://www.engrbookstore.
com/
engrbook@mindspring.com

Georgia Tech Bookstore
225 North Ave. NW
350 Ferst Dr. NW
Atlanta, GA 30332-0001

Heritage Bookstore
2375 Wesley Chapel Rd.
Suite #10
Decatur, GA 30035-2819
MicheleTF@aol.com

Ka'Lors Bookstore
4112 Maple Ln.
Powder Springs, GA 30073-
1988
KaLors@mindspring.com

Two Friends Bookstore
598 Cascade Rd.
Atlanta, GA 30310

Wizard of Odds
211 Alabama St.
Carrollton, GA 30117
seshat@bellsouth.net

HAWAII
Hawaii Children's Book World
Multicultural Resource Center
1132 Bishop St. Ste 1404
Honolulu, HI 96813-2830

ILLINOIS
Afrocentric Book Store
333 S. State Street
Chicago, IL 60604-2287

Barbara's Bookstore
9500 South Western Ave.
Evergreen Plaza–#G12C
Evergreen Park, IL 60805

Black Authors
533 Tiffany
Waukagan, IL 60085
http://www.blackauthors.com

Dusable Trading Post
Dusable Museum
740 E. 56th Place
Chicago, IL 60637-1408

The Epicenter Bookshop—
UIC
750 S. Halsted St.
M-C048
Chicago, IL 60607-7008

Free Your Mind Bookstore
35 South LaSalle St.
Aurora, IL 60505

I Dream In Color, Inc.
5309 South Hyde Pk. Blvd.
Chicago, IL 60615

Madras Company Inc. dba
Reading Is Fun
1720 N. Orchard St.
Suite D
Chicago, IL 60614-5167

U.S. Catholic Bookstore
160 N. Wabash 1st Floor
Chicago, IL 60601
uscbooks@claret.org

INDIANA
Von's Book Shop
315 W. State St.
West Lafayette, IN 47906-3591

KANSAS
Bashawn's Afrocentric
Expression
6100 E. 21st St N. Ste 150
Wichita, KS 67208

Downtown News & Books
204 S. Santa Fe Ave.
Salina, KS 67401-3999

LOUISIANA
The Afro-American Book Stop
5700 Read Blvd. Ste 275
New Orleans, La 70127

The Afro American Book Stop
8924 Jewella Rd. # 07
Shreveport, LA 71118

MAINE
Bookland of Maine
78 Atlantic Pl.
South Portland, ME 04106-
2316

MARYLAND
Essence of Thoughts
785 Washington Blvd.
Baltimore, MD 21230

Heritage Unlimited
19417 Live Tree Way
Gaithersburg, MD 20879-5706
http://www.erols.com/
hubooks/
cenchasl@erols.com

Karibu Company
3500 East/West Hwy.
Hyattsville, MD 20782-1916

Learning Ideas, Inc.
5570 Silver Hill Rd.
District Heights, MD 20747-
1100

Pratt Place, The Library Shop
400 Cathedral St.
Baltimore, MD 21201-4484

MASSACHUSETTS
Cultural Collections
754 Crescent St.
Brockton, MA 02402-3343
http://members.aol.com/
culcol/home.htm
culcol@aol.com

Food for Thought Books
106 N. Pleasant St.
Amherst, MA 01002-1703

Harvard Book Stores, Inc.
1256 Massachusetts Ave.
Cambridge, MA 02138-3820
http://www.harvard.com/
hbs-info@harvard.com

New Words, Inc.
186 Hampshire St.
Cambridge, MA 02139-1320
newwords@world.std.com

St. John Books
13 Honey Pot Rd.
Southwrick, MA 01077

Signals WGBH Educational
Foundation
125 Western Ave.
Boston, MA 02134-1098

SISTAHS'
Washington Park Mall
330 Martin Luther King Blvd.
Roxbury, MA 02119

Treasured Legacy
Copley Place 100 Huntington
Ave.
Boston, MA 02116

MICHIGAN
Apple Book Center
7900 West Outer Dr.
Detroit, MI 48235
apple001@aol.com

Books & More
21729 Constitution St.
Southfield, MI 48706-5520

First Edition Bookstore
7 Center St.
Muskegon Height, MI 49444-2151

LaCeter Book Service
16345 Melrose St.
Southfield, MI 48075

The Live Press
5727 Dunmore Dr.
West Bloomfield, MI 48322-1613

Marwil Bookstore
4870 Cass Ave.
Detroit, MI 48201-1204
marwilbk@mail.ir.net

WMU Bookstore—Bernhard
Center
Western Michigan University
Kalamazoo, MI 49008
http://www.wmich.edu/
bookstore/

MINNESOTA
Culturally Ours Books
A Division of Culturally Ours
7421 W River Rd.
Brooklyn Pk, MN 55444

MISSOURI
Eternal News Book & Music
Stop
2905 Washington
St Louis, MO 63103

First World
429 N.W. Plaza
St. Ann, MO 63074

Left Bank Books
399 N. Euclid Ave.
St. Louis, MO 63018-1245

Missouri Historical Society
Museum Shop
PO Box 11940
5700 Lindell and Debaliniere
St. Louis, MO 63112-0040

The Swiss Village Book Store
Shop # 107
707 N 1st St.
St. Louis, MO 63102-2526

NEW JERSEY
Black Pearl Books Plus
P.O. Box 5688
Englewood, NJ 07102-1702

Montclair Book Center
221 Glenridge Ave.
Montclair, NJ 07042-3542

New Jersey Books
59 Market St.
Newark, NJ 07102-1702

Theological Book Agency
P.O. Box 821
Princeton Theological
Seminary
Princeton, NJ 08542-0803

Watchung Booksellers
33 Watchung Plz.
Montclair, NJ 07042-4117

NEW MEXICO
Page One
11018 Montgomery Blvd. NE
Albuquerque, NM 87111-3962
http://page1book.com/
sheimann@page1book.com

NEW YORK
All Africa Books
81 Crisfield St.
Yonkers, NY 10710

Beyond Words
186 Fifth Ave.
Brooklyn, NY 11217

Black Books Plus, Inc.
702 Amsterdam Ave.
New York, NY 10025-6903

Briscoe Brown Books
3907 Dyre Ave.
Bronx, NY 10466
LShing@aol.com

The Bronx County Historical
Society
3309 Bainbridge Ave.
Bronx, NY 10467-2801

264   *Great Books for African-American Children*

Brooklyn Museum Shop
200 Eastern Pky.
Brooklyn, NY 11238-6052

Empire Plaza Books
PO Box 2094—Justice
Building Conc.
Empire State Plaza
Albany, NY 12220-0094

Genesis Books
154 S. 4th Ave.
Mount Vernon, NY 10550

Hacker Art Books Inc.
45 W 57th St.
New York, NY 10019-3408

Literary Tea Ltd.
23 E. 3rd St, Suite 102
Jamestown, NY 14701

Mental Health Resources
346 W. Saugerties Rd.
Saugerties, NY 12477-3152

Mood Makers Books & Art
Gallery
274 N. Goodman St.
Village Gate Square
Rochester, NY 14607

The Museum Shop @
American Museum of the
Moving Image
36-01 35th Ave.
Astoria, NY 11106-1226

Talking Leaves Inc.
3158 Main St.
Buffalo, NY 14214-1395
http://www.tleavesbooks.com/
talklvbk@fcs-net.com

Unity Book Center
237 W 23rd St.
New York, NY 10011-2302

Urban Center Books
247 Madison Ave.
New York, NY 10022-6830

NORTH CAROLINA
Newsstand International Plus
5622-128 E. Independence
Blvd.
Charlotte, NC 28212-6209

Quail Ridge Books
3522 Wade Ave.
Raleigh, NC 27607-4048
qrbooks1@aol.com

The Regulator Bookshop
720 9th St.
Durham, NC 27705-4803
http://www.regbook.com
mail@regbook.com

Special Occasions
112 N. Martin Luther
King Jr. Dr.
Winston Salem, NC 27101-4407

Wake Forest University College
Book Store
PO Box 7717
Winston Salem, NC 27109-7717

OHIO
MKK International's Black
Book Warehouse
6761 Springport Way
Dayton, OH 45424

University Bookstore
Kent State University
Kent Student Center
Kent, OH 44242
http://auxiliaries.ba.kent.edu/
top@ba.kent.edu

OREGON
Mother Kali's Books
720 E. 13th Ave.
Eugene, OR 97401-3753

PENNSYLVANIA
Allegheny College Bookstore
520 N. Main St.
Meadville, PA 16335-3903

The Basic Black Bookshop
9th & Market Streets
Gallery 1 Mall Level
Philadelphia, PA 19107

Children's Literacy Initiative
2314 Market St., Ste 4
Philadelphia, PA 19103-3017
clibooks@aol.com

Intermission, Ltd.
8405 Germantown Ave.
Philadelphia, PA 19118-3301

Robin's Book Store
108 S. 13th St.
Philadelphia, PA 19107-4532

Saint Elmo's
2208 East Carson St.
Pittsburgh, PA 15203-2108
http://www.SaintElmo.com
sales@saintelmo.com

Svoboda's Books
227 W. Beaver Ave.
State College, PA 16801-4819
http://epicom.com/svobodas/
svobooks@aol.com

SOUTH CAROLINA
Mirror Images Books & Toys
946 Orleans Rd. # B-3
Charleston, SC 29407-4889

Whitlaw Books
102 Heritage La.
Simpsonville, SC 29681

TENNESSEE
Afrobooks
1206 Southland Mall
Memphis, TN 38116

Pink Palace Museum Stores
3050 Central Ave.
Memphis, TN 38111-3316
http://www.memphismuseums
.org/giftshop.htm
shoppink@memphis.magibox.
net

TEXAS
Afro Awakenings Books Etc.
2419 S. Collins
Arlington, TX 76014-1226
http://www.bookweb.org/
bookstore/afroawakenings/
tj849@flash.net

Black Images.Book Bazaar
230 Wynnewood Village
P.O. Box 41059
Dallas, TX 75224
blackimages@juno.com

Frontier Press
10 Cadena Dr.
Galveston, TX 77554
http://www.doit.com/frontier
/frontier.cgi
kgfrontier@aol.com

Maxwell Books
900 N. Polk St., #144
de Soto, TX 75115-4000

Nu-World of Books
3250 Washington Blvd.
Beaumont, TX 77705-1324

VIRGIN ISLANDS
Dockside Bookshop
PO Box 8648
St Thomas, VI 00801-1648

VIRGINIA
Cooks' Books & More
610 N. Sheppard St.
Richmond, VA 23221

Cultural Expressions
P.O. Box 6464
Newport News, VA 23606-0464
http://www.INEED2READ.com
INEED2READ@aol.com

New Leaf Bookstore, Ltd.
43 Main St.
Warrenton, VA 20186

WASHINGTON, D.C.
Frederick Douglass Home
Bookshop
1411 W. St. SE
Washington, D.C. 20020
http://www.parksandhistory.
org/bookshops/
FDH@parksandhistory.org

Isson's Books & Records
1200 F St. NW
Metro Center
Washington, D.C. 20004-1203

Lammas
1607 17th St. NW
Washington, D.C. 20009-2403
lammers@zzopp.org

Lincoln Memorial Bookshop
126 Raleigh St. SE
Washington, DC 20042
http://www.parksandhistory.
org/bookshops/
Lincoln@parksandhistory.org

National Archives Museum
Store
7th & Pennsylvania Ave NW
NWCP Room G9
Washington, DC 20408-0002

Parks & History Association
126 Raleigh St. SE
Washington, D.C. 20032-1550
http://www.parksandhistory.
org/bookshops/
Parks_and_History_Association
@nps.gov

Reprint Book Shop
455 L'Enfant Plz. SW
Washington, D.C. 20024-2192

Sisterspace And Books
1515 U St. NW
Washington, D.C. 20009-4445
sistersp@erols.com

Vertigo Books
1337 Connecticut Ave NW
Washington, DC 20036-1801

Yawa Books
2206 18th St. NW
Washington, D.C. 20009-1813

WASHINGTON
Brother's Books
11443 Rainier Ave S
Seattle, WA 98178-3954
brobooks@aol.com

Elliott Bay Book Co.
101 S Main St
Seattle, WA 98104-2581
http://www.elliottbaybook.
com/ebbco/
queries@elliottbaybook.com

Red and Black Books
Collective
432 15th Ave E
Seattle, WA 98112-4505

WISCONSIN
Canterbury Booksellers
315 W. Gorham St.
Madison, WI 53703-2000
http://www.madison-
canterbury.com
books@madisoncanterbury.
com

The Cultural Connection
Bookstore
3424 W Villard Ave
Milwaukee, WI 53209-4710

Rainbow Bookstore Coop.
426 W. Gilman St.
Madison, WI 53703-1009
rbc@supranet.com

The Readers' Choice
1950 N. Dr. M.L.King Jr. Drive
Milwaukee, WI 53212

Roots and Vision
4829 N. 76th St.
Milwaukee, WI 53218

Sinsinawa Mound Bookshop
General Delivery
Sinsinawa, WI 53824-9999

AUTHOR-TITLE INDEX

Aardema, Verna, 109–10
Abby, 29
Abiyoyo, 29–30
Adoff, Arnold, 40–41, 198
Adventures of Sparrow Boy, 114
African American Family Album, The, 167–68
African-American Poetry, An Anthology, 1773–1927, 167
African Drawing Book, The, 30–31
Afro-Bets Book of Colors, 16
Afro-Bets First Book about Africa, 115
Agard, John, 18–19
Aida, 115–16
Ajeemah and His Son, 168–69
Alvin Ailey, 116–17
Always My Dad, 31–32
Amazing Grace, 32
Anderson, Debby, 20
Angelou, Maya, 85–86, 186, 205–206
Annie's Gifts, 33
Another Way to Dance, 169–70
Armstrong, Robb, 124, 125, 208–209
Armstrong, William H., 214
Ashley Bryan's ABC's of African American Poetry, 34

At the Crossroads, 34–35
Aunt Flossie's Hat (And Crab Cakes Later), 35
Aunt Harriet's Underground Railroad in the Sky, 36

Baby Grand, the Moon in July & Me, The, 117–18
Baby Jesus Like My Brother, 36–37
Baby Says, 17
Baldwin, James, 181–82
Bang, Molly, 23, 24
Barnes, Joyce Annette, 117–18
Beat the Story-Drum, Pum-Pum, 37–38
Ben's Trumpet, 38–39
Berends, Polly Berrien, 121
Berry, James, 168–69, 218, 239
Big Friend, Little Friend, 17–18
Bigmama's, 39
Bitter Bananas, 39–40
Black Cowboy, Wild Horses, A True Story, 118
Black Dance in America, 237
Black Diamond, The Story of the Negro Baseball League, 170
Black History for Beginners, 171

Black Ice, 170–71
Black Is Brown Is Tan, 40–41
Black Snowman, The, 119
Blessing in Disguise, A, 172
Block, The, 172–73
Bluest Eye, The, 173
Book of American Negro Poetry, The, 174
Book of Black Heroes: From A to Z, Volume One, 119–20
Boundless Grace, 120
Brenner, Barbara, 106–107
Bright Eyes, Brown Skin, 18
Bronzeville Boys and Girls, 41
Brooks, Bruce, 224
Brooks, Gwendolyn, 41
Brown, Margery Wheeler, 16, 36–37
Brown Angels, 41–42
Bryan, Ashley, 34, 37–38, 43, 230–31
Bunting, Eve, 160–61
Butler, Octavia, 205

Caines, Jeannette, 29, 67–68, 75–76
Calypso Alphabet, The, 18–19
Cameron, Ann, 159–60, 191–92
Campbell, Bebe Moore, 215–16
Caribbean Alphabet, 229–30
Carousel, 42–43
Carroll, Rebecca, 215
Carson, Ben, 131
Cary, Lorene, 170–71
Case of the Elevator Duck, The, 121
Cat, Christopher, 145–46
Cat's Purr, The, 43
Chalk Doll, The, 44
Chambers, Veronica, 195
Cherries and Cherry Pits, 44–45
Children of Color Storybook Bible, 46
Chinye, A West African Folk Tale, 46–47
Christmas in the Big House, Christmas in the Quarters, 121–22
Clifton, Lucille, 58–59, 235–36
Climbing Jacob's Ladder, Heroes of the Bible in African-American Spirituals, 47–48
Coker, Deborah Conner, 66
Color of Water, The, 174
Colors Come from God . . . Just Like Me!, 48–49
Come Sunday, 49
Contender, The, 175
Cooper, J. California, 190
Cornrows, 50

Cosby, Bill, 103
Coudert, Jo, 123
Craft, Jerry, 147
Creation, The, 51
Crews, Donald, 39, 95
Crews, Nina, 87–88
Cullen, Countee, 145–46
Cummings, Pat, 22, 42–43
Curtis, Christopher Paul, 223

Daddy and Me: A Photo Story of Arthur Ashe and His Daughter Camera, 51–52
Daddy Is a Monster . . . Sometimes, 230
Daly, Niki, 87
Dancing Granny, The, 230–31
Dancing with the Indians, 122–23
Dark Thirty: Southern Tales of the Supernatural, The, 175–76
Dave and the Tooth Fairy, 52–53
Davis, Ossie, 126, 237
Dennis, Denise, 171
Diakité, Baba Wagué, 65–66
Diop, Birage, 232
Distant Talking Drum, The, 53–54
Ditch-Digger's Daughters: A Black Family's Astonishing Success Story, 123
Dove, The, 231
Down the Road, 54–55
Draper, Sharon M., 179
Dream Keeper, The, 55
Drew and the Bub Daddy Showdown, 124
Drew and the Homeboy Question, 125
Drylongso, 177

Ear, the Eye and the Arm, The, 178
x 56
Eberle, Sara, 107
Ellis, Veronica Freeman, 115
Emerald Blue, 56–57
Equiano, Olaudah, 191–92
Escape to Freedom: A Play about Young Frederick Douglass, 126
Evan's Corner, 57–58
Everette Anderson's Goodbye, 58–59

Faithful Friend, The, 127–28
Fallen Angels, 178–79
Farmer, Nancy, 178
Fast Sam, Cool Clyde, and Stuff, 128
Father and Son, 59–60

Feelings, Muriel, 72–73
Feelings, Tom, 196, 213
Fingers, Nose and Toes, 19
First Pink Light, 60
Five Great Explorers, 61
Flournoy, Valerie, 88–89, 104
Follow the Drinking Gourd, 129
Forché, Carolyn A., 48–49
Ford, Bernette G., 18
Forged by Fire, 179
Friendship, The, 130
From a Child's Heart, 61–62
From Slave Ship to Freedom Road, 180
Front Porch Stories, At the One-Room School, 180–81

Gates, Henry Louis, Jr., 201
Gershator, Phillis, 234
Gifted Hands: The Ben Carson Story, 131
Giovonni, Nikki, 76–77
God's Trumbones, Seven Negro Sermons in Verse, 182
Gorrell, Gena K., 200–201
Go Tell It on the Mountain, 181–82
Grampa's Face, 62–63
Gray, Libba Moore, 82–83
Great African Americans in . . . , 131–32
Great Women in the Struggle: Book of Black Heroes, Volume Two, 132
Greenfield, Eloise, 17–18, 22, 60, 62–63, 79, 94, 149–50, 150, 153–54, 158, 162
Grifalconi, Ann, 233
Grimes, Nikki, 49, 61–62, 68–69, 80, 96

Halala Means Welcome!: A Book of Zulu Words, 63–64
Halliburton, Warren J., 184
Hamilton, Virginia, 78, 89–90, 177, 216
Hansen, Joyce, 187–88
Harlem, A Poem, 183
Harriet Tubman, Conductor on the Underground Railroad, 183–84
Harris, Jacqueline, 222
Harwood, Ronald, 238–39
Haskins, James, 237
Havill, Juanita, 70, 71
Hayes, Sarah, 56
Heide, Florence Tarry, 235
Herron Carolivia, 86
Hill, Elizabeth Starr, 57–58

Historic Speeches of African-Americans, 184
Hoffman, Mary, 32, 120
Hogan, Paula Z., 234
Hoobler, Dorothy, 167–68
Hoobler, Thomas, 167–68
Hopkinson, Deborah, 99
Howard, Elizabeth Fitzgerald, 35, 102–103
How Sweet the Sound: African-American Songs for Children, 64
Hru, Dakari, 74–75
Hudson, Cheryl Willis, 18, 64, 141–42, 189
Hudson, Wade, 61, 64, 72, 119–20, 141–42, 189
Hue Boy, 64–65
Hughes, Langston, 55, 172–73
Hundred Penny Box, The, 133–34
Hunterman and the Crocodile, 65–66
Hurston, Zora Neale, 219
Hyppolite, Joanne, 155, 203–204

I Can Count, 19–20
I Can! God Helps Me from A to Z, 20
. . . If You Lived at the Time of Martin Luther King, 135
Igus, Toyomi, 108–109, 132, 186–87
I Hadn't Meant to Tell You This, 185
I Have Heard a Land, 134
I Know Why the Caged Bird Sings, 186
I Like Me!, 66
I Love My Hair, 67
I Need a Lunch Box, 67–68
In My Daddy's Arms I Am Tall: African Americans Celebrating Fathers, 136
Inner City Mother Goose, The, 188–89
In Praise of Our Fathers and Our Mothers: A Black Family Treasury by Outstanding Authors and Artists, 189
In Search of Satisfaction, 190
Isadora, Rachel, 34–35, 38–39
I See the Rhythm, 186–87
Island Christmas, An, 136–37
I Smell Honey, 20
I Thought My Soul Would Rise and Fly, The Diary of Patsy, A Freed Girl, 187–88
It's Raining Laughter, 68–69

Jackson Jones and the Puddle of Thorns, 137–38

Jafta and the Wedding, 69–70
Jaha and Jamil Went Down the Hill, An African Mother Goose, 21
Jamaica's Find, 70
Jamaica Tag-Along, 71
Jamal's Busy Day, 72
Jambo Means Hello: Swahili Alphabet Book, 72–73
Jasmine's Parlour Day, 73–74
John Henry, 138–39
Johnson, Angela, 75, 101–102, 107–108, 221
Johnson, Delores, 164
Johnson, James Weldon, 51, 174, 182
Jordan, Denise, 161–62
Joseph, Lynn, 73–74, 136–37
Joshua's Masai Mask, 74–75
Journey to Jo'Burg: A South African Story, 139–40
Julius, 75
Junebug, 190–91
Justin and the Best Biscuits in the World, 140–41
Just Us Women, 75–76

Keats, Ezra Jack, 24, 25
Kidnapped Prince, The Life of Olaudah Equiano, The, 191–92
Kids' Book of Wisdom, 141–42
King, Casey, 202–203
Knoxville, Tennessee, 76–77
Kroll, Virginia, 21
Kwanzaa, 142

Langstaff, John, 47–48
Langston: A Play by Ossie Davis, 237
Last Days of Uncle Remus, The, 143–44
Lauture, Denizé, 59–60
Lessac, Frané, 229–30
Lester, Julius, 93, 118, 138–39, 143–44, 180, 194–95, 220
Levine, Ellen, 135
Lewin, Hugh, 69–70
Like Sisters on the Homefront, 192–93
Linden, Anne Marrie, 56–57
Lipsyte, Robert, 175
Little X, Growing Up in the Nation of Islam, 193–94
Liza Lou and the Yeller Belly Swamp, 144
Long Hard Journey, The Story of the Pullman Porter, A, 237–38
Long Journey Home, Stories form Black History, 194–95
Lost Zoo, The, 145–46

McBride, James, 174
McKay, Nellie Y., 201
McKissack, Federick, 121–22, 170, 206, 212–13, 237–38
McKissack, Patricia, 77, 81–82, 121–22, 148, 170, 175–76, 206, 212–13, 237–38
Ma Dear's Aprons, 77
Make a Joyful Sound, Poems for Children by African American Poets, 146
Mama's Boyz: As American as Sweet Potato Pie!, 147
Mama's Girl, 195
Mandela, 238–39
Many Thousand Gone: African Americans from Slavery to Freedom, 78
Mathis, Sharon Bell, 133–34, 151–52
Max, 21
Maya Angelou, Journey of the Heart, 195–96
Mayer, Mercer, 144
Mead, Alice, 190–91
Me & Neesie, 79
Medearis, Angela Shelf, 33, 122–23, 157, 233–34
Meet Danitra Brown, 80
Mendez, Phil, 119
Merriam, Eve, 188–89
Middle Passage, White Ships, Black Cargo, The, 196
Miller, WIlliam, 152–53
Million Fish . . . More or Less, A, 148
Minty, A Story of Young Harriet Tubman, 81
Mirandy and Brother Wind, 81–82
Miss Tizzy, 82–83
Mitchell, Margaree King, 105
Mitchell, Rita Phillips, 64–65
Molly the Brave and Me, 83
Morrison, Toni, 173
Mother Crocodile, 232
Motown and Didi, 197
Moutoussamy-Ashe, Jeanne, 51–52
Mufaro's Beautiful Daughters, 149
Murphey, Cecil, 131
My Aunt Came Back, 22
My Black Me: A Beginning Book of Black Poetry, 198

My Daddy and I, 22
Myers, Walter Dean, 41–42, 97–98, 128,
    178–79, 183, 197, 201–202, 207,
    211–12, 224–25, 227
My First Kwanzaa Book, 84
My Mama Needs Me, 84–85
*My Painted House, My Friendly Chicken,
    and Me,* 85–86

Naidoo, Beverly, 139–40
Nappy Hair, 86
Nathaniel Talking, 149–50
Newton Chocolate, Deborah M., 84
Nightjohn, 199
Night on Neighborhood Street, 150
Nine Plays by Black Women, 239
*North Star to Freedom: The Story of the
    Underground Railroad,* 200–201
*Norton Anthology of African American
    Literature,* 201
Not So Fast Songololo, 87
*Now Is Your Time: The African-American
    Struggle for Freedom,* 201–202

O'Connor, Jane, 83
Oh, Freedom!, 202–203
Olaleye, Isaac, 39–40, 53–54
Ola Shakes It Up, 203–204
Once on This River, 204
One Fall Day, 23
One Hot Summer Day, 87–88
Onyefulu, Obi, 46–47
Osa's Pride, 233
Osborne, Linda Barrett, 202–203
Our People, 233–34

Parable of the Sower, The, 205
Patchwork Quilt, The, 88–89
Patrick, Denise Lewis, 19–20, 92
Paulsen, Gary, 199, 209
*People Could Fly: American Black Folktales,
    The,* 89–90
Petry, Ann, 183–84
Pettit, Jayne, 195–96
*Phenomenal Woman, Four Poems
    Celebrating Women,* 205–206
Pinderhughes, John, 19
Pink and Say, 150–51
Pinkney, Andrea, 20, 23–24, 116–17
Pinkney, Brian, 20, 23–24, 114
Polacco, Patricia, 150–51

Pomerantz, Charlotte, 44
Porter, A. P., 142
Pretty Brown Face, 23–24
Price, Leontyne, 115–16
Psalm 23, 90–91

Quattlebaum, Mary, 137–38

Rain, Rain Go Away, 91
Raschka, Chris, 111
Rata-Pata-Scata-Fata, 234
*Rebels Against Slavery, American Slave
    Revolts,* 206
Red Dancing Shoes, 92
Red Dog, Blue Fly: Football Poems, 151–52
Reed, Teresa, 91
Richard Wright and the Library Card,
    152–53
Righteous Revenge of Artemis Bonner, The,
    207
Ringgold, Faith, 36, 100–101
Robinson, Amindah Brenda Lynn, 98
Roll of Thunder, Hear Me Cry, 207–208
Rosa Parks, 153–54
Runnin' with the Big Dawgs, 208–209

Sam and the Tigers, 93
San Souci, Robert, 100, 127
Sarny: A Life Remembered, 209
Schertle, Alice, 54–55
Schroeder, Alan, 81
Sebestyen, Ouida, 225–26
Secret of Gumbo Grove, The, 154–55
Seeger, Pete, 29–30
Seth and Samona, 155
Shaka, King of the Zulus, 156
*She Come Bringing Me That Little Baby
    Girl,* 94
Sherman, Joan R., 167
Shimmershine Queens, The, 210–11
Shortcut, 95
Singing Man, The, 157
Sister, 158
Slam!, 211–12
Slier, Deborah, 146
Snowy Day, The, 24
Sojourner Truth: Ain't I A Woman?,
    212–13
Something on My Mind, 96
Sometimes I Don't Like School, 234
Song of the Trees, 159

Soul Looks Back in Wonder, 213
Sounder, 214
Sound of Sunshine, Sound of Rain, 235
Southgate, Martha, 169–70
Stanley, Diane, 156
Steptoe, Javaka, 136
Steptoe, John, 17, 97, 149, 230
Stevie, 97
Stewart, Dianne, 231
Stories Julian Tells, The, 159–60
Story of the Three Kingdoms, The, 97–98
Stowe, Harriet Beecher, 222–223
Street Called Home, A, 98
Sugar in the Raw, Voices of Young Black Girls in America, 215
Summer Wheels, 160–61
Susie King Taylor: Destined to Be Free, 161–62
Sweet Clara and the Freedom Quilt, 99
Sweet Summer, 215–16
Sweet Whispers, Brother Rush, 216–17

Talk About a Family, 162
Talking Eggs, The, 100
Tap-Tap, 163
Tar Beach, 100–101
Tarpley, Natasha Anastasia, 67
Taste of Salt, 217–18
Tate, Eleanora, 154–55, 172, 180–81
Tate, Sonsyrea, 193–94
Taylor, Mildred, 130, 159, 207–208
Tell Me a Stroy, Mama, 101–102
Temple, Frances, 217–218
Ten, Nine, Eight, 24
Their Eyes Were Watching God, 219
Thief in the Village and Other Stories, A, 218
Thomas, Joyce Carol, 134
Thornton, Yvonne, 123
Three Wishes, 235–36
To Be a Slave, Thirtieth Anniversary Edition, 220
Toning the Sweep, 221
Train to Lulu's, The, 102–103
Treasure Hunt, The, 103

Tuskegee Airmen, Black Heroes of World War II, The, 222
Twins Strike Back, The, 104
Ty's One-Man Band, 104–105

Udry, Janice Mary, 236
Uncle Jed's Barbershop, 105
Uncle Tom's Cabin, 222–23

Vennema, Peter, 156

Wagon Wheels, 106–107
Walter, Mildred Pitts, 84–85, 104–105, 140–41
Watsons Go to Birmingham-1963, The, 223
Wesley, Valerie Wilson, 119–20
What Hearts, 224
What Is Love?, 107
What Mary Jo Wanted, 236
When I Am Old Wtih You, 107–108
When I Dance, 239
When I Was Little, 108–109
Whistle for Willie, 25
Why Mosquitoes Buzz in People's Ears, 109–10
Wilkerson, Margaret B., 239
Wilkings, Verna Allette, 52–53
Williams, Karen Lynn, 163
Williams, Sherley Anne, 110–11
Williams, Vera B., 44–45
Williams-Garcia, Rita, 192–93
Wilson-Max, Ken, 21, 63–64
Winter, Jeanette, 129
Won't Know Till I Get There, 224–25
Woodson, Jacqueline, 185
Words by Heart, 225–26
Working Cotton, 110–11
World of Daughter McGuire, The, 226
Wyeth, Sharon Dennis, 31–32, 204, 226

Yarbrough, Camille, 50, 210–11
Young Landlords, The, 227
Your Dad Was Just Like You, 164
Yo! Yes, 111

MVP/THEME INDEX

Abuse:
    coping with, 185
    triumphing over, 179, 186
Achieving dreams, 131
Adjusting to change, 94, 203, 220
Adoption, 29
Adventurous spirit, 75
Adversity, triumph over, 195
Affection for grandparents, 87
African-American folk tales, 143
African American literature, 201
African-American poetry, 34
African-American songs, learning
    traditional, 64
African-American values, appreciating,
    142
African culture:
    appreciating, 39
    learning, 115
African family values, appreciating, 84
African-inspired rhymes, 21
African life, appreciating, 53
African words, learning, 63, 72
Animals, love for, 118
Appreciating African-American values,
    142

Appreciating African culture, 39
Appreciating African family values, 84
Appreciating African life, 53
Appreciating a mixed heritage, 226
Appreciating family history, 41
Appreciating multiracialness, 40
Appreciating other black cultures, 229
Appreciating other cultures, 85
Appreciating our forebears, 121
Appreciating our history, 61
Appreciating our Native American
    roots, 122
Appreciating our tradition of
    storytelling, 180
Appreciating simple things, 87
Appreciating the contributions of black
    women, 132
Appreciating unique gifts, 29
Art, 183
Assumptions and blame shifting,
    avoiding, 109
Avoiding assumptions and blame
    shifting, 109

Babies, learning about, 56
Bad choices, triumphing over, 192

Being adopted, 29
Being alert to danger, 95
Being in love, 197
Being just like Dad, 59
Being loved, 29
Being nonjudgmental, 160
Being open to new relationships, 224
Being willing and available, 227
Believing in yourself, 32, 157
Biblical wisdom, 46
Black beauty and strength, 146
Black cultures, appreciating other, 229
Black history, 135, 167, 194, 202, 206
    primer, 171
Blackness, loving our, 119
Black poetry, 239
Black women, appreciating the
    contributions of, 132
Blame shifting and assumptions,
    avoiding, 109
Boy-girl friendship, 155
Bravery, 83, 144
Brotherly love, 105
Building self-esteem, 18

Caribbean culture, 218
Change, adjusting to, 94, 203, 220
Chasing your dreams, 197
Cherishing good memories, 56, 221
Children understanding parents, 230
Child's look at life's hard realities, 150
Christmas, keeping Christ in, 36
City, growing up in the, 41
City children appreciating country life,
    39
Cleverness, 230
Colors, learning, 16
Communication, 111
Community spirit, 73
Compassion, 71
Confidence, 81, 211
    in God, 20
Conversations with God, 61
Convictions, courage of one's, 153
Coping with abuse, 185
Coping with father's absence, 215
Coping with loss, 31, 58, 185, 215
Coping with separation, 120
Coping with serious illness, 51
Cost of keeping secrets, 204
Count, learning to, 24

Counting objects, 19
Courage, 152, 183, 190, 191, 217, 222,
    225
    of one's convictions, 153
Covetous, result of being, 115
Creation of the world, 51
Creativity, 44, 231, 233

Dad, *see* Father(s)
Dance, history of blacks in, 237
Danger, being alert to, 95
Delayed gratification, 34
Determination, 52, 78, 81, 99, 138, 139,
    152, 154, 201, 212, 215
    to succeed, 195
Dignity, 130
Disappointment, handling, 42, 54
Discipline, 175
    importance of, 193
Discovering snow, 24
Divorce, coping with, 224
Draw, learning to, 30
Dreams, 117, 123
    achieving, 131
    becoming reality, 38
    chasing your, 197
    importance of, 55

Elders:
    honoring, 88
    learning from, 35
    listening to our, 232
    valuing your, 108
Empathy, 133
Envy, perils of, 93
Escape of enslaved blacks to the North,
    200

Facing up to past mistakes, 216
Faith, 49, 100, 130, 222
Families:
    importance of, 189
    relationships, importance of, 57,
        223
    strong, 167
Family history, appreciating, 41
Father(s):
    being just like Dad, 59
    coping with absence of, 215
    -daughter love, 51
    dealing with longing for, 172

Father(s): *(cont.)*
  honoring, 136
  importance of a, 31
  longing for, 120, 172
  love for, 60
  /son relationship, 22, 168
Feeling needed, 84
Feelings, understanding our, 198
Finding yourself, 169
Finding your talents, 33, 103
Folklore, historical, 177
Folk tales, African-American, 143
Foolishness of pride, 233
Forebears, appreciating our, 121
Forgiveness, 225
Frailties, human, 145
Freedom, tales of, 89
Friendship, 75, 80, 97, 128, 137, 175,
    208, 235
  boy-girl, 155
  interracial, 127, 150
Futuristic adventure in Africa, 178

Generation gap, overcoming the, 164
Gifts:
  appreciating unique, 29
  valuing, 92
God:
  conversations with, 61
  creation of the world, 51
  protection by, 90
Grandparents:
  affection for, 87
  love for, 62
Great achievers:
  inspiration from, 119
  in sports, 170
Great men, 206
  in our history, 237
Growing up, 17
  in the city, 41

Hair, loving our, 50, 67, 86
Handicap, living with a, 235
Handling disappointment, 42, 54
Handling responsibility, 54
Hardship, overcoming, 168, 186
Hard work, 110, 123
Harlem, tribute to, 172
Helping out at home, 136
Historical folklore, 177

History, 183
  black, *see* Black history
  of blacks in dance, 237
Holding on to good memories, 56, 221
Holidays, specialness of, 136
Honesty, 49, 70
Honoring elders, 88
Honoring fathers, 136
Hope, 129, 134, 190
How enslaved blacks escaped North, 200
How God made the world, 51
How to show love, 107
Human frailties, 145
Humorous life lessons, 147

Illness, coping with serious, 51
Imaginary friends, 79
Imagination, 205, 234
  using your, 36, 44, 114, 148
Importance of a dad, 31
Importance of a strong self-identity,
  173
Importance of being thorough, 140
Importance of discipline, 193
Importance of dreams, 55
Importance of family, 189
Importance of family relationships, 57,
  223
Importance of reading, 126
Independence, 102
Ingenuity, 98, 137
Inhumanity of the slave trade, 196
Inner beauty, 149
Inner conflicts, 178
Inspiration, 116, 184, 231
  from great achievers, 119
  spiritual, 182
Interracial friendship, 127, 150

Jealousy, the result of, 43
Joy of a wedding/African traditions, 69
Justice, 217

Keeping Christ in Christmas, 36
Kindness, 82
Kitchen routines, learning, 20
Knowing your self-worth, 124

Leadership skills, 156
Learning about biblical heroes through
  song, 47

Result of jealousy, 43
Rewards of obedience, 100
Rewards of patience, 190
Rooms in a house, 21

Secrets, cost of keeping, 204
Self-confidence, 64, 205, 210, 219, 226, 233
Self-esteem, 210
Self-identity, 158
    importance of strong, 173
    maintaining, 170
Self-image, 18, 23, 66, 149
Selflessness, 81
Self-worth, 48, 124
Sensitivity, 88
Showing love, 107
Siblings, love for, 139
Simple things, appreciating, 87, 108
Single-mindedness, 81
Slave trade, inhumanity of the, 196
Snow, discovering, 24
Souvenirs from travels, 22
Spending time together, 107
Spiritual inspiration, 182
Sports:
    great achievers in, 170
    as a metaphor for life, 151
Storytelling, appreciating our tradition of, 180
Strength of character, 125
Strong families, 167
Sweetness of childhood, 23

Talents, finding your, 33, 103
Tales of freedom, 89

Thoroughness, importance of, 140
Thoughtfulness, 99
Tribute to Harlem, 172
Triumphing over abuse, 179, 186
Triumphing over bad choices, 192
Triumphing over hardship, 186
Triumph over adversity, 195
True boy-girl friendship, 155
True friendship, 80, 128
Trust, 160

Understanding one's racial identity, 174
Understanding our feelings, 198
Understanding parents, 162
Understanding war, 178
Uniqueness, 104
Unspoken thoughts of children, 96
Urban poetry, 188
Using your imagination, 36, 44, 148
Value of hard work, 123
Values:
    appreciating African-American, 142
    living, 141
Valuing friendship, 97
Valuing gifts, 92
Valuing your elders, 108
Vision, 134

War, understanding, 178
Wedding, joy of a/African traditions, 69
Whistle, learning to, 25
Wild West, 207
Wise planning, 156

Learning about life, 37
Learning African culture, 115
Learning African words, 63, 72
Learning colors, 16
Learning from elders, 35
Learning kitchen routines, 20
Learning new words, 18
Learning to count, 24
Learning to draw, 30
Learning to listen, 235
Learning to talk, 17
Learning to whistle, 25
Learning traditional African-American
    songs, 64
Learning what babies do, 56
Learning what body parts do, 19
Life's hard realities, a child's look at,
    150
Listening to our elders, 232
Living values, 141
Living with a handicap, 235
Longing for father, 120
Loss, coping with, 31, 58, 185, 215
Love, 115, 215
    for animals, 118
    being in, 197
    for Dad, 60
    for grandparent, 62
    how to show, 107
    of nature, 159
    of reading, 152
    for siblings, 139
Loving life, 68
Loving our blackness, 119
Loving our hair, 50, 67, 86
Loving your family and friends, 76
Loving yourself, 74
Loyalty, 214

Maintaining self-identity, 170
Making do with less, 44
Making holidays special, 136
Memories, holding on to good, 56,
    221
Men, great, 206
    in our history, 237
Mistakes, facing up to past, 216
Mixed heritage, approaching a, 226
Mother-child love, 77
Mother-daughter bonding, 163
Multiracialness, appreciating, 40

Native American roots, appreciati
    our, 122
Nature:
    love of, 159
    respect for, 65, 91, 159
New relationships, being open to,
New responsibilities, 72
New words, learning, 18

Obedience, 46
Obedience, the rewards of, 100
Overcoming hardship, 168
Overcoming loss, 58
Overcoming the generation gap, 1
Overcoming tremendous odds, 20

Parents:
    -child bond, 101
    children understanding, 230
    understanding, 162
Passion, pursuing your, 237
Patience, 67, 187
    rewards of, 190
Peer pressure, 172
Perils of envy, 93
Perseverance, 105, 146, 161, 175, 2
    213, 238
Planning, 105, 156
Plays by black women, 239
Poetry, 167, 174, 183
    appreciating, 198
    black, 239
    urban, 188
Positive self-image, 23, 66
Practice makes perfect, 121
Practicing what you preach, 193
Pride, foolishness of, 233
Problem resolution, 234
Problem-solving, 39
Pursuing your passion, 237

Racial identity, understanding c
Reading, importance of, 126
Reading, love of, 152
Resourcefulness, 97, 104, 106,
Respect, 118
Respect for nature, 65, 91, 15
Responsibilities, 236
    handling, 54
    new, 72
Result of being covetous, 11